Being Up for Grabs:
On Speculative Anarcheology

New Metaphysics

Series Editors: Graham Harman and Bruno Latour

The world is due for a resurgence of original speculative metaphysics. The New Metaphysics series aims to provide a safe house for such thinking amidst the demoralizing caution and prudence of professional academic philosophy. We do not aim to bridge the analytic-continental divide, since we are equally impatient with nail-filing analytic critique and the continental reverence for dusty textual monuments. We favor instead the spirit of the intellectual gambler, and wish to discover and promote authors who meet this description. Like an emergent recording company, what we seek are traces of a new metaphysical 'sound' from any nation of the world. The editors are open to translations of neglected metaphysical classics, and will consider secondary works of especial force and daring. But our main interest is to stimulate the birth of disturbing masterpieces of twenty-first century philosophy.

Hilan Bensusan
Being Up for Grabs:
On Speculative Anarcheology

O
OPEN HUMANITIES PRESS
London, 2016

First edition published by Open Humanities Press 2016
Copyright © 2016 Hilan Bensusan
Freely available at http://openhumanitiespress.org/books/titles/being-up-for-grabs/

This is an open access book, licensed under a Creative Commons By Attribution Share Alike license. Under this license, authors allow anyone to download, reuse, reprint, modify, distribute, and/or copy this book so long as the authors and source are cited and resulting derivative works are licensed under the same or similar license. No permission is required from the authors or the publisher. Statutory fair use and other rights are in no way affected by the above. Read more about the license at creativecommons.org/licenses/by-sa/3.0

Design by Katherine Gillieson
Cover Illustration by Tammy Lu

The cover illustration is copyright Tammy Lu 2016, used under a
Creative Commons By Attribution license (CC-BY).

Interior images copyright Gisel Carriconde Azevedo used with permission.

PRINT ISBN 978-1-78542-028-3
PDF ISBN 978-1-78542-029-0

OPEN HUMANITIES PRESS

Open Humanities Press is an international, scholar-led open access publishing collective whose mission is to make leading works of contemporary critical thought freely available worldwide. More at http://openhumanitiespress.org

Contents

Acknowledgements   11

1. Being up for grabs – the preliminaries   15
2. Anarcheologies   61
3. Fragments   95
4. Doubts   137
5. Rhythms   163
6. Contingency and its galaxies   195

Notes   209

References   223

*To Denise Paiva Agustinho
and Devrim*

Acknowledgements

The gestation of this book took pretty close to nine months. Its conception, to be sure, took much longer. Both processes were collective and I'm grateful to a large number of people, places and institutions for ideas, inspiration and support.

The idea came up in a bus ride with Fabiane Borges somewhere close to Arba Minch, Ethiopia, in January 2012. It was first sketched in a talk at the American University of Beirut, organized by Ray Brassier in June 2012.

Parts of the book have nonetheless had previous lives. Anarcheology is an older endeavor I have been pursuing with Leonel Antunes and Luciana Ferreira since 2009. The chapter on fragments is much indebted to the course I taught at Paris 8 in 2011, and I'm thankful to many students and colleagues there, especially Eric Lecerf, Stéphane Douailler, Zouzi Chebbi, Marie Bardet, Andres Vahos, Jean-Sébastien Laberge, Romain Flizot and Julie Alfonsi. While in Paris I also had important conversations with Lise Lacoste and Quentin Meillassoux. The chapter on doubts was developed in parallel with my interactions with the Neo-Pyrrhonism work group in Brazil and its meetings around 2012 and 2013 where the argument of the chapter took form. It benefited from discussions particularly with Oswaldo Porchat, Eros Carvalho, Alexandre Noronha, Michael Williams, Luiz Eva and Plinio Junqueira Smith. The chapter on rhythms was bred in my courses in Brasilia in 2012 and 2013, the conference on Performance Philosophy at Guilford, the one on Diverse Bodies in Rio, both in 2013 and in exchanges I had in events about ontology and speculation around this time. I'm thankful to

André Arnaut, Barbara de Barros, Tomás Ribeiro, Guilherme Moura, Lucas Kaeté, Jéssica Franco, Rômulo Fontinelle, Gena Pulino, Juliana Bramatti, Marcos Chagas, Gabriela Lafetá, Bernardo Tavares, Otavio Maciel, Gerson Brea, Herivelto Souza, Ana Miriam Altmayer Wünsch, Wanderson Flor, Loraine Oliveira, Agatha Bacelar, Agnaldo Portugal, Cecília Almeida, Laura Cull, Ana Cristina Chiara, Johnny Kemp, Marcus Gabriel, Graham Harman, Cesar dos Santos, Rodrigo Nunes, Steven Shaviro, John Protevi, Eduardo Viveiros de Castro, Déborah Danowski, Alexandre Nodari, Erick Felinto, Erick Lima, Paulo Abrantes, Julio Cabrera and Eclair Filho. Work on galaxies has been carried out together with Alexandre Costa-Leite (and more recently with Edelcio Souza and Rodrigo Freire). Furthermore, I've rehearsed some of the ideas in the book on my blog (*No Borders Metaphysics*) and I'm grateful to comments and suggestions I received.

The writing season started early in 2014 in Xalapa where Juliana Merçon and her house in Zoncloantla, close to the Pixquiac river, provided the right environment for the embryonic book. Its birth also owes much to her. From Veracruz, I moved to Vienna, Graz, Innsbruck, Granada, Paris, Brighton, Berlin, Lisbon and back to Brasilia. During these nine months I was helped in many ways by my sister Nurit and my nephew Ariê, Alfonso de Pablos, Flor Rothschild, the Coatepec organic market, Grego Queiroz, *Universidad Veracruzana Intercultural* (for hosting my course on ontographies and modes of existence and the invitation to talk in Tajin), Helio Garcia, Eckhart Boege, Irlanda Villegas, Luisa Paré, Adriana Menassé and our great conversations at Parochia and Chiquito, the *Universidad Veracruzana* (where I ultra-sounded parts of the book), the *Biblioteca Carlos Fuentes* and the adjacent street Ursulo Galván, Carol Sobreiro, Edla Eggert, Gerardo Alatorre, Shantal Mesenguer, Crisanto Bautista, Roberto Penedo, Ignacio Marcué, Barbara Hardcore, Witek Jacorzinsky who helped me with the Sahagún Colloquia and invited me to talk at *CIESAS*, Daniel Paiva, the Österreiches Nationalbibliothek, Cristina Borgoni, Marian David, Guido Melchior, the *Karl-Franzens-Universität Graz* (where I talked on the ontology of doubts), Manuel de Pinedo and his friends and colleagues at the *Universidad de Granada* (where I talked about logical galaxies), Mar Muriana, the Genil river, Filipe Chipe, Monica Udler, Aurèle Crasson, the Paris 8 library, the Buttes Chaumont park, Aharon Amir, Olga Shaumyan, the North Laines Library in Brighton, Katie Bailey, Oli Sharpe, Tom Beament, Benjamim Noys, Dariush Sokolov, Claudia Freire, Guida Chambel, Caroline Marin, Nuno Oliveira, Aia Hipácia, Joana Barata, Filipe Ceppas, Kelly Heitor, Laura Ovidio, Poncho and everyone from the community where I live: Gisel Carriconde Azevedo, Phil Jones, Laura Virginia, Judith Zuquim, Hannah Prado, Tina Nunes and Treps. During these (roughly) forty weeks Denise Paiva Agustinho was very much by my side, gestating Devrim. The book is dedicated to them both.

The text was much improved by conversations with Jadson Alves, especially concerning monadologies in general. I also thank Stephanie Mitchell and Kaio Rabelo for their careful help in preparing the final manuscript.

To conclude, I would like to thank my Department at the University of Brasilia, which made it possible for me to go on leave to write this book, the two grants that supported the investigation: one from CNPq, Brazil (CNPq/486635/2013-9) and one from the Spanish Ministry of Science and Innovation (FFI2010-19455), as well as the two anonymous reviewers for Open Humanities Press. I'm happy that this book is appearing in the New Metaphysics Series – reading its mission statement was a key factor in my decision to write this book.

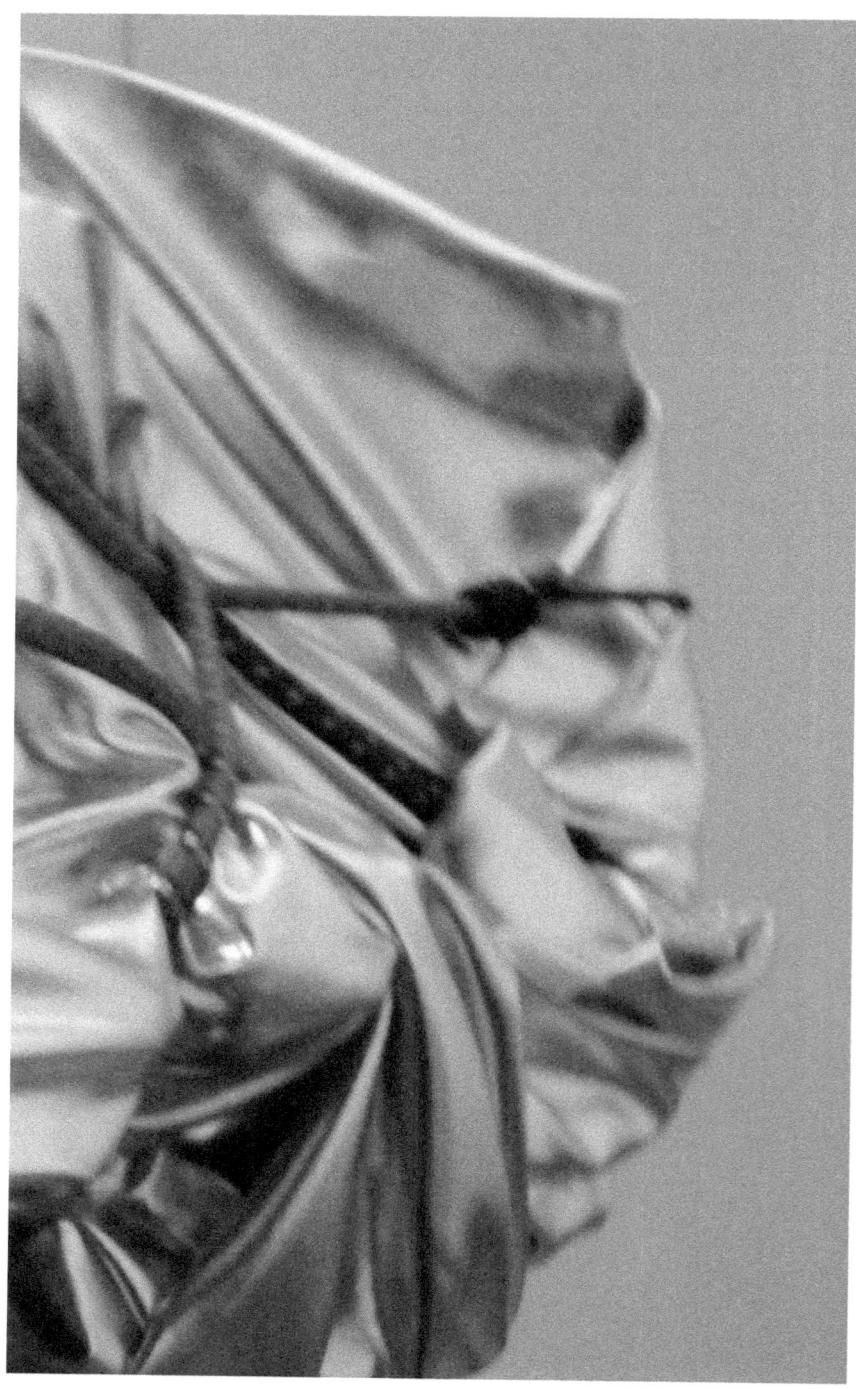

Wrapped-up   Gisel Carriconde Azevedo, Digital photography, 2011

Chapter 1
Being up for grabs – the preliminaries

Up for grabs

This is a book about what ain't necessarily so. It is about how we can grasp, assimilate or come to terms with what could have been otherwise – or might not be at all. Aristotle claims that we cannot know the impermanent.[1] It can be argued, from that perspective, that thought itself requires a measure of fixity. After all, if thought has a format akin to predication, it requires a subject for that predication. Indeed, metaphysics has classically been associated with necessities of some sort. It has typically resorted to substances (which endure modifications and provide reality to what is perceived), to substrata (*hypokeimena* underneath different qualities and predications) and to fixed principles and necessary connections: in a word, to one kind of *arché* or another. If resorting to what is necessary is unavoidable, there would be no metaphysics without an appeal to necessity.

This book, drawing on the growing philosophical attention to the accidental, attempts to develop a metaphysics of the non-necessary. It is, in this sense, an exercise in *anarcheology*. The book's main contention is that *contingency* is what we should primarily look at in order to ultimately come to terms with the sensible or the concrete. In other words, metaphysics should first engage with the contingent. In doing so, it attempts to provide positive accounts of contingency – not taking the compulsory as basic, or the accidental as primarily the unsubstantial. In that sense, it contrasts sharply with Aristotle's metaphysical project. (We will see below that it is an Aristotelian project in other senses.) The project is not to treat the accident itself as an absolute principle or an ultimate element to which everything else is to be reduced, but rather as a key to unveiling things: a key to a renewed, well-informed metaphysics. In other words, the idea is not to state the sovereignty of contingency – not even to claim merely that the accidental has the upper hand – but rather to spell out the details that makes possible its governance. Contingency is not the upper hand, but it is a primary component of what there is. As such, it counters Aristotle's premise that metaphysics cannot exist unless there is some necessity in the sensible.[2]

Aristotle's starting point is a rejection of (what he takes to be) the Heraclitean image that "everything flows" in the sensible and that therefore there is no room for necessities of any kind.[3] According to Aristotle, it was Plato's adherence to this Heraclitean image of the sensible that made him look for (metaphysical) knowledge elsewhere, because he could see no necessity in matters of fact and therefore no possibility of knowledge of those matters of fact. The Aristotelian move was to bite the bullet and reject the idea that the sensible is always insubstantial. There ought to be sensible substances constituted by their form and matter, carrying proper potentialities.[4] Because they carry potentialities, some of the ways in which they can change are necessary – they subsist in time – whereas others are accidental. They undergo changes while retaining what makes them what they are. In contrast, accidental beings cannot undergo generation or corruption for there is nothing substantial being achieved or lost. (*Met.* E, 2, 1226b21-23) Permanence and the regular order of things are condensed in substances which themselves are primarily what constitute matters of fact. This is, in a nutshell, the Aristotelian conception of sensible substances. If sensible things have no substance, no change is necessary, and therefore nothing remains what it is.

The Aristotelian diagnosis was that either there are substances in the sensible, among concrete things, or else everything is in flux. This book accepts the wager but rejects its thrust: it claims that there is a metaphysics of this flux. It holds that we have enough access to the non-necessary to enable something more sound than substance metaphysics. We don't have to choose between finding necessities and abandoning metaphysics. The book is, in this sense, a Heraclitean endeavor.[5]

The goal of this first chapter is twofold. While I introduce some elements for a metaphysics of contingency, I try to make the project of the book clearer. The objective is to bring together elements from several sources to build a mosaic where features of the inherently impermanent and contingent appear. As we will see, the project is Aristotelian in the sense that contingencies won't appear as the building blocks everything is made of – like Aristotle, I don't believe that substance is the only form of existence. However, I don't approach contingency with the intent of building a general theory that would map onto some ultimate furniture of the universe. Rather, I take the contingent to exhibit itself to us in various, contrasting pictures. Also in a rather Aristotelian vein, these pictures relate to the accident, just as Aristotelian substance presented itself *qua* several things (*qua* matter, *qua* forms, *qua synolos*, etc.). The metaphysics of the unnecessary has to be investigated with care. It engages with the vulnerable realities of things that can be otherwise and aims at understanding what it means for something to be, down to its marrow, up for grabs.

Turning ontologically towards contingency

Metaphysicians have been engaging with the accidental for quite some time. Hume hinted at a world without necessary connections, Leibniz was led by Arnauld to present an account of contingent events in terms of the rest of the possible world in which they belong. Schelling explored the connection between nature and sufficient reason, Whitehead developed a philosophy of process with no room for sensible substances where the creation of agents performs the constant production of the concrete. These voices were often obliterated by the overwhelming conviction that metaphysics should either deal primarily with necessities or boil down to thin air. A possible response is to equate metaphysics with thin air and attempt to move thought away from matters of existence. Philosophers of this persuasion have made an epoch by trying to exorcise all attraction to ontological issues and to find their ways without looking into how things are. This may be called the Era of the Correlate.[6] Or rather, to use an apt phrase of Derrida's, the Age of *Hauntology*,[7] wherein ontology became no more than a specter. Such conviction forced philosophers to circumvent ontological preoccupations and find alternative ways (semantic, epistemological, textual or scientific) to deal with issues that were once considered metaphysical. Maybe this age is now over. It has nevertheless contributed to our mounting intimacy with contingency– deconstruction, analyses of knowledge and various scientific endeavors have detected how the accidental *haunts* everything that exists.

That such an age is maybe coming to an end is the importance of several *ontological turns* that have taken place in the last thirty years or so. Philosophers of many traditions have cast new eyes on metaphysical issues, increasingly less ashamed of doing so. The work of Saul Kripke opened up a new wave of metaphysical interest triggered by his account of how terms refer in modal contexts.[8] Kripke introduced the idea that something can be contingent *and also* known a priori. This has consequences for disentangling epistemic and semantic issues from those related to necessity and its absence. Kripke's work showed how there could be genuine necessity that doesn't simply arise from analytical (or conventional) definitions. He presented reference-fixing as a procedure that could be distinguished from providing a description. The subsequent analytical ontological turn[9] made frequent use of Kripke's modal framework. Meanwhile, a speculative turn[10] was gestating in less analytical traditions, introducing several new ways of approaching ontological issues and raising issues about the absolute and how to attain it.

As we will see in a moment, a great deal of speculative attention has been paid to accidents, facticity and impermanence. They are in dialogue with several developments in other areas. Anthropologists have convinced themselves that differences among peoples are to be found in the way that the non-human is part of their common life. Human cultural diversity is not always the stable site of difference – but the very way the non-human is treated and become part of the collectives is itself diverse. Anthropologists discussing this issue found themselves swimming in ontological waters: the very divide between the natural and the cultural – and the ontological and the political – is at stake when we meet people who are unlike us.[11]

Philippe Descola shows how three other dispositions concerning the non-human in its relation to human communities can be found apart from the current one embraced in modernity – where nature is the site of common physicality and humanity is the site of interiority. The site of impermanence could be not interiority, but physicality itself. Similarly, political sciences (and political projects) have brought in the realm of the non-human, partly prompted by the demands of political ecology that address the import of things often thought to be beyond the communities of humans.[12] There is no substantial nature out there, no matter the politics (or cultural devices) we contingently adopt. An important factor that prompted attention to what is beyond the human is the work of Bruno Latour, who conceives the effort of science as taking place genuinely in a realm shared by humans and other actors, in order to rethink the divide between the scientific communities and their objects of investigation.[13]

In the same vein, philosophers are called upon to rethink, from an ontological point of view, the divide between what seems substantial and what is deemed accidental, what is necessary and what is contingent, what is permanent and what is flexible. Maybe the divide itself – like that between nature and culture – is not established once and for all. In any case, the idea is to explore the ontology of the non-substantial – the non-permanent, the non-necessary. What would the world really be like if there were no substantiality – or no necessity of any sort? The task of metaphysics no longer seems to stop where the contingent starts. That there are more than substances in heaven and earth, Horatio, is now a matter of philosophical concern.

Contingency has always been on the various intellectual *menus du jour*, often appearing solely as the opposite of the absolute. Latour himself suggests that our preoccupation with how permanence and transformation intersect is universal.[14] Rather than taking the opposing pair of necessity and contingency as a starting point, he inquires into different *modes of existence*– a term he inherits from Etienne Souriau,[15] indicating the several ways in which things can exist and where substantiality (or necessity, permanence) is only one mode among others, as we'll explore below. Among these modes is *metamorphosis*, which exists as disruption and not as anything that subsists. This mode is best understood by the peoples who make room in their images of the world for things that can appear and disappear, things that are passing and whose existence is not always easily spotted. Latour claims that if we insist on stability as the sole or fundamental mode of existence, we lose contact with the things that don't subsist (examples would include crises, transitions, interruptions or climate changes, which exist only as long as they don't subsist). Latour understands permanence and stability in terms of a mode of existence that reproduces itself. He then holds that

the thing the least well distributed in the world is not reason [...] but rather the subtle elaborations invented by all the collectives to explore the crossing between the beings of reproduction and those of metamor- phosis.[16]

The contrast, therefore, between these two modes of existence is a shared preoccupation.[17] Those beings of transformation have to find room somewhere among those that subsist. They are akin to accidents, to the surprising, to what appears suddenly. We can address the non-necessary as something that exists as a spark.

The non-necessary is indeed revealing. It uncovers, at least, something about the limits of the substantial. In fact, the borders between permanence and disruption play a role in most attempts to look metaphysically at the necessary. The phrase "law-like" contrasts with "undetermined." "Principled" contrasts with "unruly." "Causal" contrasts with "casual." The accidental, in its contrast with what subsists, can inform us about how things are stable. Maybe things endure or subsist only with respect to things that don't. It is perhaps something like a Doppler effect. The frequency of a wave, Doppler noticed, changes only for an observer moving relative to its source. Change is relative to the thing that spots the change. The sound of a car passing is only heard by those standing still or moving more slowly. Perhaps, similarly, something can be other than what it is only with respect to something else that cannot, or at least not at the same pace (or in the same way). It is this contrast that is brought to light by a metaphysics of contingency; maybe it is not possible for everything to be non-necessary, or rather, for everything to be equally non-necessary. But if so, what is the (metaphysical) nature of this injunction?

I have been intentionally lax about terminology thus far. I hope to remedy this fact throughout the chapter, but a few remarks on language are now in order. I use *contingency* as a general term. It is neither contrary nor contradictory to necessity, for what contradicts *necessarily P* is clearly *possibly not-P*.[18] Rather, something contingent is neither necessary nor impossible and, therefore, lacks the weight of necessity. It contrasts with the absolute.

Impermanence, variability and accident are symptoms of the lightness we're talking about, the lightness of being that appears when, according to the *motto* made famous by Kundera's novel, *einmal ist keinmal*[19] – whatever happens just once didn't really happen, for it carries no weight.

This lightness has *spatial* symptoms – the variable, the local, the particular[20] – as much as *temporal* ones – the temporary,[21] the passing, the unstable. It also has *modal* symptoms – the peculiar, the merely actual, the accidental. We can discuss lightness in terms of lack of resilience: lack of resilience against space variations – things that become something else in a different place; lack of resilience against time changes – things that become something else with time; and lack of resilience against variation in qualities and relations – things that become something else when their qualities and relations are removed.

The contrast between substantial and accidental is key to understanding the lightness of being. The accidental lacks resilience. It doesn't subsist on its own, as will become clearer below. Another related contrast is worldly versus trans-worldly; the worldly is a denizen of a single possible world, the trans-worldly inhabits more than one possible world. The latter is often thought to point at the substratum, a *hypokeimenon* that underlies all qualities and relations.[22] Now, things can be resilient against time and yet denizens of a single world (like Leibniz's monads or Lewis's individuals); they can enjoy some sort of worldly substantiality. In contrast, Socrates may exist in worlds where there is no philosophy while being himself time-bound. These two dimensions point at two interwoven features of the metaphysical lightness we're looking at: what is contingent on time (or space) and what is contingent on qualities and relations. In fact, lightness of being appears in several formats, and it shows itself in the impermanent and in the particular as much as in the accidental and in the merely actual. In all these cases, we find an element of existential fragility.

The accidental invokes the idea of the coincidental. *Incident* comes from *cadere*, what happens (just happens) or what "falls," the way things land at random. Two or more things coincide if they fall somewhere together. A coincidence, therefore, has to do with plurality – more than one event happening at the same place or time. These events chance to fall – or to happen – together. We often find coincidences in the unplanned, when two or more things *lightly* co-occur. Accidents have a measure of the unexpected – coincidences are, in a sense, accidental.

When Hume takes all succession of events to be accidental, he asserts that any expectation we may have of that succession is merely psychological (not based in reason or experience).[23] Maurice Blanchot, who thinks of the disaster as what has been separated from its fate (*astrum*), conceives it as being out of all expectation.[24] There is no future to disaster, he says, as it is under the sovereignty of the accidental. If the future has to do with what can be expected – with what is associated to the stars that govern calendars – accidents are not in the (foreseeable) future.[25] We can at most say that, if there are accidents at all, accidents will happen. They have no place in the future, because by their nature, we cannot predict them based on the past. It is in this vein that Catherine Malabou writes, in her *Ontology of the Accident*, that such an ontology is a "philosophically difficult task: it must be acknowledged as a law […] that does not allow us to anticipate its instances."[26] She goes on to say that the law of the accident is "surprised by its own instances."

Because of this element of surprise, it might seem that knowledge (or discourse) about the accidental is impossible. In any case, even before the contemporary drive toward rethinking the contrast between what is necessary and what is not, we witnessed some systematic studies of (certain realms of) accident. Schelling famously heralded the historical sciences as starting where laws go silent: for Schelling, that which follows a necessary law, as he conceives it, is not an object of history. Nature was then taken historically by the endeavors of *Naturphilosophie*, which paved the way for evolutionist biology and was in line with Huttonian geology – both historical to the core. In both cases, what is explored is the accumulation of accidents, the development of the coincidental.

Accidents constrain each other – they help some things to happen while pre-empting others. A contingent event could be like Blanchot's disaster – surprised by its own instance – but a succession of contingent events display a connection, even if they cannot provide proper expectation (or a foreseeable future). Discourses on history – as the history of accidents – are known for explaining without predicting. They provide no covering laws, but still offer a sort of explanation, at least as much as lightness allows.

Stephen Jay Gould, in his *Wonderful Life: The Burgess Shale and the Nature of History* explores this lightness by showing how, in our narrative of the evolution of organisms, the crucial corners are accidents: unrepeatable both in time and in the closest possible worlds.[27] Manuel Delanda studies how geological, biological and linguistic histories have interacted in the last thousand years on Earth, plotting the history of the planet.[28] He shows how indeterminacies mix together into a concatenation that, while being more than a series of random independent events, is less than a determined trajectory where each event falls as the previous event ordained. Contingencies coincide to weave a plot that make some events more likely than others. The weaving is triggered by the sheer accumulation of accidents, as twigs shape into a nest. This unveils something about contingencies: lightness somehow builds up toward a sort of gravity.

To look at this lightness is to look at something elusive. The metaphysics of the accidental has a family resemblance to that of the *je ne sais quoi* that Jankélevitch endeavored to bring about.[29] In fact, philosophers have often tried directly or indirectly to engage with that which lacks solidity and seems to be approachable only on tiptoe. That is why this book tries to address a metaphysics of contingency from different angles. It looks for alternative ways to see the contrast between that which carries necessity and that which doesn't. The lightness of being contrasts with what comes necessarily, for it is precisely what exists only by the skin of its teeth, not consolidated but lying open, exposed to the elements.

The dismissal of necessary connections

When Hume exorcised necessary connections from an image of the world constructed around experience (aided by analytical judgments about matters of reason), he brought back the specter of a Heraclitean image of the sensible that Aristotle had put aside, and the message rapidly spread that there was no longer any business for metaphysics. Hume saw matters of fact as lacking any necessary connection or substantiality, or possibly any modality at all. Among matters of fact, he said, things *just happen;* there are nothing but actual events. In this actualist picture of the world, necessary connections are alien to a realm of inert distinct objects and qualities. They have to be found elsewhere, for this is a realm where no event necessarily follows any other. The coupling of objects and qualities with necessity requires alien elements like human observers trained by events they perceive as displaying succession, concomitance or commonality. These observers are affected by the repetition of events – whatever is necessary is necessary solely to them. They introduce necessity into a realm of pure actuality. Metaphysics cannot be about the sensible, about matters of fact alone. It could perhaps be about matters of fact coupled with their observers, but then necessary connections migrate from ontology to psychology.

Kant felt the need to look for necessities somewhere else, if they couldn't be found in the sensible. His move was to resolutely reject any appeal to psychological needs, habits or instincts and rather find some sort of rational basis for what we perceive as necessary connections in the world. He looked at how our concepts intrinsically and necessarily respond to norms and thus make binding necessity – invoked by duties and obligations – replace the appeal to a necessity that is taken to be true in the world, the so-called alethic necessity. His insight was that metaphysics could be built on normative necessity, which itself is (at least sufficiently) universal, instead of postulating necessary connections in the world. In so doing, he attempted to regain the lost substantiality not in the supra-sensible but rather in the infra-sensible, the transcendental. Substances are not sensible, but we can find substantiality among the concepts that make the sensible possible. Kant then heralded a revamped metaphysics postulating no necessity in the world. The idea seemed to be: metaphysics must go where necessity is – if necessity is nowhere, metaphysics should be abandoned; if it dwells in concepts, metaphysics should revolve around a description of how concepts operate.

In the last few centuries of hauntology, many philosophers have explored ways of abandoning metaphysics, only to find several pitfalls and red herrings. In fact, the Humean challenge (and the ensuing Kantian response) alters the landscape where metaphysics had its place and makes the end of metaphysics a tempting possibility. A less-explored response to the challenge is to rethink the ties between metaphysics and necessary connections between concrete things. There are at least two strategies, then. First, one can posit that there are *necessarily* no necessary connections. In the same vein, one can say that, *necessarily*, nothing is substantial. There may be something inherent in the structure of concrete things that make substances or necessary connections impossible. If so, metaphysics would look at necessary *principles* instead of necessary things or relations among things. This would be a metaphysical (or maybe speculative[30]) explanation of why and how, as is written everywhere in Lars von Trier's *Antichrist*, *chaos reigns* – or rather, why and how the lightness of being is itself not accidental, capricious or light. Necessity is necessarily absent, and it matters why this absence is necessary. This book, by contrast, intends to address the issue of sensible contingencies head on, relying neither on a general principle nor on an ultimate absolute. A second strategy is to stop treating the contrast between what is necessary and what is not as a primordial divide, a structuring stricture of all metaphysical horizons, a privileged vocabulary central to all things ontological.

Maybe the divide can itself be illuminated, if we stop taking it as the starting point. Contingencies can be approached as basic, as ontological primitives. This book is an attempt to move in this direction. It tries to find ways to think about that which is up for grabs without using necessity as a fixed metronome. It makes use of images not oriented by a contrast with necessity while keeping an eye on how the absence of necessary connections (and of substantiality) sheds light on the lightness of being. It seeks to understand what is not contingent in terms of what is up for grabs – and not the other way around. Meillassoux argued that a factual world admits of apparent law-like events by exorcizing the charge of a cosmic coincidence – that would leave regularities unexplained.[31] His exorcism involved appealing to the difference between what is under judgments of probability and what is not. Regular events are not under such judgments, and therefore there is no sense in saying that only miracles can explain them. This book provides a different solution for a slightly different problem. Facticity itself is elaborated, so that the verdict is not merely that hyperchaos reigns. Further, what is regular is accounted not in terms of the scope of probability arguments, but rather in terms of a metaphysics of what is up for grabs.

Hume himself may have indicated ways in which this can be done. In a world of contingencies, habits are built from actual repetition that has an impact on what is affected by it. Repetition creates permanence in the eye of the beholder. Indeed, repetition could be enough to emulate much of what is ascribed to necessity. Repetition and expectation form a matrix very different from that formed by the necessary and the contingent. I explore this matrix below in a rhythm-oriented ontology (see chapter 5).

Humean actualism is driven by a temptation to equate the real with the actual. There are no real connections but the non-necessary ones. Actualism is sometimes understood in opposition to dispositionalism[32] – the idea that there are tendencies, capacities, potentialities in the world. Actualism postulates a world without powers, without tendencies, without capacities. Interestingly, here there is no room for contingency, because everything is equally contingent; the actualist world is modally flat. Indeed, Humeans think of actuality as a thin layer composed only of what happens. However, it can also be conceived as something denser, encompassing a tectonics between multiple strata. We can approach a multilayered actuality through Aristotle's distinction between a first and second actuality.[33] First actuality is related to capacities or abilities one is not exercising – like knowing a language one is not speaking at the moment – while second actuality appears when an ability or capacity is exercised. Potentiality underlies these actualities – second potentiality is a capacity to acquire a capacity, while first potentiality coincides with second actuality. This gives us three layers; the top two are layers of actuality. Such a tectonics can be understood in different ways. It gives rise to tendencies and dispositions as much as to finks and antidotes, understood as actual events that prevent some capacities to be ever exercised.[34] We can think of muscle strength that is never exercised – never put to work, if we think of Aristotle's word *en-ergeia*, often translated as 'actuality'.

We can also include a tectonics of *urge*. An urge, like a capacity or ability, is actual and can be found in the pressure of a tree root against a road or in the drive of sugar to melt in water. It can be contained or diverted into something else, but it does exert an influence on the course of events. Urges are not necessities, but events can be explained in terms of urges created by other events.[35] As with tectonic plates, the movement of events creates new urges that will make other things happen. Urges are products of accumulated tension built up by events, and simultaneously, they are what fuels events, what provokes things to happen. Lightness of being appears in the absence of any urges; on the other hand, an accumulation of a critical mass of light events can generate urges. A multilayered actuality is a way to understand what is light as what is not under gravity – as *out of the blue*. To be sure, the very presence of enough things from out of the blue generates some weight, as the mere assembling of a number of people walking in a crossroad would require some of them to change their path.

Three speculative accounts of contingency

To start broadening the metaphysical horizon of contingency, I will briefly sketch three recent speculative perspectives. The recent speculative turn has pulled the discussion, whether directly or indirectly, toward the insubstantiality and contingency of things. Some of the ideas guiding several of these thinkers, such as immanence and flat ontology – about which we will talk later in this introduction – revolve around how to conceive of being as light. This is why I see these perspectives as accounts of what it is to be up for grabs. What is interesting for our purposes here is that these three speculative perspectives are not often thought to be compatible with each other, yet they all capture elements of what contingency may be. This book enters into dialogue with these accounts because we are exploring ways to think about being up for grabs, and because this book dwells in speculation.

Speculation. These three recent perspectives are speculative in the sense that they share a method or procedure that can be traced back to Alfred North Whitehead. For him, speculation is a procedure to expand what is known or experienced. It proceeds by taking a starting point – a discovered or established particular – as an example of something larger, more general, closer to the universal. To speculate is to enhance general knowledge by using particular items of knowledge as tools. According to an image put forward by Whitehead in the opening pages of *Process and Reality*, speculation is

> like the flight of an airplane. It starts from the ground of particular observations; it makes a flight in the thin air of imaginative generalization; and it again lands for renewed observation rendered acute by rational interpretation. [...] The success [...] is always to be tested by the applicability of its results beyond the restricted locus from which it originated. [...] In other words, some synoptic vision has to be gained.[36]

When Whitehead extends the subjective forms associated with the Cartesian *cogito* beyond the realm of the mental, he is engaged in a speculative flight. Whitehead praises high flights over those that simply look over the airport runway. Importantly, he notices that speculation is always at risk of excessive ambition, which should lead not to more caution but rather to frequent self-correction. Speculative results are not all true, but whenever they are self-corrected (by other philosophical systems), they elicit some grains of truth. Whitehead says that speculative philosophers "do what they can in the way of systematization, and in the event achieve something. The proper test is not of finality, but of progress."[37] In that sense as well, this book is a speculative exercise. It tries to broaden the particulars we know about what is up for grabs so that we can view the issue through a wider lens.

The first speculative perspective on contingency I would like to mention comes from Whitehead himself, and from the so-called philosophy of process. There has recently been a remarkable surge in interest in both Whitehead and process philosophy in general.[38] I take the central idea in terms of processes: reality itself is nothing but the processes that sustain it. This is an idea put forward not only by Whitehead's notion of organism but also by Gilbert Simondon's notions of transduction and meta-stability,[39] Souriau's notion of *instauration*,[40] and Latour's conception of gradients of resistance.[41] The reality of anything can only be explained in terms the processes that make it possible – there are no ultimate principles that are out of the reach of existing processes. Nothing is separate from the processes that maintain it; maintenance is typically not internal to a thing but rather dependent on something external. There are no substances *causa sui*, but rather the model of being is what after Souriau, calls "being-as-other".[42] As a consequence, being is always in the hands of the processes that maintain it – it relies on the rest of the world. There are no permanent (concrete) things; something sensible can be permanent only if it is sponsored[43] to be so by external processes.

Simondon's diagnosis is that Aristotle was wrong when he claimed that conceiving sensible substances was the only alternative to Heraclitus's view of matters of fact as in flux. Meta-stability – the idea that bits of the flux stabilize others – is an alternative to both the stability of substances and the unruliness of flux. Substances are replaced by something else – called actual entities, or actors, or even monads (see chapter 1 below) – that are what they are only while relevant sustaining processes are taking place. Nothing is either destined or disposed to last over time – everything is simply actual, existing only while sponsored. Whitehead conceives his actual entities to be basic, but they are concrete things constantly becoming other actual entities under the influence of other, contemporary actual entities. To trace what becomes concrete – in his words, to trace the routes of concrescence – one has to focus on actual entities and their actions. Latour prefers to look at things as relative to tests of resistance – any actor can dissolve into a network of actors given sufficiently stringent tests of resistance that makes its unity collapse, and analogously, a network can act as a unit given less stringent tests of resistance. In any case, it is subsistence that needs to be explained, because substantiality – that some things tend to subsist – is not taken for granted.

Process philosophy has no room for either substantiality or for necessary connections. Nothing exists by itself or without the concourse of a (concrete) sponsor. This doesn't mean that each actual entity – or each actor – is under no determination. Necessary connections are replaced by maintained connections – and these need sponsors. Substantiality is replaced by enforced subsisting. This move, championed by Simondon, is an indispensable tool for a metaphysics of contingency. Not that anything goes, nor that nothing holds, but rather that there is a cost for things to be as they are – a worldly cost. (Simondon's word is *allagmatics*, which comes from the Greek *alagma*, a word that translates into English as "costs.")

Lightness of being, process-philosophy style, is something akin to what Sartre called *pour soi* – that which does not have an essence preceding its existence. In fact, in his analysis of bad faith, he takes it to be double-edged: we deceive ourselves by treating ourselves as transcendent as much as by treating ourselves as objects of pure will, not shaped by facticity.[44] Similarly, actual entities are light not because anything can happen to them but rather because they escape both substantiality and pure flux. Interestingly, Sartre talks about a transcendence-facticity meta-stability – bad faith is found both in not recognizing ourselves as our own sponsors and in taking ourselves to be our only sponsors.[45] Process philosophy can be regarded as coming from this kind of speculative step: from the meta-stability of human consciousness to the sponsored character of all connections. Latour captures this last idea through his principle of irreduction.[46] It states that nothing is in itself either reducible or irreducible to anything else. Anything can be reduced or taken to be peculiar or irreducible, but either way, there is a cost – there is a process behind it. In other words, someone or something has to go through the process of reducing one thing to another. Exorcising reducibility (and irreducibility) is itself a way to approach a world without necessary connections – nothing boils down to anything necessarily, and if a reduction is available, it is provided (or sponsored) by something else. All reductions (and irreductions) are contingent on something.

The second speculative perspective on contingency is the idea of a principle of unreason or insufficient reason. Sufficient reason is often taken to be what swings things toward a given state of affairs. A principle of insufficient reason holds that nothing swings anything toward any state of affairs. Meillassoux defends this principle as necessary; he also calls the principle *facticity*.[47] He holds that, necessarily, there are no necessary connections. Things are not contingent on other things, but rather they are unmoved by anything and therefore can be consistently one way or another. Philosophy, he says, has been trapped by correlationism – the idea that there is no way out of the correlation between a subject and the world, that we cannot *access* anything beyond such correlation or perhaps even *think* beyond it. Starting from Hume's criticisms of necessary connections, Meillassoux advocates that a world without them is a world without any form of sufficient reason for anything. Kant's reaction to Hume was to recoil upon an environment determined by the correlation between thought and world. Such correlation displays a primacy over anything else we can access (and therefore taints every access) and a facticity, as they are simply matters of fact, no correlation is necessary. These are two features of correlations – they can neither be dismissed, nor treated as absolute, as necessary.

Meillassoux applies the speculative method not to correlations themselves but to their facticity. This is crucial, because it parts ways with process philosophy: through a speculative procedure performed on correlation itself, correlation is made absolute. Process philosophy therefore betrays the lessons of correlationism, because no correlation –

human or otherwise – is to be taken as a necessary piece in the furniture of the universe. Meillassoux's alternative speculative step – beginning in the facticity enjoyed by any correlation, according to the lessons of correlationism – enables him to justify his principle of unreason. Everything is necessarily up for grabs, except that very principle. The principle of unreason is, therefore, the only absolute that speculative reason can attain. It follows that a principle guarantees the contingency of things. Things are not factual because they are left to their own devices with nothing sustaining them; they are made contingent by a necessary principle.

Meillassoux's unpublished manuscript *The Divine Inexistence*[48] contains further contributions to the philosophy of contingency. He makes explicit some of the consequences of his principle of unreason – especially the eventual birth of God and a subsequent advent of a "World of Justice." The advent of God changing everything in the world can happen at any moment and we can hope for it because, everything being factial, nothing prevents it. The principle of facticity runs above the eventual advent of God and cannot be overruled by no fact in the world – including the advent of God. Meillassoux explores the possibility that God is not a necessary being under which everything is contingent – God can render necessary truths false – but rather that God himself is under a principle of facticity. Facticity is not up for grabs, not even God can dispel it. Meillassoux takes it to be absolute, a genuine *anarchiste couronné*, a guarantor that nothing else will prevail. Facticity is the very fabric of things. Through it, Matter was followed by Life, Life by Reason – each one forming what he calls a World – and Reason can be followed by Justice. The lightness of being is what makes things emerge – it acts as a transcendent principle that imposes itself on everything.

After Whitehead and Meillassoux, the final speculative perspective on contingency I will mention for now is the appeal to a history of light beings. Iain Hamilton Grant has used the sciences of the accidental, mentioned above, to establish a speculative image of layers of contingency.[49] He draws on Schelling's image of natural history to place nature as the home of the undetermined, and he says that it cannot be approached without taking its layers into consideration. It is like a floor, it grounds and it keeps track of what it has grounded through the marks that constitute it. Further, it is not an ultimate, necessary layer that grounds all the others, but merely actual layers that hold all the others. There are sufficient reasons in these layers – not necessary connections, but elements that lead the state of affairs to lean one way or another. For Grant, nature itself is the principle of sufficient reason. There is no reason to be found anywhere but in nature and its history. Nature is subject to a tectonics where each layer depends on the previous one. Contingency is not a principle that assures the lightness of everything, nor something that is itself up for grabs, but rather an embodiment of nature. To be natural – which amounts to being sensible – is to exist under the embodied principle of sufficient reason, the very stuff of which every ontogenesis is made.

Such an embodied principle – of sufficient reason – makes a contrast with the other two speculative perspectives. Grant appeals to the unconditioned (Schelling's *Unbedingt*) – which is both the unconstrained and what is not a thing – as a general framework for contingency. Nature itself is therefore substantial and, as the unconditioned, it is not sponsored by anything – except itself. It is substantial, albeit ever-changing and built on non-necessities. In this sense, we are closer to Meillassoux's principle of facticity than to process philosophy. However, unlike speculative facticity, this perspective takes the lightness of being to have a genetic element. Any (concrete) ontogenesis – the coming to being of things, relations or events – takes place within nature, where all contingencies have left their mark. Grant explores the line from Meillassoux's position to his own endorsement of nature as sufficient reason. He comments on Meillassoux's thesis that contingency is the only necessity, according to which there is no single reason for what exists and how it exists. Apparently denial of the Principle of Sufficient Reason, Meillassoux's claim is in fact expressly designed to satisfy it, albeit paradoxically. Yet the character of the question is irrevocably altered if it is asked what grounds any particular satisfaction of the principle; or again, as Meillassoux notes, what necessitates contingency in nature. Now this recursivity or regress might be held to afflict any putative satisfaction of the Principle of Sufficient Reason; but it indicates that although the Principle [...] is logically satisfied, it is not, nor can it be, really or materially satisfied by reason alone.[50]

Natural history is a series of accidents that disfigures whatever is taken to be particular substances. However, it is, crucially, a series. The principle of facticity is untenable without appeal to sufficient reason, because any facticity originates in facts of nature. There is a fully historical place where things happen, and there is no reason beyond it. Being up for grabs is being open to history, because the up for grabs is fully at home in the aggregate of layered contingencies that makes up nature.

Communitas and immunization

Being up for grabs is related to an expression frequently used by Bataille: *mettre en jeu*.[51] This phrase could be interpreted as meaning to put at risk, or rather to dare or to go beyond one's own will to subsist or conserve. Daring, in this sense, is the opposite of protecting and therefore of maintaining something that subsists. It can be thought of as going beyond substance, or beyond what subsists. Bataille would have it that the serf is someone who prefers not to *mettre en jeu* her life – would prefer to conserve it, and by doing so engages in a relation of subservience in order to be immune to threats on her life. Serfdom appears as a device where one's life is preserved in exchange for some service – for the performance of some task, some duty. Looking beyond life, facing death on its face, one reaches beyond serfdom by a *mise en jeu* of one's preservation. Such *mise en jeu* contrasts with immunity: to take risks is to be affected and not protected.

Roberto Esposito explores the difference between connection and independence in terms of *communitas* and *immunitas*.[52] His purpose is to analyze associations and how external ties constitute individuals. His work is based on the Latin etymological origin of both these words – *munus* (or *munia*). *Munus* translates to "task" or "law," or rather to "duty," in the sense of binding obligation. It is not about any non-constitutive relation, but about a binding necessity, something akin to a law that is intrinsic to something communal. It is about ties that constitute an individual as dependent on something else. To be in a community, Esposito stresses, means already to be bound by a law that makes sure the community members provide a *munus*. *Communitas* is something reciprocal, intrinsically capable of both affecting and being affected. *Munus* is a two-way road: its law requires something from both parts. If someone is in a community, she has duties over others and others have duties toward her.

By contrast, to be immune is to be out of the scope of any *munus*. Someone is immune if no *munus*, no reciprocal lawful duty, applies to her. To be immune is to be out of the scope of a community. Typically, this means not being affected by the community, being out of reach, because there is no *binding* law making the connection. Immunity means not having to be affected by the community – it therefore spells detachment, independence and indifference toward what takes place elsewhere. To be out of the reach of a community is to be free of any binding interference from it, and also to be closed to it.

Esposito's remarks about the difference between community and immunity – and about the process of immunization, through which someone gains the means to subsist on her own – are addressed to biopolitical issues concerning common life. Now, although they are framed as pertaining to human associations, these categories can illuminate issues concerning modal ontology, in particular ascriptions of necessity and contingency. I believe they can be applied to any association whatsoever, as there is an ontological dimension to *communitas* and *immunitas*. Consider how Gabriel Tarde understood societies in general: non-human beings such as bees – but also molecules, stars and even objects in general – form societies with different degrees of internal cohesion.[53] Cohesion will soon prove relevant to an ontology of contingency: whenever there is a great degree of cohesion, we can say that things are contingent on each other's existence. Objects, events, relations and qualities can be intrinsically at the mercy of others – and hence under the effect of a *munus*.

On the other hand, if they are somehow untouchable then they are immune to anything else. To be sure, something can be immune to others and have an effect on them, but such effects are not bound by reciprocity. The effect would therefore not be affected by any (temporal or modal) difference in the community. If something is immune to everything – say, a principle or a necessary connection – it is not under any influence and, if it interferes with something else, it does so irrespective of what is under its influence. It would interfere in whatever is under its scope. It is not sensible to any difference in the community it can affect, and is not up for grabs.[54] Indeed, the contrast between community and immunity unveils some features about the lightness of being. While *communitas* involves openness to others, necessity – and necessary connections – seems to have something important to do with immunity. Something is necessary if it affects things while not being affected by them (and not being affected by the way it affects things). Necessity seems, in fact, to be close to indifference, to unreachability. But notice that only what is under a necessity is immune: what imposes the necessity is not immune. In order for something to impose necessity – provided that it doesn't do so out of necessity – a certain freedom of action is required. A non-necessary start, as we will see in the next chapter, is one that could have been otherwise. As such, it can be affected and is exposed to the elements – it is up for grabs. This is a central issue for the purposes of this book: what is up for grabs contrasts with what is immune. It can be affected.

To gain more intuition into how close necessity is to *immunitas*, I'll consider some simple examples where we ordinarily distinguish cases of necessity and non-necessity. I'll make oversimplifying assumptions that will ignore, for the moment, the bite of Quine's criticisms of the analytic-synthetic duality and its consequences for a distinction between facts and meanings.[55] Consider these two sentences:

1. A triangle has three angles adding up to 180 degrees, and
2. Adam has sinned.

The first is ordinarily taken to be necessary, while the second is not. Now, 1 is independent of any fact (except, of course, facts about how to define triangles or how to measure degrees, but we are assuming the fact/meaning divide that Quine appropriately criticized). Sentence 2, on the other hand, depends on facts about the serpent, Eve, the apple tree, God, and all sorts of other things about Eden (and beyond). Sentence 1 can be taken as a fact immune to the influence of any other fact in the world – it doesn't depend on the color, the texture or the components of any triangle. It also affects triangles irrespective of their color, texture or composition. It is thought to be necessary because it is thought not to be up for grabs, to be unreachable, so that nothing can change it. An epistemological consequence of this is that no fact about our empirical knowledge – no way of carving the world or measuring quantities – will affect our acceptance of it. Interestingly, one of Quine's points can be rendered like this: our belief in Sentence 1 (or our capacity to safely commit to Sentence 1) is not really immune. Rather, we immunize it by protecting it from the verdict of a tribunal of experience that can impose beliefs on us only to the extent that they don't affect Sentence 1. In other words, the verdict of experience is such that it can be deflected so as not to hit Sentence 1. There is a protective veil around it that needs to be maintained – its immunity requires sponsors. Quine's image is that we place Sentence 1 in the center of a sphere whose edges touch experience, and we protect Sentence 1 from being revised by experience by making the verdict challenge instead whatever we have placed closer to the edge of the sphere.[56] It is a process of immunization.

On the other hand, Sentence 2 is often taken not to be a necessary but rather a contingent matter of fact. That Adam sinned was once up for grabs by the serpent, Eve, or whomever else. There is no immunity, no unreachability. I choose this example because it comes from Leibniz, especially in his correspondence with Arnauld.[57] Leibniz argues that Sentence 2 is tied to the rest of the world by a modality that he understands as co-possibility – Adam is tied to sin by the world in which he is. Therefore, Leibniz emphasizes, God doesn't create an Adam who is a sinner, but rather He creates a world where Adam has sinned – not an immune fact, but something that was in a community with everything else in its world.[58] The creation was of a community, and not of isolated, unreachable facts.

Deleuze in his book *The Fold*, echoing a movement already present in *Difference and Repetition*, makes use of a notion of virtuality connected to contingency.[59] Something is virtual when it depends on everything else in the world – for example, that metal expands when heated depends on several other contributing factors; it is only when we take it in isolation from everything else that we can say it is the case. Most laws of physics depend on supporting conditions (i.e., atmospheric states, gravitation, friction, etc.); they are virtual and therefore often only strictly true in lab conditions.[60] The virtual is contingent upon many things, just as "Adam sins" is, for Leibniz, contingent upon the (rest of the) world. We can then reckon that knowledge of the virtual is always tentative, as it depends on knowing everything else, which is unlikely. Knowing something virtual is not enough to make predictions, unless they involve *ceteris paribus* conditions. This is a way to link the contingent, the virtual – what lacks in *immunitas* – on one side and *a posteriori* knowledge on the other.

Indeed, *a posteriori* knowledge is typically regarded as revisable. It relies on experience and, as such, it gathers information from particular events and occurrences. Before Kripke established the possibility of necessities *a posteriori*, empirical knowledge was generally considered to be knowledge of contingencies, and therefore only applicable to things that are accidental.[61] Accordingly metaphysics, understood as an endeavor about the necessary, could not rely on any empirical knowledge. To the measure that it attains contingency, *a posteriori* knowledge is knowledge of virtualities. I know that the sun will rise tomorrow, but only based on my expectation, which can be met with disappointment from any corner of the world. Something I am not aware of can change the movement of the planets: an asteroid, a distant celestial body, a cosmic phenomenon, a God or even a Mallarméan throw of the dice, which Meillassoux interprets as an episode of his own concept of hyperchaos. In any case, something else affected the rising of the sun; it is not immune to everything. It is up for grabs.

The so-called knowledge of necessary truths (if we disregard Kripkean *a posteriori* necessities for a bit longer) is knowledge of a content that nothing can affect. Logical (and semantical or analytical) truths are thought to be truths that nothing can overcome. If we attain them, nothing can affect our knowledge; it is knowledge of something fully immune to all facts, and that knowledge is fully immune itself. From a Humean point of view, these immune pieces of knowledge are about matters of reason, knowledge of which no fact can interfere with and no tide of randomness can disrupt. Except, of course, Meillassoux's facticity – but then, of course, Meillassoux claims that nothing but his principle of facticity displays full immunity. *Immunitas* is missing in anything up for grabs. To know something with *immunitas*, if it is possible at all, is to know something distinct and apart from the rest of the world, knowledge that stands alone. Because it is about something independent from anything else, it is sheltered, protected from erosion by facts.

The vocabulary of *immunitas* and *communitas* has an important feature that can help us understand contingency. It admits of degrees: something can be more immune than something else. We might say, for example, that Sentence 1 above is more immune than Sentence 2. To accommodate lessons from Quine about no fact grounding the distinction between matters of fact and matters of reason, we might say that Sentence 1, taken as a sentence or a belief, is immunized by language-users who protect it from easy revision via experience. Similarly, we can consider Kripkean *a posteriori* necessities such as:

3. The morning star is the evening star.

It surely depends on the way the reference of "morning star" and "evening star" is fixed. Given what we refer to with these terms, Sentence 3 is, according to Kripke, a necessary fact. It is immune to anything except changes in the ways the terms denote. The notion of immunity can provide, in this case as in others, a fine-grained way to determine what facts and propositions are contingent upon. Necessity can be taken as a matter of degree, as Paul Churchland among others has suggested analyticity should be treated.[62] Things are contingent upon some things but not upon others. If we find a way to fix the denotation of the terms in Sentence 3, we immunize Sentence 3 from anything else. If "morning star" refers to Phosphorus and "evening star" to Phosphorus, they are the same, come what may.

Immunization is a procedure by means of which something is protected from (some) risks; it is made more secure by the provision that whatever elements are doing the immunizing endure. Degrees of immunity can be conceived in terms of *instauration*, as an effect of sponsors. We can also think of them in terms of meta-stability: something is meta-stable if it is not immune in itself but it is immunized by something else. Degrees of immunity, the vocabulary of *communitas* notwithstanding, can also be seen in terms of brute likelihoods; something is more immune if it is simply less likely to change (or not to repeat itself), independent of any other fact or event in the world. In any case, relative immunity is a way to deal with lightness of being as a quantity. It also fits into the Doppler effect analogy drawn above: things can be more or less contingent with respect to a reference element. The more contingent something is, the less strongly it is tied to what it is; it follows the trends. We can understand to what degree it is up in the air and to what degree it stands on its own in terms of immunity.

Substances and substrata can both also be understood in terms of immunity. The former are sometimes taken to be what subsists in time, while the latter are what subsists when qualities and relations are removed – what subsists when moved to another possible world. The former is trans-temporal, the latter trans-worldly. Substances are whatever is immune to the passing of time. They keep their identities, immune to change. Events occur without affecting the substance, which is sheltered and resists whatever happens. Thus, the substance of a wooden chair is constant, no matter its changes in color. Substrata are whatever is immune to qualities and relations and their possible changes. The wooden chair would keep the same substratum if it had a different color altogether. A substratum, accordingly, is what often makes something retain its identity in different possible worlds. Thanks to a substratum immune to any properties, a particular is the same no matter what universally applicable predications it acquires. It is immune because it lies under any of its properties – a *hypokeimenon*. As I mentioned above, Leibniz's substances have no substrata; they are worldly, even though they subsist in time. There is something in each monad that is immune to events while attached to a particular world.

The same distinction can be drawn concerning relations. Some relations are trans-temporal and subsist no matter what accompanies them. Causal relations are often thought to be substantial in this sense – and it is arguable that this was primarily the target of Hume's attacks. We can say, nevertheless, that "metal expands when heated" is a virtuality that endures through changes in time, even if it does not hold in all possible worlds. It may be contingent upon the rest of the world, but if it stands as a virtuality, it resists changes in time; it is at least strongly immunized.

Other relations are trans-worldly and subsist in all possible worlds. These are thought to be logical (and sometimes semantical) necessities like Sentence 1 above or *a posteriori* necessities like Sentence 3. They are immune to circumstances – or at least immunized to their effects. The difference between these two types of immunized relations – we can call them substantial and *substrating* relations – is the crux of the difference that Kit Fine defends between natural and metaphysical necessity.[63] Natural necessity, like substantial relations, is typically worldly, while metaphysical necessity holds in all possible worlds. Kripkeans tend to suspect that at least some natural necessities – some laws, for example – are metaphysical necessities discovered empirically. Fine argues that this can sometimes occur, but he doesn't generalize. In any case, we can understand the distinction in terms of *immunitas*: relations that are only immunized against travels through time and those that are further immunized against travels through the world.[64]

Being up in the air

It is clear by now that lightness of being, even apart from whether it is a matter of degrees, admits of modes. Something can be up for grabs, for example, if compared with an immunized substance or if compared only with an immunized substratum. As there are varieties and modes of necessity, there are corresponding types of non-necessity. Further, as we will see, there is a lightness of being that doesn't fit into the contrast with necessity. For our main purpose in this book, we will look at the contrast to find out what makes it hold. One piece of this jigsaw puzzle is the notion of self-abandonment – being in something else's hands. (We will see below how this notion is related to Plato's rejection of the Parmenidean idea that to be at all is to be substantial.) Self-abandonment means that something is not specially protected by its own nature but rather *mise en jeu*. Rainer Maria Rilke, in the letters from Muzot[65] rendered famous among philosophers by Heidegger's commentaries[66], depicts it well:

> [...] Nature gives other creatures over
> to the venture of their dim delight
> and in soil and branchwork grants none special cover [...].[67]

In Rilke's image, nature leaves its creations up for grabs, not giving them any special cover against the ventures he mentions. Rilke continues by saying that our nature doesn't give us any special cover against risk, either. It is not that we are forsaken by something external; it is rather a case of self-abandonment, a theme that Rilke explored for example in his *Duino Elegies*, where he talks about the *Verlassenen – the forsaken*. Heidegger has also elaborated it under the category of *Verlassenheit* – a sort of solitude of being but also a lack of protection. Heidegger talks about the opposition between *cura*, that which needs care, and *sine cura*, that which does not – that which is secure.⁶⁸ Security relates to immunity, while the insecure requires (sponsoring) care to continue being what it is. It is not especially protected by something like a substance or a necessary connection; it rather requires care of what is abandoned. There is, nonetheless, another element to *Verlassenheit* – it points at a tonality of inertia. Even without care – without, say, the work of its sponsors – a forsaken being can carry on, in sheer availability. Something can persist in a fragile state, abandoned, vulnerable and up for grabs. This is why mortality falls within the horizon of what doesn't subsist on its own.⁶⁹ It involves a measure of being up in the air.

There is a dimension to *immunitas* of not being exposed, of being closed, locked in and somehow protected. When something is fully determined, it is protected, sheltered, immunized. Substances (and substrata, necessary connections) display a kind of aloofness where nothing around them matters – for they are *causa sui*. Lack of *immunitas*, by contrast, comes with this openness, this exposure to the elements and this measure of availability that Rilke is considering. Being light is being at something else's disposal, as if there were a weight that could not be carried on one's own. Too light to persist, and yet persisting. Indeed, if we take immunity as a protection, whatever is not immune displays a sort of availability, a being left to the world. Up in the air.⁷⁰ Things left available are unsecured, like something that was thrown away and has nothing holding it. It is being in the *Offene* – the Open– that Rilke also often refers to in his poems.⁷¹ To be in the Open is to be in a state of availability where there are no ontological locks or fences. Whatever exists in the Open co-exists – being there is being *in* co-existence. Therefore, nothing in the Open has a fixed, inborn upper hand. It is a realm of what Jonathan Schaffer calls priority nihilism: nothing is metaphysically prior to anything else.⁷² We can put it in terms of government, of *arché*: what is at other things' disposal is not under anything else in particular; nothing *governs* it and therefore everything *can* govern it.

This being up in the air, with its openness or availability and this sense of being thrown into the world, can also be said to constitute a space of interdependence. Things are abandoned if anything can take control over them. An ontology of contingent things is akin to what Manuel DeLanda calls a *flat ontology*: the elements of the world differ in spatio-temporal scale but not in ontological status.⁷³ The absence of necessary connection leads to an open world, with no priorities or differences in ontological status to shape a previously structured landscape. This flat space where things are equally at stake turns up in many accounts of contingency. Tristan Garcia crafts a *plan d'égalité* – a plane of equality – where things are present not as what they are but rather because they all harbor a *n'importe quoi* – no matter what – that enables everything to be something else.[74] This plane is a surface on which all things are at the same footing.

The notion recalls many aspects of what Deleuze and Guattari termed the *plane of immanence*, a plane where all different plans are executed.[75] The plane is like an ontological street everything has to pass along in order to do its business. While in the street, it is exposed to the elements.[76] The upshot here is that everything has to go through a space of contingencies in order to be what it is. In order to have an effect on the world, a thing must become available in order to be affected. The lesson can be explored in many ways – and it will throughout the book. In any case, to be thrown into the world – into the sensible, concrete world – is to be thrown among the accidents. Even a substance has to dwell in accidents if it is to reach the realm of concreta. It is as if anything must first meet the force of contingencies before it can affect the sensible – either Plato's intelligible substances play no part (*metexis*) in concrete things or they come down corrupted by accidents. The pull of these accidents is the scope of an ontology of *Verlassenheit*.

Automaton

Another dimension of contingency has to do with what is not subsumed, what is not under anything else. The not-subsumed is what contrasts with what is in serfdom – and therefore is *mise en jeu*. Considering necessity in terms of subsumption makes explicit the political character of the ontological discussions concerning contingency – what is under a government is also protected, put in security, safeguarded because it is governed (as chapter 2 explores). Thinking in terms of *arché*, what is not (especially) protected is not subsumed. It follows that what is thrown into the world is left to its own devices. Something is light if it doesn't have the pull of a determination immunizing it from further interferences, but by the same token, something is light because it is not determined. This double-aspect character of contingency can be seen more clearly if we think of it in terms of the ungoverned. Something ungoverned has to fend for itself – it is not immunized, not *sine cura* – and at the same time it is left unruled, without *arché*.

In Book Z of the *Metaphysics*, Aristotle considers how substances are generated out of other substances and says that such transformation (*gignomenon*) can take place due to *physis*, to *techné* or to *automaton*.[77] This last is a very interesting word – it is sometimes translated as "chance," sometimes as "spontaneity"; things can be generated by chance or spontaneously.[78] *Automaton* is also the origin of the automatic; indeed, sometimes we consider that which is not controlled to be automatic. According to Aristotle, whatever is not generated by nature or manufactured by people is brought up by something, not subsumed by anything else. It is planned neither by manufacture nor by a natural process – therefore, it happens in an ungoverned manner. Excluded from the produce of nature and manufacture, it is an accident.

The word *automaton* points at processes that are either indeterminate (associated with chance) or self-determined (associated with spontaneity). We can indeed draw a line between things that are self-governed, and therefore autonomous, and things that are thoroughly under no government, and therefore in anomy. For some reason, Aristotle clusters together what seems to be two different cases. It is interesting to notice that something that is generated by *automaton* is somehow originated *motu proprio*, that is, without an external need. What seems to be important for Aristotle is that those *gignomenon* are not ruled either by *physis* or by *techné* – these external bodies do not govern them. In any case, there is no heteronomy, either by humans or by nature – nothing governs the *automaton*, even though it can be susceptible to interference from elsewhere. Is it up for grabs?

Aristotle opposes *automaton* to *physis* (and *techné*). *Physis* governs a thing's nature, and if something follows its nature it is acting *causa sui*; a nature holds it as it is. Aristotle clearly doesn't conceive of *physis* as abandonment. In contrast, generation by *automaton* is not governed by any nature, and it is under no rule, except for self-imposed ones. But then if X imposes a rule on itself, X, as a ruler, is not governed (it is self-determined; nothing external causes it). X, as a ruler, is left to its own devices and is not *causa sui*, not immune. By contrast, X as the ruled is immune to anything apart from its ruler, that is, itself. X, the ruled, is governed, while X, the ruler, is susceptible. Overall, X is not governed except by itself. This is also what is meant by absence of government: nothing rules, except if we consider self-rule. The *automaton* X, whether governed by itself or not, is up for grabs.

To be sure, this flies in the face of some central Kantian doctrines. Kant made a lot out of the difference he drew between indetermination and self-determination. He would say that if X, the ruler, is free, it would respond to a deontic *necessity* – a moral law. It is therefore not contingent on anything but the moral law. If this is so, it seems an *automaton* is not up for grabs, as it cannot be affected by any (non-moral) element. But this is because X, the ruler, is then (morally) governed, as another necessity has been introduced. (One could say that the nature, the *physis*, of whatever is free is to follow its moral law. If it is so, Kantian self-determination falls short of being a case of a genuine *gignomenon* through *automaton*.)

The parricide

When we look at what is up for grabs, we face the legacy of the Stranger's parricide in Plato's *Sophist*: something can *be*, full-bloodedly, while not being substantial. Parmenides held that being cannot come in more than one variety: substantiality.[79] To exist at all, a thing must be self-standing, unchangeable and tied to necessity. In fact, the description of being in Fragment 8 presents arguably all the features of a substance:

> [...] what is is uncreated and indestructible; for it is complete, immovable and without end. Nor was it ever, nor will it be; for now it is, all at once, a continuous one.

There is no change or transformation in being; nothing affects it, nothing moves it, it is inviolable. It has no dealings with any other thing, nor does it relate to nothingness, and so it could never have come into being, for if "it came into being, it is not; nor is it if it is going to be in the future." It follows that the flow, whatever is in flux and not permanent, does not exist. Existence doesn't come into being. It has no origin. Parmenides proceeds:

> [...f]or what kind of origin for it wilt thou look for? In what way and from what source could it have drawn its increase?

> [...] And, if it came from nothing, what need could have made it arise later rather than sooner?

Only being creates being. Any other origin of being is outside the scope of what can possibly be. Therefore, existence admits of no degrees, no varieties, no modes, no gradations, for it must "either be altogether or be not at all." Being is described as compact, with no parts and no division, nor is there a divide between what falls within its border and what does not. It is pure interior, for "everything is full of what is." In contrast, nothingness has no interior – it is like complete emptiness, with nothing inside anything. One of the corollaries of Parmenides's allegiance to being as substance can be expressed in a motto: to be is to have a (compact, dense and self-standing) interior. The connection between existence and substance is an ontological privilege of what comes from inside as opposed to what is affected by the outside. Because its substance lies in its interior, being is self-sufficient, and "rests in the self-same place, abiding in itself." Hence, he takes it to be

> [...] complete on every side, like the mass of a rounded sphere, equally poised from the center in every direction; for it cannot be greater or smaller in one place than in another.

He proceeds:

> [...] it remains constant in its place; for hard necessity keeps it in the bonds of the limit that holds it fast on every side. Wherefore it is not permitted to what is to be infinite; for it is in need of nothing; while, if it were infinite, it would stand in need of everything.

Being, therefore, is neither an assemblage of what there is nor the origin of everything, but rather what is kept in place by "hard necessity."

This necessity – which arguably has to do with enabling predicative thought – is what makes substance what it is. It both constitutes being and keeps it as it is. Parmenidean being (or substantial being, as we can call it) is not an *automaton*, for it is driven by an internal necessity that doesn't admit gradations. Western metaphysical thought and imagination have been so strongly committed to the parricide – the rejection of Parmenides's theses in Fragment 8, and the disentanglement of being and substance – that it is hard to figure out what Parmenides might have meant. The parricide made it possible to consider existence beyond substantiality – something Aristotle learned very well from Plato, for while he concentrated on substances and took them to enjoy some ontological primacy, he also took accidents, for example, to full-bloodedly exist. Emanuele Severino has been trying to package a neo-Parmenidism that rejects the parricide and returns to the unity of being.[80] He intends to critique and reject what he sees as the nihilism that follows from admitting that anything but being is. To consider the substantiality of all being is indeed an important breakthrough in post-parricidal thought. To be sure, the unity of being – expressed in what Souriau calls existential monism[81] – is still widespread[82], and plurality has seldom made an impact on, for instance, the copula that makes up predication. The predication of any subject is often conceived as the same operation no matter what is attributed to what. In that sense, the parricide is perhaps still incomplete. However, the parricide was successful in claiming that unsubstantial being is possible (which is, I believe, the *leitmotiv* of Severino's complaint).

The Stranger's parricide essentially allows for the "other" to be. Breaking with Parmenides's injunction to think of being beyond unity – to affirm the existence of anything but the substantial – made room for things other than uncreated, indestructible, complete-yet-finite being to exist. Plato's effort is to determine that being itself has no opposite. The Stranger says:

> [...] the opposition of the nature of a part of the other, and of the nature of being, when they are opposed to one another, is no less truly existence than is being itself, if it is not wrong for me to say so, for it signifies not the opposite of being, but only the other of being, and nothing more.[83]

To be is plural enough to admit varieties while encompassing all of them. The Stranger continues:

> Just as we found that the great was great and the beautiful was beautiful, the not-great was not-great and the not-beautiful was not-beautiful, shall we in the same way say that not-being was and is not-being, to be counted as one class among the many classes of being?[84]

If nothingness is, there is something non-substantial that reaches to existence. The parricide opens the way for the existence of that which has no self-sufficient interior maintaining its being; if something as empty as nothingness can exist, existence makes no requirements for what is inside. Impermanent and occasional things that cannot subsist on their own – either like Simondon's meta-stable individuals or Latour's entities of the mode of existence of metamorphosis (see above) – acquire the status of being as much as what is substantial. Substantiality is no more than one class among many classes of being, for being is not univocal. Plato's parricide, positing more than one mode of being, addresses the issue of whether all modes are on equal footing. As we will see, for Aristotle, who was thinking within the realm of the parricide, some beings exist because other beings are substantial.

The parricide opens the Pandora's box of the diversity of being. It introduces plurality in the very kernel of being, and it shows how it relates to what is up for grabs (see also, in chapter 2, Anarcheology E 1/J-N).[85] The parricide precipitated the distinction between the different ways something can be on the one hand, and its very being or existence on the other. It made it possible for an S that is not P to be P – possible for a chair that is not white to be white. That is, it established a distinction between matters of existence and matters of predication. The former is about *whether* something exists, regardless of in what ways, while the latter is about *how* it exists – provided that it can exist in different ways. Things can be very different from what they are while still being. (In fact, it became possible for existence to be conceived as a predication.) For Parmenides, in contrast, if S is not P, it is impossible for S to be P; an S that is P would be like a nonbeing that is (like the white chair that does not exist). Meillassoux puts a lot of weight on the capacity to be other in his argument for absolute facticity. He claims that whenever we appeal to a distinction between the "in itself" and the "for us," we are tacitly appealing to the "absolute's capacity-to-be-other relative to the given"[86]. Because everything has this capacity, I can think of myself as not existing in-itself. He writes:

> We are able to think – by dint of the absence of any reason for our being – a capacity-to-be-other capable of abolishing us, or of radically transforming us. But if so, then this

capacity-to-be-other cannot be conceived as a correlate of our thinking, precisely because it harbors the possibility of our own nonbeing.[87]

The capacity to be other while still being itself may indeed be required for the distinction between the "in-itself" and the "for-us." (We could maybe face Kant's transcendental distinction between phenomena and things in themselves as a distinction between different modes of being.)[88] For Meillassoux, however, it also grounds an absolute principle of facticity according to which everything could be other. The principle seems to imply that everything is *equally* under facticity – and therefore nothing stops anything from being anything else. If it is so, it seems the plurality of modes of being attained by the parricide is lost: everything is equally unsubstantial. It verges on an inversion of Parmenides's formula: to be is to be capable of not being.

Aristotle's lesson from the parricide was that there are many modes of existence. His metaphysical project was indeed to counter Heraclitus and find substances in the sensible. The project, however, was neither to say that everything is substance nor even to say that in the sensible everything is substantial. It was rather to explain the existence of what is sensible by means of some substances: *ousiai protai ton onton* – substances are primordial to all modes of being.[89] (*Met.* Λ, 6, 1071b.5). That is, substances enjoy a primacy among what exists. Aristotle realized that the sensible had room for accidents – as much as for relations, qualities, etc. There is as much being in the substances as in the accidents, and it is only under the light of substance that accidents can be understood at all. Things are elucidated and can be known through careful examination of *ousia*. Aristotle held that there were more things in the world than substances – parts of substances, for example, were not thought to be substances themselves – and yet, without substances, we cannot understand the sensible. Substances are not the only thing that exist, nor the ultimate ingredient, but rather they are existence's central character, much like the central events in a history narrative or the central geographical accidents in a region. For Aristotle, some things cannot be otherwise, and it is on the basis of this sensible necessity that we ought to examine other modes of being.

Symbebeka prota ton onton

The present book is Aristotelian in several respects. It maintains that what is up for grabs has a primacy in a sense close to that which Aristotle ascribed to substances. To formulate this as a proposition in Aristotelian terms, we can say: *symbebeka prota ton onton*. This has to come with a caveat: it is not the accidental itself that is prior, but rather what is up for grabs – that is, what makes accidents possible. Also, to be clear, the primacy of what is up for grabs does not explain anything else away, but it is crucially a starting point to address how things are. It enjoys a non-reductive (and non-eliminative) primacy. Not that everything is up for grabs, but rather that a picture of the sensible should start out depicting what is. The proposition can be read as addressing Aristotle's project in his own terms: we don't have to start out with *ousiai* but rather with *symbebeka*. Therefore, Heraclitus would be on the right track if he claimed that the sensible was full of flow, but not quite so if he meant that everything was equally in flow – or flowing at the same speed. The current project, albeit Heraclitean in an important sense, takes seriously Whitehead's remark that "pure chaos is intrinsically impossible".[90] Contingency is primary but it is neither all-encompassing nor all-pervasive. The claim in this book is that the sensible is the realm of accidents, but accidents can be instrumental in sustaining things that endure – they sponsor things at different levels of subsistence.

The methodological similarities with Aristotle go further. I take one of the main points of the *Metaphysics*, and explicitly so in books Z and M, to be the introduction of aspects: substances have many aspects (form, matter, etc.). He makes important use of the particle *hé* (translating "as" or "qua"). In Book M, he claims that mathematical entities are aspects of sensible things; in geometry, it is an accident that a circle is white but not that it is circular, while if we study the whiteness, the shape is to be treated as accidental.[91] Aspects are thought to be fully external, independent of the examiner, and thus we can have perfect knowledge of them. Mathematical entities are not something other than sensible substances (as opposed to Plato's view of them as abstract or intelligible objects), but neither are they sensible substances *tout court* (as opposed to the Pythagorean view that numbers are among sensible things). Instead, they are aspects of sensible substances.

Analogously, in this book, being up for grabs appears in many aspects; these aspects are neither fully independent from each other nor reduced to a single one. Nor are these aspects mere ways of seeing contingency – they are rather, as we shall see, ways in which contingency shows itself to us, or ways in which it is expressed. There is no univocal way to present contingency. In particular, it is not to be thought univocally in terms of a contrast with necessity. It presents itself under many disguises: echoing Aristotle once more,[92] it can be said in many ways. There is no ultimate, non-contingent aspect of contingency, but contingency can at most be partially unveiled as it shows itself in its aspects. The present book considers several aspects of being up for grabs, only to show how it enjoys primacy without being overarching. We will consider being up for grabs as if it were flowing, with its many aspects, through the sensible.

Contingentism and haecceitism

The parricide introduced issues of existence and predication. They appear when we consider contingency. What, in something, is up for grabs? *That* something is, or rather *how* or *what* it is? To be up for grabs can itself be understood in these two different manners: either in terms of non-necessary *existence* or in terms of non-necessary *predication*. Something can exist necessarily while taking contingently different forms – acquiring different qualities, being in different relations. Something can also exist contingently while necessarily having some form, some qualities or relations.

Existence is sometimes thought to contrast greatly with predication: it is sometimes thought not to be a predicate like any other. There are debates of all kinds concerning this contrast, and it may be useful to note a few of them. First, whether "exists" is a predicate like "is a horse" – Meinongians[93] and adepts of a general theory of objects, including some variants of object-oriented ontology[94], believe it pretty much is – or rather like "is here" or "is now" – modal realists like David Lewis[95] would say "to be actual" functions like a demonstrative. Second, whether existence is a real predicate, as opposed to an indication of a position – a modal position, for example, whether something is real or merely possible. Kant denied that it is real – which gave him resources to refuse all ontological arguments for the existence of God.[96] Third, whether existence is a first-order predicate (or rather a higher-order predicate, a predicate of predicates) – Russell denied it is first-order in order to deal with Meinongism.⁹⁷ Fourth, the debates around what Quine labeled Plato's beard: whether there can be predicates of something which doesn't exist, a question which stems from Plato's parricide.⁹⁸ Fifth, and most importantly for our purposes, debates around what makes something exists. In particular, whether a thing is more than a bundle of qualities and relations, whether something independent of any predication must also exist; whether, for instance, there is a substratum or a *haecceitas* – a non-qualitative *thishood* – to a particular.⁹⁹ These are, to be sure, just four debates among many others, including most debates about reference and descriptions or about *de re* and *de dicto* modalities.

If existence contrasts with predication, then it can be up for grabs that something exists *and also* that something is what it is. Contingency can affect a thing's existence and its predicates. To say that something is contingent on its circumstances might mean that it wouldn't exist without them (it is worldly, a denizen of a single possible world) or alternatively that it would be something entirely different without them (it inhabits more than one world). If existence is contingent, there could be more things than there actually are – looking at an empty doorway, there could be a possible bald man in that doorway and a possible fat man in that doorway.¹⁰⁰ (If existence is not contingent, there is something that could be the bald or the fat man in that doorway, even if it is not actually anything concrete.)

The issue could maybe be presented in terms of what is up for grabs *de re* and what is up for grabs *de dicto*. It is arguable that the structure of predicative thinking favors considering the latter more easily than the former.¹⁰¹ The former concerns the lightness of moving between existence and non-existence, that nothing holds things on either side. I mentioned above Latour's attention to metamorphosis as a mode of existence – things that don't remain in being yet exist, though they are impermanent. Such beings would be temporary by nature and, arguably, would be naturally conceived of as having a contingent existence (they couldn't be anything but beings of metamorphosis).

Timothy Williamson presents the debate about whether what exists is necessary in terms of two positions, *necessitism* and *contingentism*:¹⁰²

Call the proposition that is necessary what there is necessitism and its negation contingentism. In a slightly less compressed form, necessitism says that necessarily everything is necessarily something; still more long-windedly, it is necessary that everything is such that it is necessary that something is identical with it.[103]

He defends necessitism while making clear that his defense has no consequences concerning whether things are necessarily how they are – that is, whether predications are necessary.[104] Necessitism and contingentism are about what exists and not about how it exists. (He also presents the distinction between permanentism which holds that everything is always something, and temporaryism that negates this thesis.) Williamson's necessitism holds that the *dramatis personae* involved in whatever happens are fixed, although each of the characters could take a very different form in order for something else to happen. Indeed, very different forms for something concrete (or sensible) could have been non-concrete (or non-sensible) and vice-versa, while still existing. He says that

> [...] on plausible auxiliary assumptions, necessitism requires the barrier between the concrete and non-concrete to be modally [...] permeated in both directions.[105]

If necessitism is right, contingency acts on a fixed number of items; nothing can come to existence, and nothing can cease to exist. Contingency can change things, but it can never create anything *ex nihilo* or destroy it *ad nihilum*. Necessitism holds that all things have substrata independent of any of their qualities (as permanentism holds that all things have something substantial independent of any of their changes). The necessitist talks about something that is a possible table, or a possible fat or bald man, meaning that it is not concrete. Something could be a table, or a fat or bald man, but it is actually something else, something non-concrete. A table is not necessarily a table, but it is necessarily something. Notice that a contingentism, on the other hand, could either endorse or not endorse a non-substratum view of the particular, whereby something is what it is only by virtue of its qualities. For she can say that there is a substratum to this table independent of its qualities and yet it is not necessarily something. Contingentism holds that the existence of something is exposed to contingencies, while for necessitism, existence is protected from being up for grabs – although predication is not.

Williamson connects the necessitism controversy to issues in modal logic and, in particular, issues related to the acceptance of the Barcan formula.[106] He argues that necessitism is a more convenient metaphysics to use to elucidate and explore the consequences of a classical quantified modal logic, while such a commonly accepted alternative in logic has its metaphysical advantages. The choice between necessitism and its denial is tied to the way modalities are seen and, in particular, to how contingency is conceived.

The distinction is relevant for this book, as the aspects of contingency to be considered here will have implications concerning it. In any case, the main thesis of the book, the primacy of contingency, is compatible with both necessitism and contingentism. The primacy, as considered in the last section, could be present both in a world of fixed characters – the necessitist picture – and in a world where the existence of something is itself up for grabs. In particular, in a necessitist scenario, the transit between what becomes sensible (concrete) and what ceases to be so ought to be understood in terms of the primacy of contingency; it is contingent that something (which, according to necessitism, is necessarily one thing or another) is concrete. In other words, the contingent border could either be placed at the gates of concreteness or the very gates of existence – in both cases, contingency plays a relevant bouncer role.

Although Williamson claims that the necessitism–contingentism debate is clearer than the actualist–possibilist debate, and should replace it – for it is plausible to say that all possible worlds are equally actual – it is still illuminating for our purposes to briefly consider another debate centered on possible worlds.[107] David Kaplan has introduced a distinction between *haecceitism* and *anti-haecceitism*, a distinction about trans-world identity. He defines them as follows:

> The doctrine that holds that it does make sense to ask – without reference to common attributes and behavior – whether this is the same individual in another possible world, that individuals can be extended in logical space (i.e., through possible worlds) in much the way we commonly regard them as being extended in physical space and time, and that a

common "thisness" may underlie extreme dissimilarity or distinct thisnesses may underlie great resemblance, I call Haecceitism. [...] The opposite view, Anti-Haecceitism, holds that for entities of distinct possible worlds there is no notion of trans-world being.[108]

The haecceitist is necessitist, for haecceitism assumes that, necessarily, everything is necessarily something (in all possible worlds). The contingentist, though, can embrace either an anti-haecceitist or a haecceitist view. Here again, the primacy of contingency fits with both views. If things are trans-worldly, still there is room for contingency to play a role in making them what they are – and, in particular, making them sensible. However, haecceitism suits the primacy thesis better. In fact, our interest in this second distinction lies in that it points toward the *haecceitas* of something beyond any of its qualities – its singularity. Singularity is what makes something more than the sum (or the cluster) of its qualities. A thing's *haecceitas* is not dependent on the thing's qualities. Singularities are tied to the primacy of contingency in the sensible, for sensible things are left abandoned by their qualities – by their nature (see *Verlassenheit* above). Deleuze and Guattari call their plane of immanence also a *plane of haecceities*[109]; it is formed by singularities detached from the qualities they realize. The very tie between things and their qualities is touched by contingency. The qualities of things are up for grabs, and so are things that carry on through changes in their qualities. For that reason, for the primacy of contingency thesis, it is more suitable for us to embrace haecceitism. As a consequence, the thesis would favor necessitism and the view that the gates of the sensible are the ones that contingency guards.

Transcendent and immanent contingency

In two sections above (*Three speculative accounts of contingency* and *The parricide*) I have contrasted a view like Meillassoux's, according to which there is a principle of facticity that makes it possible for everything to be something other than what it is, with those views according to which contingency is not an overarching principle. Meillassoux considers a God whose inexistence is contingent; God is up for grabs, for His existence is under the principle of facticity that is not up for grabs. (In that sense, his conception of God contrasts with the equally non-standard one held by Whitehead according to which God is what ensures that pure chaos is intrinsically impossible.) We can distinguish between contingency viewed as transcendent – as a necessary principle – and contingency viewed as immanent. In an immanent view, the lightness of being is itself light. While a transcendent view of contingency places it outside its own scope – chaos reigns by necessity or by other non-contingent reasons – an immanent view holds that contingency is itself contingent. According to this view, something can come along – like a newborn God, as we are in Meillassoux's quasi-theological territories – and revoke all contingencies; nothing is necessary, but not by necessity. A recent fragment of Heraclitus expresses what it means for a test of force to be immanent: "[...] the stronger prevails because it is stronger – and not due to any law of the strongest" (fr. 138, see ANARCH., 2/138). Analogously, immanent contingency means that it prevails because there is no *arché*, and not because there is an *arché* that makes it prevail. The immanent view is that, contingently, everything is contingent; the transcendent view is that, necessarily, everything is contingent.

The primacy-of-contingency view diverges from both of these. It doesn't hold that (necessarily or contingently) *everything* is contingent. Primacy, for us, means no universality. To be sure, it agrees with the transcendent view that there is something structural connecting the accidental and the sensible. It also agrees with the immanent view that there is no general principle of contingency under which everything lies. An objector might then wonder whether the *symbebeka prota ton onton* approach genuinely differs from taking contingency to be immanent or transcendent. In order to see the difference, we need a firm grip on the Aristotelian character of the proposition. Contingency is not meant to be the ultimate reality or a principle that rules everything. Neither is it something fully contingent itself, which disappears due to further contingent matters of fact. Contingency is central – that is, it is structurally present among the sensible. It is a main character, a key one; therefore, it is neither a single character – for there is more than one mode of being – nor a passer-by. It is transcendently present while not being transcendently unique. It is just a *sine qua non*.

The view defended in this book is that we cannot conceive the sensible itself except by ascribing a central – albeit not exclusive – importance to the accidental. Even though it is not possible at this point to give a complete picture of the central character of contingency among the sensible – this is the task of the whole book – we can now grasp some pieces of the puzzle. To begin to see why accidents are the main characters of sensible plots, we can think again of contingency as a lack of *immunitas*. In order for something to be up for grabs, it has to be open to interference; no substantial interiority and no other necessary connection protects it from being affected by something else. Interference can either come from other things, or it can come *ex nihilo* as an *automaton*, as in the Epicurean *clinamina*.[110] As we will see, the different aspects of contingency deal with interference. Interference has to do with sponsoring, with meta-stability, with dependence, with abandonment, with compossibles, with fragments, with doubts, with rhythms. It is related to a conception of existence as co-existence. There is a common plane on which things exist – a plane of what is up for grabs – that shows itself in different ways and that we will meet in the following chapters. To be sensible is to be accidental, because the sensible is the very realm of the unprotected, where any immunity is itself up for grabs. To be concrete is to be surrounded by what is less than substantial, by connections that are less than necessary. Fragility is not the only ingredient of the sensible, but without it, the stew cannot be ready.

The parricide introduced plurality into the kernel of being while making no form of being overarching. I will later mention the fallen pile of Muja (see Anarcheology 1/J-N), which explores the connection between the multiplicity of modes of existence and what is up for grabs. There (N), Idarsal Selassie writes about a discontinuity that governs the different modes; nothing can cross from one mode to another without being translated. We cannot have different things, he says, if we don't have separators. Translation is a gate where things are lost and things are found. Here again, contingency acts as bouncer. Without it – if discontinuities could be dispelled – there would be no plurality. Selassie's addressee espouses the thesis that different modes of existence co-exist.[111] Latour talks about mini-transcendences that feature in each mode, which are also like gates in that they make each mode irreducible to the others. These gates, like the modes of existence they guard, are *sui generis*. If contingency deals in gate keeping, it must somehow be in the corridor that links the different modes of existence. Such a corridor has to do with the plane I mentioned before (the *plan d'immanence* of Deleuze and Guattari, the *plane of equality* of Garcia). Etienne Souriau also has a name for this concept: *surexistence*.[112] He defines it as the crossroads of existences. This crossroads does not precede the modes of existence, but it is rather a consequence of their plurality – a consequence of there being more than one mode. If there are genuinely many modes of existence within the sensible, the gates between them cannot dispense with discontinuities. These discontinuities, in their turn, must usher in contingency. In other words, if contingency enjoys a primacy while not being overarching, it stems from the very plurality of modes of existence within the sensible. This reveals why contingency is connected to the sensible: it is a feature of genuine interference and of genuine plurality.

Anarcheologies and ontoscopies

A metaphysics of accident ought to look different from a metaphysics of substance. The former is not a one-faced endeavor. Contingency has indeterminately many faces – all of them look toward the concrete. There is no general theory of what is up for grabs; at least, there is no theory that could replace it in its gatekeeping. Doing metaphysics is not to step out of the grasp of the primacy of contingency but rather to follow its paths through its many aspects without losing sight of its consequences. This book is not a collection of arguments for the specific primacy of accident it maintains. Rather, it attempts to follow the paths of contingency by looking at its marks; it tracks some of the faces with which what is up for grabs shows itself. The arguments will eventually appear both to ground and to bend the main proposition. They will be embedded in the faces that what is up for grabs exhibits. Those faces may have something to do with us, but they also have a lot to do with contingency.

A recent fragment of Heraclitus (fr. 204, see ANARCHEOLOGY 2/204) compares the voyeurism of someone spying on a neighbor with that of the public at a peep show. The latter, but not the former, involves an important act by the people being watched: the act of selecting what is seen and for how long. Analogously, that which exists determines how it shows itself.

What we see is not our projection onto the world, but rather how the world hits us. I call the ways the world shows itself to us *ontoscopies*. As contingency has many faces, spotting it requires a measure of stereoscopy – this is why I introduce the word in the plural. Ontoscopies have to do with what we see of what there is, for they reveal what reality makes available to us. In that sense, they are what gets exhibited, what the world affords to present to us. Ontoscopies are presentations of what there is, prior to any maps, descriptions or interpretations. Still, these things always contain ontoscopies – as any account of being, any ontology, contains an ontoscopy. Hence, for the purposes of this book, we will treat ontologies themselves as ontoscopies.

Although I understand ontoscopies to be different from explicit storytelling, there is something in common between how an image is put forward in a story being told[113] and how things present themselves in an ontoscopy. A metaphysics of contingency needs to create its own images, for otherwise it will be prey to images already spread and that often obliterate the accidental as merely what contrasts with what is necessary. An ontoscopy is a way to see things. It aims at producing an image. It is an invitation to see something *qua* something, as much as what is done when a story is told. Images invoke tonalities. Thinking about the world always engage tonalities – and some of them are metaphysically fruitful. To use a Whiteheadian phrase, an ontoscopy is a lure for feeling.

The rest of this book divides into six chapters. The first explores the notion of *anarcheology*. It is a study of the absence of *archés* – and in this sense, as I said at the outset, this whole book is a study in anarcheology. However, the notion has important parallel meanings, to be explored in the chapter. One of them has to do with exploring the historical consequences of an unsanctioned version – and in that sense intervening in the thought-scenario through explicit story-telling, where truthfulness to facts is not a measure of importance. In this sense, anarcheologies dwell in story-telling but in an explicit way, not like ontoscopies where what matters is the creation of images. The chapter contains three anarcheologies in this latter sense, which we will refer to and consider throughout the book (some of them have been mentioned already always referred to as "ANARCHEOLOGY" followed by identifiers). The following three chapters present ontoscopies that look at the sensible and explore the primacy of what is up for grabs.

They relate to each other in several manners, but they are also independent aspects of contingency. They could be considered as modes of existence, but I take them to be closer to Aristotle's aspects. Each of these ontoscopies revolves around one concept and provides an image of the sensible. These concepts shed light onto what it is like to be up for grabs.

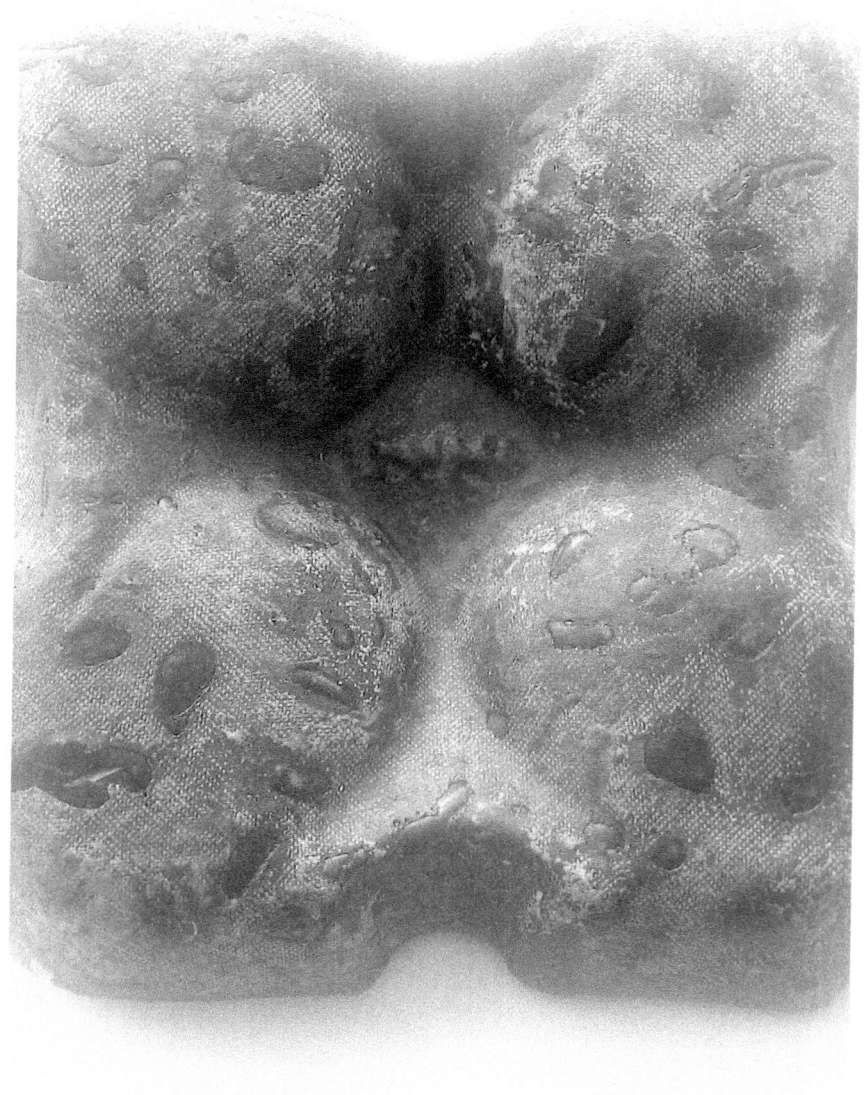

Mistudy of my traces Gisel Carriconde Azevedo, Sculpture: silicone, pigment and crystal, 2010

Chapter 2
Anarcheologies

Being out of the blue

Hector D'Alessandro tells a story about witnessing something out of the blue.[114] Stories often involve preparing, describing and accommodating rupture, depicting something that suddenly starts – or ends. In D'Alessandro's narrative, a character goes for a late breakfast in an ordinary department-store restaurant. He spots people sitting with their food and drinks, chatting or looking around and proceeding with their activities: business as usual. Eventually he notices a man and woman arguing. So far, so unremarkable. Then comes the sudden rupture. The man stands up, walks toward the toilet, goes to the balcony, breaks the glass and jumps from the seventh floor. The narrator becomes a witness. The weight of the out of the blue burdens him. It is the lightness of the casual, of *automaton*, of what is determined by itself. He bears witness to this lightness – and it proves hardly bearable. Another witness of the out of the blue is the viewer of the TV show in Saura's film *Antonieta*, which opens with a woman presenting a recipe in a cooking program only to suddenly shoot herself. There is always something sudden to any death – because something else suddenly starts. This is the strength of what is out of the blue.

Beginnings point to the core of that which is peculiar to anything sensible. The sensible is perishable, because it contains what is on the brink of beginning. Looking for the starting point is often a way to look for the commanding element, if the original holds the force of a beginning, which provides a rightful ascendency. If it is so, what merely follows exists to a lesser degree than what is followed. This is the kernel of the discussions around priority monism and its alternatives. If the whole is prior, everything depends on it. If the parts are prior, everything else depends on them. Priority, which is not what we mean in this book by *primacy*, here spells command.

Although temporal, logical and governing order seem to be tangled up here, this could be an effect of our chosen vocabulary, where to be prior is to generate and to govern. Before debunking this conflation of orders, I would just point out that beginnings, as such, display independence. Being up for grabs has something to do with the independent and with what is not ruled. That which is contingent on something else is open to interference – it is exposed to the elements. This exposure is present in what begins, for in order for anything to start, it must be capable of making its own rules. A beginning is only really a beginning if no rules are at work on it; beginnings are outside any determining scope. In this sense, what is *automaton* is open and up for grabs. *Automaton* is a determination that starts there, that is not under anything else's control. That which is under a rule is immune – that which imposes the rule is not. Whatever is immunized has its up-for-grabs feature switched off. A start could always have been otherwise. Only what is up for grabs can afford to be out of the blue.

This an-*arché* feature is at the heart of what is up for grabs. It is present in the Kantian idea of a *causality of freedom*: the starting point of a novel causal chain. The starting point is not ruled, because self-determination is by definition an independent determination. Because it is unruled, it is exposed to the elements. Only what is up in the air can genuinely start something. This independence is crucial for Kant; there cannot be another causal chain being started if everything were fully chained in a single causal connection. There are starting points because there is more than one causal chain. In fact, Kant uses our capacity to start new causal chains to introduce a moral realm in a world that is determined by us. Whether or not Kant means to introduce genuine lapses of determination in the non-moral realm, what is described morally through imperatives requires agents that can do otherwise – even though they won't if they are really acting according to the categorical imperative. The point of departure of any action that follows an imperative – that issues a causality by freedom is a freedom of action, a freedom to be determined autonomously. The Kantian agent acts morally because she genuinely chooses to be under the moral rule. Moral determination is therefore *sui generis*: it requires that what is in its scope is *not* immunized. Because the scope is not immunized, the moral agent starts a genuinely new causal chain. To be a moral agent, for Kant, is to be an initiating agent.

We often view a beginning only as the origin for what follows, considering it in terms of what it has originated. But starting points cut an edge between the out of the blue and the realm of determinations (a term I always use as meaning *hetero-determinations*; that is, something that is determined if it is under a command). A beginning is therefore an undetermined (hetero-)determiner. Disentangling beginning from mere originating is part of the plot of Heidegger's reflections on being and beginning in Über den Anfang (About the Beginning), a posthumously published manuscript. There, he holds that being has its essence in beginnings.[115] To begin is to be preserved from unveiling – there is nothing to conceal a seed when it hasn't grown into a tree. Beginnings display a peculiar transparency, whereas the things that follow are hidden in an ontogenealogical tree of ancestors and descendants. Such transparency is not the lightness of an origin, but rather its disconnection from the tree of governing and governed nodes. Heidegger's suspicion concerning the insufficiency of metaphysics shows itself as an incapacity to deal with all the power of a beginning. The luminous character of the beginning is what makes it possible, for Heidegger, to understand truth as unveiling. What is revealed when a beginning is made explicit is not what leaves a shade over whatever exists, but the strength of the out-of-the-blue. This is present in all origins only to the extent that they are ungoverned.

Arché

We can now start to debunk the idea that beginning is legitimate dominance. This is an entrenched idea and hard to debunk. The connection between being and beginning can suggest that there is an *arché* to being –

its original core that is at the same time its ultimate revelation and which ultimately governs it. Part of the force of the notion of *arché* derives from the conception of being as centrally substantial: the *arché* is the original core, the grounding or foundational stone that unveils all that can be unveiled about something. But the substantiality of being is not all there is to the connection between being and beginning – not even to the notion of *arché*. There is accident to this connection, since *arché* is the bridging point between the ungoverned and the ruled, between the starting point and what is under immunizing effects. The out of the blue requires the up for grabs. Further, the *arché* is the point where a dominion is created. It is the institution of a rule – and of its scope.

Agamben takes up the Foucauldian notion of archeology as a lever to explore what an *arché* is.[116] The original two meanings of the verb *arché* as both to commence and to command – to give rise to and to rule – are intertwined. It is an entrenched overlap: we take what genuinely starts something to be what originates a new determination. Archaic, archetypes, hierarchy: we speak of priority as carrying a power of governance. To command comes from *mandare*, "to send." What is sent has a destination and embodies a destiny. But it is also thrown – carrying an indefinition. An issued command is up in the air, for it has to find obedience, but simultaneously there is no obedience without the command. The fitting together of these two elements is perhaps a central political drama, and Agamben explores it in terms of how the present is shaped by obedience to past *arché*s. His analysis is biopolitical, but like Esposito's, it provides the right terms to consider ontological issues concerning determinations. The *arché* brings to ontology the issue of governments that need rulers and followers. It brings in determinations, and with them substance, necessity, and fixity. Aristotle's search for the substantiality of the sensible was guided by the notion of *arché*: to understand the sensible is to spot its obedience.

Agamben diagnoses a lack of reflection in Western philosophy about command. Governing is possible because of commands; it is not enough to have obedience. Yet commanding has received far less attention than obeying. The sovereignty of a commanding force hinges on its capacity to act out of the blue, its capacity to start something – no determining force can be entirely at bay. This is why weak governments rarely manage to start anything unexpected; their gambit is to stay within the boundaries of business as usual. Whatever is ultimately determining – or genuinely prior in the sense of an *arché* – has to preserve an element of the up in the air.

It because it is about commencement that the commanding word – *arché* – contrasts thoroughly with apophantic discourse, the discourse that declares how things are assuming that they are determinately one way or another. The command belongs in a different procedure with words: it intends to make them true rather than attempting to be true. It is an intervention. Consider the inextricable co-existence of normative and declarative vocabularies. Agamben ventures the hypothesis that there are not one but two interplayed ontologies inherited from Parmenides: that of "being" and that of "making it be" – *esti* and *estó* in Greek. The latter is the ontology of the ruler: it deploys the non-declarative tenses of "to be." It is ontology, albeit in another tense, only to the extent that *ontos* revolves around *arché* – and through a connection with the substance of what is. If to be is an issue in determinations, accidents can exist, but only in a peripheral way. The effect of the focus on *arché* is to center ontology on rules and commands. It follows that to be is either to determine or to be determined.

These two intertwined ontologies are therefore related to the idea of *arché* as the dominant origin. Agamben cites Nietzsche's definition of will: to want something is to command, and therefore to be ready to commence. To act according to a will, one needs to be at least somewhat outside the scope of a governing rule. One must be away from a determination and not fully immunized – a causality of freedom. Agamben raises the issue of a society of control – or a society of performance, in Byung-Chul Han's terms.[117] In such associations, there are few limitations to the will that is stimulated; in general, it is exercised without restraint. Government acts on the content of these pursuits – the content of the commandments of the will. Desires become the battlefield: government becomes the government of self-commandments. This is possible because where there is a genuine starting point, something is up for grabs – and therefore open to interference. The two intertwined meanings of *arché* show how the declarative discourse is hostage to the normative one. They both dwell in governments and, as such, they both draw from Bataille's notion of *mettre en jeu*. To describe what there is in terms of its substantiality is to acknowledge what governs things; to invoke originality is to appeal to what lies in the open.

The first ontology of Agamben – the *esti* ontology – is guided by the notion of obedience to a command to provide an ultimate account of the nature of things. The second ontology – *estó* – looks at the exercise of a command. In Elizabeth Anscombe's terms, the two ontologies work in opposite directions of fit: *estó* brings about a determination, while *esti* recalls a determination.[118] Just like desire and belief, the two ontologies can fail and succeed in opposite ways: a command fails when it is not obeyed – there is no item in the shopping trolley matching the shopping list – while a declaration fails when it doesn't obey – there is no item on the receipt matching something that is in the shopping trolley. But we can also understand these two directions of fit in terms of government: its constitutional power and its constituted power. The former makes power be, and the latter declares it. Together, they swing between the controlled and the controlling, the movable and the immutable mover. The central moment is precisely the *arché* – the advent of a command.

Arché, as a word hosting a claim, makes room for the intertwining ontologies and can be understood as follows: to disclose the world is to disclose what rules it. Archeology looks at the past to find the commanders of the present. In contrast, attention to what is up for grabs intends to reject this claim and rather look at the ungoverned. This book tries to shift the attention to the an-*arché*. Its concentration on the centrality of contingency displaces not only substance but also the *arché* toward which the thought of substance is directed. The aim is to begin to put forward a metaphysics of the non-archeological.

To be sure, it is on the ungoverned that determinations can have scope – and it is the ungoverned that can institute determinations. Both ruling and failure to rule draw on the ungoverned, because obedience always has an up-in-the-air character. The unruly lives in what can escape determination (see Heraclitus' fragments 198 and 205, ANARCHEOLOGY 2/198 and 2/205 below). This is what makes following a rule a delicate affair: an imperative has to find its way through several ungoverned obstacles. As national governments must negotiate with their citizens and institutions, imperatives must find a path of implementation between the vicissitudes of other rulings and among the resistance of the ungoverned. It is about sponsoring – the word we chose to translate Souriau's *instaurer* in the last chapter. A rule must navigate what is up in the air, negotiate with other determinations, interfere in the established order. The ungoverned makes explicit that *arché*s require allagmatics. The up for grabs harbors an an-*arché* – an absence of pull. We can see what is up for grabs in the friction between the *arché*s, in the emptiness produced by their absence or in the capacity to emulate them by commencing something else. These three loci of an-*arché* will appear in the three upcoming ontoscopies.

Three anarcheologies

Anarcheology[119] can be understood in at least three different ways, in line with three different parsings. Perhaps they are three different but entangled anarcheologies:

1. Anarche-ology: the study of the unruled, the ungoverned, the absence of command or determination and its effects;

2. An-arche-ology: the study of what is groundless and doesn't have a foundation;

3. An-archeology: the study of versions of the past independently of whether they are considered to be facts.

The first one points toward a non-*arché*-based ontology that is the main concern of this book. It looks at the unruled in contrast to the determined. It explores how something can resist determination and finds ways to access what is not ruled. Governance is considered by anarche-ology as derived from the unruled and as search deserving of explanation – and not merely posited as the name of the game (*arché*). Anarche-ology can certainly be approached in different ways; in this book, I will pursue it through the friction of ontoscopies.

An-arche-ology, by contrast, looks at what has no ultimate foundation – at the groundless. An-arche-ological excavation does not aim to find bedrock, but rather to unground further. It doesn't explore the underground as a grounding resource for the surface; it places on the same surface what is underneath and what is visible – the past and the present in the same hierarchical position. There is no hierarchical depth to the present, for that would have to refer to an ultimate foundation – the underground has no priority. An-arche-ology is close to priority nihilism, for nothing is ascribed a superior ontological status.

There is a sense in which Deleuze and Guattari's *Mille Plateaux*[120] inaugurated an-arche-ology. In the opening pages, the authors talk about transversal communications that mix genealogical trees, about our understandings of the past being submitted to all sorts of contaminations, of the parallel development of things unrelated to each other. The book presents an ontology of co-existence around the idea of a *plan d'immanence* where all hierarchies coincide. On such a plane, primacy gives place to geography: everything sensible must occupy a space (and, presumably, bicker with its neighbors). Excavating an-arche-ologically is an exercise in conjunction more than an endeavor of unveiling constitutions or tracing roots.

In this sense, an-arche-ological exploration can go together with an anarche-ological emphasis on the unruled – which has only an-ancestors. The methods of an-arche-ology are those of contiguity: infection, disruption, diversion. It doesn't look for roots, but rather exposes arbitrary associations that are themselves up for grabs. Further, an-arche-ology is the study of the unoriginal. As such, it points toward *anarchetypes*, that is, toward parodies or simulacra. Anarchetypes are anathema to (Platonic) models, which are unoriginated originators. Anarchetypes can be imitated by anything in their path – or by nothing. Imitation, simulation and parody follow from contiguity and not from any primacy. Deleuze's account of repetition draws no distinction between the originals and the simulacra – they all can be repeated.[121] He then invokes a generalized eternal return to dissolve any appeal to an original form; everything is repeating something else, there is no ultimate model. There is no prototype, no archetype, nothing but a succession of repeated parodies where nothing can have any status but that of a simulacrum. The an-arche-ological move here is to exorcise the precursor as a fixed determiner – anything can incidentally govern anything else.

An an-arche-ological archeology can be also compared to Ben Woodard's xenoarcheology[122], the ungrounding of the alien. This excavates the strange, that which produces the opposite of an explanation – xenoarcheology excavates to unexplain. As such, it replaces ontological patriarchy (or matriarchy) by a provisory xenoarchy where the unfamiliar seems to affect the present by its sudden contiguity. It is a Cthuluoid archeology, for it is – like Reza Negaresteni's ethics, which he cites – not suggested by anything but openness to the weird. The image of Lovecraft has become a figure of a call from the alien weird: Negaresteni's stance is one that makes room for the appeal of the unrecognized, of the unclassified, of what lacks a pronounceable name. Time – or the succession of eras – is no longer seen as layers approaching the familiar, but as a tortuous assemblage of alien materials. A xenoarcheological geology would be a natural history of strangeness – as an an-arche-ological geology would point toward a natural history of the incidental.

Finally, an-archeology deals with the past in the form of its versions. It is unconcerned by what we take as fact, for it assigns no preference among the versions. Zouzi Chebbi once claimed that south of the Maghreb there is no distinction between facts and versions.[123] The assignment of a privilege among versions is always tainted by the power of those who write the history books. An-archeology, therefore, excavates what could have been; it ungrounds different pasts – and provokes an-arche-ological awe in those concerned with a history of facts. If anarche-ology deals with the unruly, an-archeology uproots the past while reintroducing the (an-arche-ological) unruly in the present.[124] It takes the alien versions together with the sanctioned ones to constitute the present and future. It is a department of history – where counterfactual history lies. An-archeology invokes the power of the past as an anarchetype – as something that admits of reshaping and could be disentangled from the force of authenticity. (I have used the term *inarcheology*[125] to describe my action of inserting in the archeological site of the castle of Sappho, dedicated to Artemis, in Lesbos, a stone engraved with an-archeological fragments of Heraclitus – 144 and 210 – see below Anarcheology 2/144 and 2/210. In this case, excavation purports to ground, and not to unground, something.)

An an-archeology of philosophy aims to provide philosophy with a freedom from the chains of its actual history. It is not an antirealism about the history of philosophy but rather a tonality – one less concerned with the veracity of the past – that considers versions as capable of motivating and inspiring thought as historical facts. It intends to free thought from its archeologically approved background. It moves in a tonality in which there is no room for asking how much of a fact a version is. In this sense, it unveils the power of the counterfactual in philosophy: the different ways that thought could have gone but (in fact) has not. If Chebbi is right about what happens south of the Maghreb, it also points toward a decolonization of thought in which many versions of philosophy's past are called to the fore.

This book primarily addresses anarcheology in the first *sens*, but it eventually connects to the second and makes use of the third. The remainder of this chapter is an exploration in what we might call the an-archeology of anarche-ology. These exercises bring together some senses in which the ontological obsession with *arché* can be dispelled.

Exercises in anarcheology

History is always incomplete without its counterparts. It's not only that a grain of truth can always be found in what is rejected, but also that truth must live side by side with what could have happened. The shadow of the counterfactual on facts is what makes lightness shine in facticity. The factual is made insufficiently determined by the possibility of a counterfactual. If facts are just a counterpart, they are incomplete without the other things that could have happened. These exercises explore virtual history: what would have happened, for example, if Heraclitus had lived until our era and had had time to rethink his doctrines of the *polemos* under contemporary lights? An-archeology invites us to consider such doctrine as much as its factual absence; it is certainly harder to consider counterfactual doctrines, but that doesn't make them unimportant.

The truth of facts is always split, for the lightness of what took place cannot be fully appreciated without the alternative routes things could have taken. What could have been points toward a split that has existed from the beginning: an ontological *diaphonia* that enables things to take several directions. An-*arché*. What we call truth, as Edmond Jabès ascribes to an anonymous mouth, is truth in shards.[126] To come to terms with these shards, we must not attempt to see the hidden full thing. An-archeological history is never more than a mosaic of versions. The an-archeological tonality is one that attempts to place them together on a single surface to offer material for thought. Jabès himself is a thinker who resorted to anarcheology: in his *The Book of Questions* [127] he introduces several voices of rebs who are invoked in a dialogue where a tradition and its past has to be populated by literary characters that are as ready as fiction can be to manage some truths. As Marianne Moore once said, "imaginary gardens with real toads in them."[128]

The following three pieces of anarcheology are referred to in the rest of the book (as they have been so far) as ANARCHEOLOGIES. The pieces are called 1, 2 and 3 respectively, and their components are identified in the texts.

Idarsal Selassie and the pile of Muja (1)

Ethiopian history has many versions. Most people live there with several of those versions, making their pasts come alive with tales and endless conversations. I had one such conversation when I was in Mekele on a Sunday afternoon in early 2012, waiting for a transport to Lalibela which would depart early the next day. I sat in a café and started browsing a copy of Latour's *Irreductions*.[129] Seeing the book in my hands, a passer-by approached me, enthused. He had come across it some years back and it had made a big impression on him – or so he told me. I offered him a piece of chocolate and he sat down. Our conversation covered some of the many versions of what had happened to the dynasty of Menelick. After some hours, he told me he had recently written a letter to Latour and asked me to wait for him while he went home and fetched a copy he would like to give me. An hour later, he came back with the letter, photocopied on dirty sheets of paper.

(A) Dear Mr. Bruno Latour,

I am Idarsal Selassie and I live near Mekele, Tigray, in northern Ethiopia. I write to you because I have something to tell you, as much as you, in a piece of your writing, had something to tell me. Reading is something that disturbs me – I find it hard to understand what is not directly said to me. I enjoy books most when they are read to me – they seem more like chatting. But I read pieces of your book, as I will tell you, on my own. So I may be misunderstanding what you wrote. Plus, I don't like keeping what I understand anywhere – I don't like the stink of my thoughts rotting away. I know I cannot think them again. And yet I enjoy when they come again in my mind to visit – but only because they feel different. The thought I got from your book comes back to me very often, as I will try to explain.

(B) I traveled around my area of the world and beyond, always looking for some insight into how things are. I was looking for *hows*. I found many *becauses*, which often seem to me to amount to advice to stop scavenging. Yet I found inquiry to be able to free me from being a proud and accomplished shepherd in my village. They say I am restless.

(C) I have a job cooking for tourists in a hotel in Mekele. I'm proud of some of the things I have cooked, a *shiro*[130] that comes out tasty, some boiled beans with the right color, a tomato sauce they eat to the last drop. I cook and I find the chance to talk to people from afar. Our customers are almost always *faranjis*.[131] Most of them end up telling me something about nature and, as they like it, I often approach them asking about how nature works. Some of them talk about God, but nature is different, is all ready, as if it were created once and for all, even if it was never really created. Sometimes I have trouble understanding why they take some things as natural but not others. When I press them a bit, they get confused, but they rarely give up thinking that only some things are natural. Some tourists tell me about rituals they see in the south; they sometimes scarcely understand what the whole thing is about, but they are always certain that some of the things they see are natural – but not all. I invariably spend hours in the kitchen trying to figure out how they draw the line.

(D) My traveling has taken me to several different parts of the world and to many conversations. I have talked to all sorts of people: travelers, priests, peasants, pious folks, worshipers of animals, whores, Zulu believers in a Christian *Unkulunkulu*[132] and many others. I met the followers of Skendes back in Axum, where I was born, who told me that all that I need to know about things is that they were created by just one of them. A God. A creator, responsible for all things and who responds for all things. There are no more things, as everything boils down to one. Gods as a principle that unfolds on all things, I take it. But then they unfold on my prayers as well. I asked them why prayers should be directed to the origin of all things instead of being directed to the origins of what we want (or fear). In any case, why are origins so important? They said prayers should be directed to the ruler. I thought, aren't those prayers somehow making the rule happen? Skendes himself slept with his mother while she thought she wasn't sleeping with her son but with a stranger, and for some money. When she found out, she didn't curse the origin of all things for making her bump into her son like that, nor did she blame the son who fooled her for the sake of some investigation he was carrying out, but rather she killed herself. I have always thought there is more than one story happening in everything that manages to happen.

(E) I also met the enchanters of *Nenaunir*.[133] *Nenaunir* resides in the clouds, in the rainbow that flags water. Rainbows are in the clouds, but they live in the clouds seen from some places, not from others – and so does *Nenaunir*. Her naughty face spells peril, as she reigns over evil for those who spot her. But then I showed them the rainbow I can concoct by playing with running water in my hands. They don't quite like this kind of Abrahamic quest for what is behind their divine spirits. They went: you can make *Nenaunir* appear, but you cannot do it on your own – no spirit can, one needs water. Some told me *Mungo* is behind the rainbow and no God could make *Nenaunir* appear without *Mungo* – not even me playing with running water in my hands. Surely, kids paint rainbows with sunshine on a sheet of paper. But a painted *Nenaunir* rules only over a painted piece of land. It is all about power and dependence: who can do what they want and who depends on superior rulers. Clearly, there are gaps between the realms of all those many powerful spirits. Unless each thing is itself a god – I asked a *Mungo* worshiper once. She bowed her head and said in a low voice: there are also gaps between things, and gaps between the spirits of each gap. There is no god for the unruly.

(F) When I cook, I deal with spirits. I don't dare count them. When I count, they become too many – when I don't, they are just one, the one who makes itself present. They are the kind of thing that doesn't agree with the storekeepers. Still, sometimes I venture to count them and then decide to redo it again a minute later and the numbers end up not matching. Plus, to tell you the truth, my attention is rarely enough for more than one spirit at a time – even though I have to attend to many pots, many fires and often too many clients at once. There is no divided attention when spirits are at stake. I once thought I could decide to call them all one, but then I decided to call them many. The numbers seem to be in the eyes of the beholder. Count the stars, and the night sky will disappear before your eyes.

(G) I came across a book of yours years back. It was in a bad state, and I read the first part, about Pasteur and the microbes, only in passing. The second part, beginning with your principle of irreduction, captured my attention. The principle made me think a lot about what I have been looking for. I didn't have time to check out how you explore the principle in the book. The book was in the hands of a costumer here in the hotel when she came down for breakfast. We chatted for a while and she left it with me for the day, while she was going around for some sightseeing. She was off the next day and so was the book. I did copy some pages in the photocopy machine we have in the office, but I couldn't copy more than ten pages in one go. In any case, when the costumer came back – she was from Holland or Belgium, I believe – we discussed her interest in your work. She told me you're interested in doing what she called an anthropology of the *faranjis*. She said you want to look at them in the same way the anthropologists look at native peoples here in Africa. I thought you had something important to tell me with your principles, and I myself have long been remarking things about the *faranjis*.

(H) As I said, in my job, I end up doing a lot of talking to the *faranji* costumers in the afternoon. The *faranjis*! There are several things that call my attention to them. To be a *faranji* is not about the color of the skin, not only that. I'm not sure I know how to define these people – but most of them come with some hidden certainties that they never talk about. I like chatting with them. They have a habit of suspicion toward most things Africans tell them, and that intrigued me for a very long time. I think this is partly because they have a sense of reality and everything has to match it, otherwise it is not credible. Sometimes I see some distress in them because it seems they realize there is too little they are entitled to believe. It is as if they have to live in small places, no matter where they go. It seems that everything has to fit in the single way they conceive what exists and everything else has to be placed in some sort of garbage bin where they place things that are at most well crafted. I suspect my discomfort with this attitude has something to do with my allegiance to something like your principle of irreduction. They say polytheism is an African idea, and as for monotheism, well, I believe it all started out around here too. But I don't want to get into these controversies. I just think things in this life come in many colors. Or maybe they come in a single color – but the effort to make colors out of what is black as much as the effort to paint everything white is something that I often find too heavy to be compulsory. Do you see what I mean? Why would one really have to do the hard maneuvers needed to make many seem one? It also takes too much work to make one seem many. A sense of reality cannot distort your sense of what is true and what is false. This sense, on its own, makes things already too complicated to grasp. To get closer to truth, as my travels have told me, is a hard job, and I don't understand why it should be made harder from the beginning by adopting a general scheme for everything. You can see I read your principle in my own way – but then again, how else could I have read it?

(I) I realize you are a *faranji* yourself. Plus, I can imagine what kind of *faranji* you are: one that is a bit burdened by your lore. As I told you, restlessness has been in my veins for a long time – and I believe it somehow goes beyond the borders of ethnic or any other identity. I have met many different *faranjis*, and several who breathe genuine restlessness. I had a long-standing *faranji* friend who used to transport cash across Africa and who took me to many capitals as she traveled like a globetrotter. Anna introduced me to many books and taught me much about writing usages. We discussed your principle many times in our conversations. She was also very much into it, but used it in contexts that were very different from my own. She thought it was all about the complexity turned simple and the simplicity turned complex of the human soul. For her, everything apart from human preoccupations was very liberating yet unbearably cold. I took Anna once to travel by foot in the mountains in Semien Wollo, around Lalibela. There is much there, as you have probably heard, and I was convinced I would find something out there that would ring like an insight.

(J) At some point in our weeks walking the mountains, we met another *faranji* traveler, quite adventurous. Myriam Karmona was investigating the circumstances of the construction of Roha (nowadays Lalibela) and lived in Gondar for some years. She took us to have coffee and *injera* with a small group of men in a small nomad village close to Morora Hospital. I understand these people, not more than twenty in the village, have lived around the mountains for some time. We talked for many hours about these mountains far before Roha was built. They have ancient stories they hear from their ancestors and, you know, great ruptures are what really matter in people's lives. They feel committed to them as if they were hostages to the memories of things that have shaken too much. We arrange historical events around catastrophes – or big blessings, depending on which side of the break you are. In any case, they told us about what had been the biggest turning point for the Oromos who lived in the region. They believed that the higher the mountain, the closer to the nothingness of the sky it gets. To reach nothingness was something simultaneously feared and desired, and they used to engage some effort in building up further mounts on top of high mountains so that they could be even closer to it. To attain nothingness became, it seems, an obsession, to the point where they decided to make an organized enterprise to come up with a pile of stuff on top of a mountain in Muja. The pile was made of whatever materials they could get hold of, but the pile had to stand on its own. It was made, I understand, mainly of rocks but also of some wood and other bits of vegetation. They told us the Oromos planted trees on top of the pile and then tried to plant more trees on top of the others. It was as if they were making an artificial earth, layer by layer.

(K) The pile was a sacred site around which they performed many rituals about reaching nothingness and keeping in touch with it. I believe they were maybe trying to find ways to need less, to crave less, as life in these mountains is quite hard and starvation was probably routine. Well, a catastrophe took place when the pile came down. It must have taken part of the mountain with it, as it seems to have been a huge and probably heavy construction. It took many human lives with it also. They say that the pile eventually reached nothingness, and then its being itself crumbled into pieces, all of them contaminated with non-being, at least to some extent. Some pieces gave rise to existences that were flimsy, elusive, without substance, like liquids, while others turned stiff and stringent. In other words, they say that as the pile broke down in shards, existence became varied, a bit as if it were served in many different dishes combining being and nothingness – like various ways to season what it is with something else. Existence acquired many varieties after the pile came down. Again, what was one became many. But it was not that several things then came into being out of one, but rather that there appeared many ways to be. Ways that make things one, ways that make things several. Later, Myriam spent hours telling us how she believed in *Shekhinah* – that presence that can be found in shards, in fragments, that we ought to bring together. She somehow thought all this could have come from the pile the Oromos tried to make stand on top of the mountains. When the pile came down, significance itself was scattered on the floor and under it. And with the pile down, there were also many ways to make sense.

(L) Myriam reckons this tale of the origin of the many varieties of existence became the legend about the Tower of Babel, where different languages became spoken as a punishment for human lack of humility in trying to reach the sky. I always thought there was far more to language than the way people speak. Language is a translation of a way things are, and translations are part of how they are. I wonder, though, why the tower of Muja became the Tower of Babel – it was moved away from Africa and it was moved from the many ways things can be to the many ways we describe how they are. It seems to me, as it does too often when the African past is concerned, that the tower in Babel was a way to hide the pile in Muja. Languages are ways to reduce some things while not reducing others. But the fall of Babel left existence alone, singular; even though there are many things that exist. Beyond the fog curtain that is the conversion of a pile in Africa into a tower in the Middle East, the Oromos thought Muja witnessed the origin of a plurality in the very heart of being. Our judgments of what is true or false are always within the shards, and we never know how many there are. I think the Oromos found a way to vindicate reliance on our careful hiking around in a landscape of insecurity.

(M) You understand, of course, that I'm not sure at all if I have means to know whether anybody ever built this pile in Muja. I like what they told me. I don't mind legends. Sometimes I even suspect my memories are themselves legend-makers. But I did find some insight in my trip to the mountains in Wollo. I think Muja became for me a symbol of how things can be incommensurably different from each other. To have a sense of reality is always to have one sense of reality: we cannot judge cooking as if it is entertaining. It is really curious that Muja became Babel – if you hear me in English, my Amharic doesn't make sense. But here in Africa, we don't make these sharp distinctions between languages that I learned to make with the *faranjis*. Languages mix together all the time, and we don't listen to one language judging its grammar by the standards of another one. We get around using a mix of them. Sometimes one language is just not enough – and yet we can make it be enough; but in order to do that, we have to let something go.

(N) The more I think about it, more I find it enlightening that Muja became Babel. I did learn to transit between one language and another – and to do it quite self-consciously, like the *faranjis*. I very often think I find things in translations (even more than what I lose). I move to another language and suddenly something that wasn't there appears – it is brought up like that, suddenly, without previous notice. Translation is a curious thing – nothing can be anticipated when we move to another language. In fact, if it were otherwise, Babel – or Muja – wouldn't have had that much impact, for one could easily move from one language to another. What happens is that when we move to another language, we often discover the unfelt discomforts that we had in the previous one – and the unfelt comforts, for sure. I feel sometimes alien in Amharic, because there is a genuine gap between languages. It is a gap we cross all the time, but it is not straightforward to explain how we do it. I think there is a gap between these many ways things are that these people in Wollo told me about. This gap was brought about in Muja. A discontinuity that rules over the different ways things are – and it is an interesting kind of ruler. It makes me remember your principle of irreduction. It rules because there is always something to cross between the different ways of being. No way can just follow, as a matter of course, from any other. There is a pause in things. Things have to stop at a crossroads in order to change their way of being. The crossroads is the lore of Muja, as I understand it. (As much as translation itself was what we took from Babel.) In a sense, we cannot have different things if there are no separators. These separators, although so hard to attain directly, are what I learned to consider the main ingredient of how things are.

Well, I have written more than I thought would be suitable. I wish you luck and peace.

Respectfully,
Idarsal Selassie

New fragments of Heraclitus and the polemos (2)

Contrary to popular belief, Heraclitus survived his ailments and recovered as soon as he left Ephesus. He settled for awhile – perhaps with Hermodoros – close to Assos and then carried on traveling. This was the beginning of a millenary life, in which he lived close to the Etna and could have met Empedocles, in various parts of Italy and the rest of Europe up to the twentieth century. Then, he went to India, went to Brazil and spent his last few years in Deiral-Balah, Gaza. In early 2009, he disappeared, although there are rumors that he has been seen in various places since. This is hard to confirm, as he had a habit of living and traveling anonymously. During all his years, he reworked the very book he had deposited at Artemis's temple in Ephesus. As he left the place with no copy of the text, he resumed his work using only the fragments that emerged afterwards, and legend has it that he always carried a Diels-Kranz (DK) version of what survived of his writings.

In 2012, a book was published in Brazil[134] in which a group of anarcheologists unveil fragments of an updated version of Heraclitus's book. They claim that Heraclitus had a working copy of the revamped book with him in Gaza when the bombardments took place and he disappeared. They can only reconstruct fragments based on what was available in more than one language. (Apparently Heraclitus had started to write versions of his new book in several languages but didn't complete any.) They published these fragments in Portuguese, claiming that the philosopher had expressed this wish in the few years he lived in parts of Brazil around 1987 and 2004.

What follows is a selection of these fragments, mostly translated from the Brazilian book. In some cases, marked with a star, I have considerably changed the version appearing there based on other versions available. Their numeration is built from the standard DK numbers.

> 53. There is *polemos* when things are created by other things; it makes some believe they are gods and others believe they are just mortals. It makes some into slaves, others not.

> 128*. Not even once we can swim in the same river. Now is a passing state, but here is also a passing state. Without the passing of time, the river is not a river. Some say that they can imagine an atom of time and picture the river there – maybe even swim there. But I say there would be no river left. Cratylus corrected me clearly by saying that once is always once too much. Cratylus said that the water that arrives at one's feet is not the same that reaches one's legs. It is not the same drop. It is not the same sample. It is not the same tide.

> 130. Whenever something comes about, a *polemos* comes about, and then there is politics – a dispute between governments.

131. *Polemos* often lies where we don't expect. It lies not only in the catapults, but also in the surprise that meets the *polemos*, in the temptation for *polemos* and in the knowledge of *polemos*.

133*. I often prefer to talk about each *polemos* in turn.
Not about the beginning, not about the end. I'm not into principles. They grow old. I'm into aging instead. Even if all things are grounded in the same source, each thing ages in a different manner.

138. I liked to say that the stronger prevails because it is stronger – and not due to any law of the strongest.

139*. The route of the *polemos* is never other than the one that cuts through fringes.

141*. When *physis*, which is *polemos*, was replaced by a realm of laws – and nature stopped being strong to become merely ruling – it freed itself of wild dispositions and became merely an instrument of order and progress. What was left of *polemos* itself was then thrown into the realm of chance.

144. In order for people to reach *logos,* they should become *like rolling stones.*

145. It is quite common to exorcise *polemos* from the world by holding that each thing has its core. A core is a conquered territory where battles have already been fought and everything is properly trained and tamed. We find no cores, we find more and more things. In order to persuade ourselves that the world is rid of any *polemos*, we posit a world that has no more things than the ones that seem to be unmoving.
And then we can say, with the sort of philosophy that is most popular in the last centuries, that the *polemos* is in our heads.

147. In the beginning, there was no politics. Neither was there *polemos*. Nor beginning.

150. [...] on me live the philosophers who didn't intend to have a grip on things [...] but rather would approach everything on their tiptoes [...]

155. I keep meeting people who act as if disputes are about poles. Polarization distorts the *polemos* – *polemos* has no poles. Its force lies in the sliding of the poles. [...] only when we tire, we choose sides.

157*. P*hysis* should not be translated as "nature." I have myself used that translation sometimes, either because I was confused or because I wanted to make myself understood. But, come to it, nature cannot be hidden. It is all there, all available, all open to us – even when we don't understand it. *Physis* is rather the power or the act in all things – the blossoming of the rose, but not the rose. The former is what is hidden – even when all the roses have blossomed.

157b*. Nature, by contrast, is no more than a scapegoat.

169*. I have heard many people talking about idealism and realism. It seems there is a realm of thought without nature and a realm of nature closed in itself. [...] then they ask themselves whether they have created nature. I say that the moon created the tides. There are slow creations and fast creations. It is like a Doppler effect. Things happen because there are slower things around them.

175. [...] as with the government of the states, our control of ourselves is subject to insurrections, rebellions, strikes, civil disobedience and *coups d'état*.

177. There is no cage without an escape route somewhere. Still, we cannot escape from the *polemos* without it – for it is escape itself. It is what doesn't fit in itself. It fits no cage. It is not present, but it springs from what is somehow omni-absent.

178.* There are no *archés*. What we take to be *archés* are often no more than the slowest things to change. Like when we think we spot a turtle holding the world. Or we spot laws of nature guiding it. Or we spot a unitary cosmos grounding all its parts. What is slow is not always a metronome setting the pace for the orchestra. Often, it is another instrument. *Polemos*, by contrast, is just the lack of *arché*s – it is an an-*arché*.

196.*[...] While the river changes, it changes what it drags and what can swim in it. Nothing is necessary or contingent once and for all. The flowing of the river changes not only what there is but also what there possibly is. No law is immune to flooding. Some of them are just too costly to challenge at the moment.

197*. The world is not a stage, for a stage is an *arché*. There is always a backstage. There is also a back-*arché*. Things can be ready and ripe, but they don't stay put.

198*. [...] [On the other hand,] attachment to *arché*s springs from an interest in control: find out who is the boss and we shall deal with him. Find the laws of the land and we will strike our deals. But no empire lasts, because no realm lasts. Not even the realm of all things. There is no principle that could prevent any other beginning. Bacteria, worms and viruses as much as roaches and rats haven't surrendered to the alleged human victory over the animalia. Human gestures are themselves full of anomalies that resist the humanizing principle imposed on all things and mainly on whomever happens to be born into the human species.

202. We have been hunting the animals but not the viruses inside them – we never eat from the same plate twice. The hunted animal is a cradle. They say back to dust. They told me I'm going to go back to dust myself. I ask: which dust?

203*. *Polemos* is waged by mercenaries, war deserters, those who escape from the bright light, those who riot at more than one pace, those who rot, those immune to antibiotics.

204. Things for us, in our perspective, from our own viewpoint... I hear about this often, and often it sounds like we are the ones who possibly cannot escape the veil that covers everything with our fingerprints. It is as if the issue is whether we can go beyond the pale. [...]It sounds like we're talking like spies: how to break in, how to see beyond these limits set for us. Or, rather, we are engaged in an exercise of voyeurism (of those things in themselves). I say that things are rarely just there to be perceived. Voyeurism – but of what sort? They rarely are seen like when we look at our neighbors through binoculars. More often, they give a peep show. They decide what and when and how they will show themselves to us, and they go back home after work hours.

205*. *An-arché*: fate, like grounding, looses its grip when it becomes plural. "Everything is fated" could mean "there are fates for everything." There are grounds for everything. For each thing, there is plenty of ground, several fates, and many intersecting laws applicable. This plurality itself concocts the *polemos*: an-*arché*. Instead, people often pick a single *arché* and herd it. We cherish poles, identities and labels. We hold on to the lasting banks of the river to give a name to it – we think of what there is in terms of what can be tracked down. Yet *polemos*, leaving its traces everywhere, is always changing tracks. We asphyxiate things by trying to lock *polemos* out. [However, just] like a stone or a grain of sand, it has no doors.

207*. Eros is Eris, and Eris carries *polemos*. [...] It is a centrifugal force that rips apart what is glued together. Its centripetal antidote acts often with a quite different speed. When we look for ingredients of things, we don't find in them the craving to fragment. There are no ingredients. It is like a jigsaw puzzle that cannot be completed and yet is never in pieces.

210. While everything is connected to everything, there is no such thing as everything [no whole].

212. Borders are where the war has stopped. Being? There cannot be anything but a cease-fire.

213. [They say, someone says] that words are themselves prejudices. So are things.

214. Nature is full of dirty roads, escape routes, forgotten paths and shortcuts. There is no bird's-eye view of all those things, only groping in the occasional shining light. Each moment would require a different world map.

215*. Politics loves to hide behind the bushes of nature.

222. A friend once explained to me that ontology is politics viewed from above. I have never stopped thinking about that. But I feel the vertigo.

223. In the middle of all, there is *polemos*.

226. Who is this *polemos*? A character? I am the character; *polemos* is no more than a *façon de parler*.

228*.[...] No description of the world can afford not to stir it. Don't read me as if I were saying that there is *polemos* or *logos* or anything. I don't deal in catalogues. Everything can be ripped apart. When I talk about what there is, I want to unlock something. The unlocking matters to me. What matters is what escapes from one's words.

236. I like what needs to be thought on the tips of one's feet.

237. I hear people asking what the world is made of. It cannot be made of anything but of world, I want to say. They want a list. There are things that cannot be in a list. There are lists of things that wouldn't fit in the world, the world wouldn't fit in any of them.

252. *Polemos* doesn't do anything, but it doesn't leave anything done either.

255*. The *polemos* is a stage of *hubris:* struggle can melt each convention about ontology.

259*. The *polemos* is no demiurge. It gives birth to no chaos, to no order. It leaves a trace of exceptions behind it. Eventually, they germinate...

260. We avoid thinking about what has no government. It is as if thinking dealt with governed matters. [I have been convinced that] to think through the lack of government is not itself to provide it with a government. There are more things between chaos and order than have been dreamed of in our last anxious centuries.

263*. Things are often escaping their orbits. But we don't see them, we see the orbits. *physis* lives in unveiling. It is not in the ready-made stuff. Not the castle in the sand, but the grains of sand that are now tied to each other.

271. [It often seems as if we are] taming nature in order to tame people. The world is presented as a universe of servitude. Sometimes of inescapable servitude. The open possibilities are no more than concessions. So people fight for concessions. [But, in fact,] no one ever has anything to lose other than their chains. To win or to lose are things that happen only to those who are ruled.

274. Decrepitude is everywhere. It brings together several forces of nature – and it has no borders. Things get loose with age. And there is always more degeneration to take place; our final form is the lack of form. I always feel a new wrinkle carving out my face again, making my body more disconnected, more flexible, more trembling, more clumsy, less intended. Then come the wrinkles on the wrinkles themselves. Aging is centrifugal. It is an internal force of dilapidation. All the role models disappear with age. And I feel close to everything around. They are all very old. We cannot imagine how decrepit the things around us are that we name beautiful. We convince ourselves that they were created and therefore they are still young. They are not. They were all carved out by

wrinkles and further wrinkles. I think of each thing around me as hosting a fountain of eternal oldness.

277b*. Thought cannot strip off the garments of the world. It is itself a garment. Nothing, not even the world, is ever fully naked – nor fully clothed. P*hysis* loves to hide itself – it cannot be fully unveiled. Thought has nothing to do with the naked universe. *physis*, and the *polemos* that infests it, is rather in the undressing.

286. When I talk about the *polemos*, I'm not describing the underground of things; I'm rather inserting underground beneath them.

286a*. [...] I don't do geology. I dig tunnels.

286b.* Words are actors. So are my words, *logos*, *polemos*... They perform different characters in different acts. At most, they carry a style throughout. *Polemos* is a style of acting.

299*. I talk about what breaks up. It is no principle (and no end). If I liked units, I would say that the units of the world are wrinkles, as things are folded on wrinkles. Things are to be seen as the origami of what there is. But I don't particularly like units; I prefer to let them go.

321. No, I don't talk about an ontology of what is left loose. I talk rather about what, in ontology, leaves things loose.

327a*. Let *physis* remain hidden, and yet don't turn your eyes away from its stains.

Apocrypha from the Sahagún Colloquia and the bringers of movement (3)

In 1524, twelve Franciscan friars arrived in Mexico to make sure the conversion of the pagans was going in a suitable direction after Cortez's *Conquista*. Some years later, they convened in Tepeculco under Bernardino de Sahagún with twelve *tlamatinime*, priests and wise men of the place, to discuss, in Nahuatl, matters of how things are. The manuscript made by

Sahagún and his indigenous collaborators transcribing the colloquia came to light years later, but always in an incomplete format. The material that circulated featured subservient and easily convinced natives. But, out of Sahagún's material – composed of two books (one of thirty and the other of twenty-one chapters) – only the first fourteen chapters were available. The missing chapters included parts where the natives described their creed more thoroughly. Sahagún, himself a historian of the so-called New Spain[135] and considered one of the first anthropologists[136], has changed the structure of his book of colloquia quite dramatically throughout the years.[137] It is unclear what precise effect he hoped his transcriptions would have, but the manuscript that ended up circulating (and was later published[138]) does little more than portray the *tlamatinime* as ready to convert to Christianity.

There is a considerable amount of controversy about the historical accuracy of the document. Some say that it is no more than a piece of literature, ultimately having evangelical purposes, while an increasing number of scholars grant it historical veracity. The issue, however, has become more complicated in the last few years, as two supposed fragments of the transcriptions of the colloquia have emerged. They were found in a monastery in Popocatépetl, Veracruz, in relatively good condition. They display the Spanish version and parts of the Nahuatl version of the two fragments. They have supposedly been copied by hand from the original transcriptions and preserved for centuries, hidden in the obscurity of the monastery library. The authenticity of the fragments is under all sorts of religious, historical, ethnographical and anarcheological scrutiny. A factor in favor of their legitimacy is that they both express mostly the views of the *tlamatinime,* with almost no substantial counter from the twelve friars. This, however, is not decisive. The monks could have kept the manuscripts for several reasons unrelated to it being historically factual.

In any case, the first fragment includes two lines present in the published version in chapter 7 of the first book – lines 1017 and 1018. It seems to fit well in chapter 7, specifically between lines 1016 and 1017, and could have been removed for censorship... The lines of the fragment are therefore referred to as VII-1016-2, VII-1016-3 and so forth, VII-1016-1 being the line published as 1016. The second fragment seems to fit somewhere in the lost chapter 16, also of the first book. As the chapter is otherwise entirely lost, the lines are referred here as XVI-?-1, XVI-?-2, etc. What appears here has been translated from the Spanish version.

VII-1016-2   because every sun rises and sets,
the sun that creates a day
as much as its absence that creates a night
the sun that creates years, generations, eras.

VII-1016-6   One sun after the other.
It was in Teotihuacan
that our present horizon emerged.
This is the fifth sun,
a sun that doesn't rule by water, air, earth or fire

VII-1016-11   like the previous ones, but by movement.
Its navel nothing but the friction
of one ruler against another
and its *Chicoóztoc*[139] is not one but many.
The sacred place shines in different mountains

VII-1016-16   and in valleys, lakes, cities and holes.
The gods of the fifth sun
are moving forces, they don't have addresses,
they have roads.
They erode.

VII-1016-21   They digest. They burn. They flood.
It was the Fifth Sun that burned away the
previous four;
it is not a static sun
but one that has a different light each day.
As those who destroyed all the other stabilities,

VII-1016-26   they are liberators.
We suspect that this is why some *macehuals*,
common people, welcomed you in their spasms;
because you were also dissolvers,
destroyers of a rule,

VII-1016-31   you brought changes, shifts, alterations, new starts.
Little some of us knew
That you were bringing
a celebration of the un-moved.

	The spirit of the *huehuehlahtolli*[140]
VII-1016-36	is that a god frees us from an order,
	from another need.
	A god is what shakes the perennial.
	None of them can rule all because
	since *Nanahuatzin*[141] went to fire in Teotihuacan,
VII-1016-41	other gods have bumped into their realms.
	gods of the ancient customs
	were not those that command,
	but those that disrupt.
	We need them to displace the commanders.
VII-1016-46	We invoke them to shake what is about,
	to bring up the riot and to go away.
	We invoke them because without disruption,
	we wouldn't have been born,
	we wouldn't have grown.
VII-1016-51	They make us move.
	The *tzitzimine,* by contrast, are the keepers.
	Those who preserve.
	The gods come and exorcise
	the devils of fixity
VII-1016-56	because they come unnoticed.
	This is why gods are several –
	the world is full of chains,
VII-1016-59	full of traps.
VII-1017	That's why gods are invoked,
VII-1018	that's why we pray for them.
	So you see that your gods didn't protect you
	from the holy hands of the Conquerors.
	They couldn't because they are not out there
	and if they were, they would have recognized
XVI-?-5	the presence of a greater Force
	and perhaps they would be first to bow their heads.

	And then some priests have contested:
	Much as there are turmoil and havoc
	amid our peoples since you have arrived,
XVI-?-10	we should see your arrival as an event
	of the Fifth Sun.
	We are in the horizon of disruption
	and our gods are revered
	because they are those who unsettle the affairs.
XVI-?-15	They are those who undo the chains
	and leave things unheld
	and, as such, open to new rulers;
	for no God can both free us and protect us.
	To unchain is to erode a determination.
XVI-?-20	To protect is to cherish it.
	Whatever we worship in the Fifth Sun
	is to be worshiped not as shelter but as roads.
	Our gods are here to free us,
	and those who advertise their protection
XVI-?-25	are in deviant ways –
	even though we are entitled to wish protection
	when our land is invaded by murders like you.

	Many *tsitsimine* have come to us recently.
	They advertise security
XVI-?-30	or redemption, or a superior order.
	They cannot resist the heat of the Fifth Sun.
	Yet they make their bites,
	like you do with all this small *tsitsimine*
	that you brought to infect us
XVI-?-35	and kill us and make us feel unprotected.

	The *huehuehlahtolli* is all for what unchains,
	for holier is what makes us escape,
	and sacred is forgiving.
	Our gods are those who forgive,
XVI-?-40	forgo and forget.

	Like in your Bible the debt is cancelled
	after a number of years
	and promises are forgotten.
	Such are the acts of our gods in the Fifth Sun.
XVI-?-45	They are forgivers.
	They are many, they are everywhere
	because they don't dwell in small numbers,
	and because this sun brings dispute,
	our ancient *tlamatinime*
XVI-?-50	had different liturgies
	and they spot movement
	in different places
	and fixity in different places
	depending on taste, season, transport.
XVI-?-55	For movement itself cannot be caught,
	except in movement.

	This is why, as you have noticed,
	hesitation, deception,
	lack of decision and of certainty
XVI-?-60	are appreciated by some of us, priests.
	Under the Fifth Sun, they are virtues,
	because they manifest movement.
	Even though they are painful
	they bring about what redeems us
XVI-?-65	and show us the road out.
	So I advise you: beware.
	We live in the horizon of uncertainty,
	and no Conquest will dispel it.
	As for us, we seek and treasure
XVI-?-70	what we don't know.
	It is less heavy on us.
	We distrust what seems to merely repeat,
	for the Fifth Sun is the sun
	of what is loose.

Out of Jesmonite   Gisel Carriconde Azevedo, Sculpture: resin and jesmonite, 2010

Chapter 3
Fragments

Leibniz on contingency

Antoine Arnauld famously gave Leibniz a hard time because of what he deemed the excessive role Leibniz ascribed to necessity. He accused Leibniz of leaving little room for either human free will or God's freedom to create future events disconnected from present ones. In fact, Leibniz envisaged a way to consider concrete things as very much like abstract ones – he dreamt of a *mathesis universalis* that would bring the sensible into the scope of calculation, at least in principle.[142] He thought that what divided the abstract and the concrete – the sensible – was simply the line between infinite and finite mathematics. These steps, feared Arnauld, placed Leibniz dangerously close to a Spinozist image of the world as ruled by immanent necessity, with space neither for human nor divine freedom nor for contingencies, except perhaps for those that boil down to human ignorance. The danger was that, in order to fit the connections between events into a basically mathematical analysis, the first casualty would be the possibility of genuine accidents in the world.

Louis Couturat attributed to Leibniz a proposition he called the principle of reason: a proposition is true if and only if it is analytical.[143] An analytical truth was taken by Leibniz to be one where the predication brings in only what is already present in the subject. In other words, in any true judgment, the predicate is contained in the subject; no truth is other than an unpacking of a definition. An event can be no more than a consequence entailed by a true predicate of a subject. This seems to leave no room for surprises, nor for human or divine decisions that are not predetermined. The principle of reason makes it sound as if the appeal to monads and the insistence that this is the best of all possible worlds were no more than a roundabout way to dismiss everything but necessity and determination.

Yet I believe Leibniz laid the basis for a very useful route to think about what is up for grabs. Several features of his system pave the way for a conception of contingency by exploring the consequences of metaphysical dependence.[144] Leibniz conceived of his monads as substances and, as such, they endure and subsist through changes. Following a tradition inaugurated by Descartes (and followed by Spinoza), his substances had nevertheless no substrata; nothing assures their identity but the infinite discernible predicates that indicate the events they go through. This is an important departure from the Aristotelian notion of substance. First, because there is no such thing for Leibniz as primary substance.[145] Second, because although substances are thought as self-standing, or rather dependent only on God – like in Descartes[146] – they are intimately related to all the other substances in their world. Substances are intrinsically worldly. In fact, there is nothing to substances but their infinite predicates that connect them to the world where they are. Hence, indiscernibles are identical – as much as identicals are indiscernible (that indiscernibles are identical *and* identicals are indiscernible is often called Leibniz's Law).

Arnauld accused Leibniz of ascribing to God the creation of Adam, who is by definition a sinner. For Leibniz Adam has to be a sinner, but nothing forced God to create him – Adam is the product of a choice God made. Adam was chosen in virtue of all the other items in the best possible world and given all that, Adam has to be a sinner but he doesn't have to exist. In other words, Leibniz appeals to the plurality of worlds: there is a world for Adam that happened to be the best according to the judgment of God. It is contingent that this is the best possible world – although God necessarily chooses the best of all possible worlds. Adam existed because of the (wisest possible) choice made by God. Spinoza would have it that every thing exists necessarily, but not Leibniz. In Williamson's terms (see chapter 1,

Contingentism and haecceitism), Leibniz embraces contingentism, although he is to a large extent close to permanentism. Each monad is worldly – God created the world in which there is Adam, and Adam is a sinner. God is a creator of worlds, not of individuals.

Each monad in the world depends on all the others through their dependence on God.[147] Because a monad is attached to all the others in the world, its being is distributed throughout the world through the reach of their perceptions and the scope of their actions. In fact, Leibniz's monads are places in a world in two distinct senses: they are connected to the others in a concerted manner, and they are authorities over a body attached to them. These two senses have to do with two dimensions: *c)* the *institution* of a scope of government and *b)* the *exercise* of governance over this already instituted scope. This body that expresses a monad is where its governance is exercised as it is under its authority. The province of a monad is itself infinitely divisible in chunks that are governed by (other) monads no matter how small they are,[148] and are under the jurisdiction of other monads that in turn have to *institute* a scope and *exercise* their government. Leibniz's substances can be understood like a generalization – or a speculative flight – from souls in the human relation between bodies and souls. The former is under some sort of government by the latter. The matter under a monad's authority is like its feud – its territory. Monads are compossible, possible together with others – a possible world is an aggregation of compossibles. It is with the other monads in a worldly relation that each monad *institutes* its scope of jurisdiction – those scopes have to be compossible. Compossibility has something to do with *communitas*, in Esposito's terms (see Chapter 1): nothing is safe from the rest of the world, except, of course, the world itself.

Leibniz's worlds are ultimately composed of simple substances that are each different from all the others – each has a specific place in both senses mentioned above. They are infinitely many. Monads can belong to different types – some of them have apperceptive capabilities and are rational souls or spirits, whereas others are ordinary or sensitive souls – but all of them are on the same ontological footing. Ontology, in that sense, is flat (at least within a possible –and real– world).[149] To be sure, a world of monads is not a world of atoms, for there is an infinite divisibility of areas of jurisdiction for different monads. Each monad reigns over a (variable) part of matter[150] and as matter divides, each piece of it is the expression or the body of a substance. Monads enjoy from birth a family resemblance with infinitesimals. In matter, there are no atoms – and because of this substances are infinitely many, like infinitesimals. Schaffer and Bohn have recently introduced the idea of a *gunky* and a *junky* world – in the former everything has a (proper) part and in the latter everything is a (proper) part.[151] In these terms, a monadological world is clearly gunky (but notice that Leibniz's worlds are not junky for they compose a whole). Flat ontology entails that there are no ontological hierarchy between the entities – in Leibniz's monadology substances are not such that any of them has by its nature the upper hand over others. All of them are worldly and enjoy the same ontological status.

Each monad is both a part of the world and a part of experience. Each simple substance has perceptive capabilities while the events they go through are determined by their predicates and therefore by their perspective on things. There is a general perceptive capability that enables each monad to have a mental pole capable of sensing the rest of the world – although in different intensities. Because each monad experiences the world, experiences are themselves constitutive of the world – there is a sense in which each substance is a piece of experience that is itself determined by all of its other world-mates. The spread of perception makes experience with the rest of the sensible dispense consciousness – apperception is therefore a type of perception. Leibniz understands perception in the broader context of how different entities co-exist while taking into consideration the others. His monads need no windows because what they ought to perceive is already within their inner constitution; and still they perceive and the act of perception is itself an event. Perception is a crucial element in the life of a monad, for monads are closer to processes than to materials. They are what will occur, more than they are building blocks of matter.

Leibniz's monads have no location in space (as they are presented in the *Monadology*[152]), and although each one has an area where it is expressed, this feud is not itself the monad. The feud is primarily where the monad exercises its authority. The appeal to monads give rise to ontologies in which materials have no major role – materials, as such, are not protagonists. Typically, monads are not part of a materialist recipe – except when matter is equated with processes or potentialities and not with materials.[153]

The concrete is instead explained in terms of monads. The ultimate reason for things appeals to monads and their interaction – together with compossibility within a world and the appeal to the pre-established harmony that makes clocks work in synchrony without consulting each other. However, the sufficient reason for something to happen is spelled out in terms of monads, in terms of simple substances in their being part in the world. The possibility is open for contingency to be thought, therefore, in terms of the actualities that compose the world.

On the other hand, no entity is disconnected from its world-mates. Interconnectedness of all monads is achieved through perception: every monad perceives others that in turn perceive others. Interconnectedness is therefore experience-based. Leibniz considers that for whatever is concrete, existence depends on being perception.[154] There can be no worldly vacuous actuality; that is, there is no worldly actuality that fails to affect (or have an effect on) anything. Because every worldly event boils down to existing entities while no such entity is fully disconnected from all the others, Leibniz is neither a standard priority monist nor a typical priority pluralist.[155] He does ascribe to actual simple substances all the events in the world as pluralists would do, but he also take monads to be all interconnected in a way that prefigures a whole as the monist would claim. Leibniz's monadology is a system where monads are responsible for everything worldly while they are themselves intrinsically interconnected.

For a monad, each event is dependent on infinite others; it is reliant upon its world. It may seem that contingency is no more than ignorance – no monad can foresee everything, because each has a partial, distorted view of the world. Notice, however, that even if contingency is no more than an expression of ignorance, it is not simply an affair of human ignorance; rather, it has to do with the constitutive ignorance of each monad. Ignorance is a feature of all simple substances – monads – and therefore contingency constitutes each of them. They are themselves incomplete and dependent on the rest of the world for their satisfaction – Adam would have no place in a world with no apple trees, for instance. To be in the world is to be in the open, for one's government is measured by all the others. Only when the whole world is taken into account, where all monads come together, ignorance subsides. Contingency is conceived as a feature of the trajectory of each monad, given that such trajectory depends on infinite other monads. Only from a world-encompassing point of view that can deal with this infinity is a monad's fate not up for grabs.

Monadologies

Leibniz conceives of substances as governing authorities at the mercy of their world-mates. We can separate Leibniz's conception of contingency from his other assumptions about an available omniscient perspective on the world and on the articulation of all substances in a pre-established harmony. It is fruitful to disentangle the idea of a monadology and the particular use Leibniz made of it. In this sense, his doctrines can be divided in two groups: those that propose a general and systematic (monadological) way of thinking about the sensible and those that have to do with his particular engagements and commitments. I don't intend to provide an exegesis of Leibniz's work in terms of this division, and in the previous section I did no more than highlight some features of Leibniz's system that point towards a monadological approach to contingency. I do think that the idea of a monadology contains interesting elements to apply to contingency – and some general dimensions of the idea can be isolated from other tenets of Leibniz's metaphysics.

These dimensions come with blanks that can be filled in different manners. I take at least three thinkers to have developed the central tenets of a monadological ontology further: Tarde, Whitehead and Latour.[156] While Tarde explicitly acknowledges the influence of Leibniz on his speculative system, Whitehead intends his philosophy of organism to be an alternative to other systems of modern philosophy, including Leibniz's. Whitehead's explicit inspiration was Descartes and Locke, and a metaphysical path they opened but could not follow since they were prey to the attractions of a metaphysics of substances and qualities. His system, I claim, is nevertheless to a large extent a monadology. Latour, for his part, is more explicit about it as he realizes that his basic entities, actants, can perfectly well be called monads.[157] The three of them have made different uses of the general ideas of a monadology without committing themselves to the entirety of Leibniz's system. They provide existence proofs of monadologies that are not fully Leibnizian – and show that we can hope to make sense of a monadology in general. Such monadology provides interesting insights about contingency in terms of world-dependence and, as we saw, the insufficiency of each monad without all the others.

A monadology, therefore, is something broader than Leibniz's system (or any system in particular) and therefore it is possible to separate a monadology in general from a system in particular. In order to appreciate the more general character of the idea of a monadology, I will enumerate some of what I believe to be the features that must be present in any such system. These are related and yet separated features and, while they are central components of Leibniz's thought, they are by no means sufficient to make up the core of his system. I propose these as features of all monadologies, although in different and – we will see – sometimes deviant forms. In the last section I presented Leibniz's account of contingency highlighting precisely these features. I take the five defining features of a monadology to be:

1. Flat ontology – Monadologies posit entities that are responsible for what goes on in the world. They stand on the same footing – none of them is ontologically superior to any other. They affect things through their position, either by instituting with the other monads a scope for their expression or by exercising their governance in this scope (see *a* and *b* above). Leibniz conceives of his monads as substances that are compossible within a world – they are part of a concerto where each of them play a part.[158] Tarde conceives of his monads as articulating in equal footing associations whereby they can exercise their beliefs and desires. Whitehead posits actual entities as the prime component of what is actual and they interact more like an improvisation than like a scored piece of music. Latour conceives his actants (or actors, or monads) as making alliances and forming networks to resist tests of strength and subsist.[159] In all cases, these entities are such that no prior ontological structure makes any of them stronger than any other.

2. Perception is everywhere – Monadologies are ontologies of perception – all entities perceive others. Perception is not

a privilege of conscious beings or organisms but is crucial in the glue between the different entities. This is a reason why monadologies are often accused of panpsychism: they extend to everything a feature associated with mentality – that of perceiving their surroundings. To perceive, at least in a monadological understanding, is not something that requires a full-fledged (human) mind. Monadologies could also seem anthropomorphic,[160] but perception can be very different from what humans do with their sensorial capabilities. Monadological perception has to do with the capacity to be affected. Leibniz takes all his monads to be affected by the presence of the others – although only some of them are capable of (conscious) apperception. Whitehead considers perception to be the central connection between actual entities – efficient causation is itself a form of perception where the effect is what is perceived. For him perception provides a general scheme for metaphysics to think through how things relate. Latour, in a Tardean move, conceives his actants as guided by how they perceive things to craft alliances and be part of networks in their turn affected by what happens in other actants and networks. In monadologies, to be is strongly linked to being both perceived and perceiving.

3. There are entities behind anything – In monadologies, an explanation always boils down to a matrix of responsibilities ascribed to the basic entities. There are no general principles or necessities that dispense being supported by actual units. Nothing subsists without sponsoring and those sponsors are, ultimately, what explain both regularities and whatever lies behind them.[161] Monadologies are ontologies of agency, although in Leibniz monads have their capacity to act bound by their internal constitution. In any case, the action of a monad – and events are always traced down to predicates – is behind anything worldly. In Tarde, monads have to be behind associations and their permanence in time. The basic tenet of Whitehead's philosophy of organism is his ontological principle: no actual entity, no reason.[162] Latour's actants compose networks, translations, orders

and time.¹⁶³ He inherits Whitehead's conception of *concrescence* whereby concrete features are always a product of the interaction of agents. It is a very monadological idea, for it allows for no element to be a scenario for existing entities unless it is itself built and maintained by existing entities.

4. No vacuous actualities – Monadologies conceive of their basic entities as interconnected; they affect and are affected (typically through perceptual links). There is nothing like a worldly entity enclosed in itself and unaffected by anything else. Monadologies are about interconnectedness, compossibility and an intrinsically distributed character of being. Basic entities are engaged in a worldly solidarity that encompasses everything that exists: to exist, in a monadology, is to co-exist. In Leibniz, monads are not chosen or created one by one but only attending to the compossibility that makes a world possible. Tarde is a prince of associations: nothing subsists on its own. In fact, this feature of monadologies is the counterpart of the previous one in the sense that both are related to sponsors: sponsors are required for everything and nothing stands without sponsors. Whitehead rejects vacuous actualities explicitly by considering a principle that no actual occasion subsists without affecting anything else.¹⁶⁴ Latour resists thoroughly the idea that something could subsist on its own and even that something can be known without being affected.¹⁶⁵ In all cases, nothing actual can dispense co-existence.

5. No substrata – The idea that indiscernibles are identical is central to any monadology for the basic entities posited are not identified through a substratum, but rather by what connects them to other entities. It is their position with respect to other entities that make them what they are – and these positions are all different and infinitely many. Basic entities are therefore worldly and enjoy no trans-world identity that would enable them to be something completely discernible in a different possible world. The reverse is also part of what a monadology is for a single entity cannot operate as something discernibly different – they cannot

be another entity when seen as something else. Leibniz is clear about his rejection of substrata and of discernible identicals – unsurprisingly, he espouses what we have called Leibniz's Law. Tarde and Latour hold that monads are to be identified by their history of associations. Latour believes that actants are not quite infinitely many but come in an indefinite number – as many units as there are calculating forces.[166] It seems like he could be departing from the idea that identicals are indiscernible, but he is in fact just emphasizing that there are indefinitely many monads that appear through different counting procedures (themselves sponsored by actants or networks). In any case, even if Leibniz's Law is not accepted in both of its senses, there is no room for substrata. Whitehead conceives his actual entities as having a real and an abstract essence, where the former is specified in terms of other actual entities.[167] He holds that no two actual entities could have the same real essence. The dismissal of substrata is the Cartesian element in monadologies: entities are not conceived of independently of what they do, of how they appear or act. As an immediate follow-up from this feature, monadological systems are contingentist.

Several additional features could be added to these basic ones. I believe the following four features would be corollaries of these six above. A first consequence of the previous features (1, 2 and 4) is that the most important modality in a monadology is *compossibility*. This is an important element for being up for grabs; no monad is strictly necessary and none is possible on its own. They are all compossible. This is because of the thoroughly mundane nature of all monads. Compossibility is the monadological tactic to deal with contingency: things are contingent on other things to their bones. In a monadology, events happen because it is compossible for them to happen. Compossibility is a modal relation, and in monadological terms it is a relation of infinitely (or indefinitely) many *relata*. This is one of the most crucial of Leibniz's insights about contingency: it is a matter of dependents, and of a number of them not easily counted.

A consequence of 3 and 4 is the second feature: *neither priority monism nor priority pluralism* in monadologies, at least not in any straightforward way. There is an emphasis in the plurality of different actual existents understood as basic entities as the pluralist holds but at the same time these entities are interconnected is important senses and none of them stands alone in a way that insinuates a whole – as the monist would have it. Schaffer, as I said, takes Leibniz to be a priority pluralist but it is clear at the same time that his world is gunky and everything has a (proper) part – every area of jurisdiction of a monad has subareas where other monads govern. In other monadologies, the actual world could be not only gunky but eventually junky – where everything is a (proper) part. Latour's actant is distinguished from networks only through tests of resistance that determine whether the network stands together or its composing actants split. It is reasonable to assume that all networks are themselves parts. In Whitehead all actual entities form a nexus that is itself part of a gunky concrescence – his cosmology is one where space and time enjoy no boundaries others than those crafted by the exercise of the actual entities.

An important feature of all monadologies – which follows from features 2 and 4 above – is that ontology is thought in terms of *governments* and jurisdictions. This is the third feature. A monad for Leibniz, Tarde or Latour – as an actual entity for Whitehead – can be understood as an authority; it is associated with an area of jurisdiction, its feud – or body. As Whitehead puts it, each actual entity has a mental and physical pole that can be seen as what institutes government (and does diplomacy) and on what it is exercised. Prehensions – perceptions and perceptions of absences – also can be physical or mental and various forms of integration of these forms of prehension enable various forms of experience. For Leibniz, a monad is not the materials under its authority, but rather the authority over them. Monads are centers of command, and also of commencement as every event is somehow written in them. This is why they have variable areas of jurisdiction in matter: authorities can be exerted over different governed bodies. Monads are particles of authority. A monadology depicts the world more as a collective of subjects than as a collection of objects.

Further, when we say that there are monads inside the jurisdiction of a monad, we mean that there are other authorities within an area of jurisdiction. It's like a feudal system or, in a sense, a federal government with jurisdiction over more than one state area, which all have many municipalities inside their areas, and so on, all the way to individuals and beyond. While in other monadologies – such as Tarde's or Latour's – federal governments negotiate with the subaltern authorities within their jurisdictions, in Leibniz's they all act together in a concerted way. Leibniz indeed thought that a general concert involved all authorities and no monad would act irrespective of this concert – he postulated a pre-established harmony. This was his way to tackle the problem of how a general design is implemented for the pre-established harmony is achieved by distributing governing tasks to an infinite number of local authorities. These authorities fulfill their tasks perfectly, and so the general harmony is maintained. The problems of interaction in any monadology are problems of relations between governments; monadologies always involve some form of diplomacy. A general concert of all authorities is one diplomatic solution – something akin to a global government solving everything ahead. In a monadology, entities act as units of local government, and their diplomatic ties – including ties with the subaltern authorities they have within their jurisdictions – shape their actions.

Finally, Leibniz conceives of a monad as dependent on its world, and it acts in its picture of the world. This picture is always distorted, because no (worldly) monad can have a non-located position; they each have a point of view. This distortion makes things that are closer look distinct, while other things look blurred because they are farther away. This is why units of a monadology have the feature that they can be described as *units of perspective* and what is more distant appears to them as non-individuated, non-discrete things. These blurred bits of a monad's picture can be compared with Whitehead's extensive continuum. The notion satisfies the obligation of transmutation, which Whitehead deems important to explain Leibniz's idea that monads have confused perceptions of the whole universe. Transmutation is the transformation of a set of actual entities into others. Each actual entity starts out on the extensive continuum and brings about further actual entities, which are the starting points for the next round of actual entities. Whitehead conceives the production of new actual entities as a result of the distorted view each entity has. Here, the congruence with Leibniz is striking: each entity acts to the best of its (necessarily distorted) knowledge. In Leibniz, no two areas of jurisdiction coincide, no two monads are the same and no two pictures of the world are identical. No monad has a view from nowhere, but each of them has a (unique) picture. For Tarde, each monad acts according to its beliefs – none is in a neutral doxastic state. In fact, in monadologies there is always some knowledge in the basic entities; nothing is fully knowledge-free. Neither can it know only about its own interior, for there is no interiority without exteriority. Thomas Nagel attributed to Donald Davidson a version of the Cogito with only one letter changed: *je pense donc je sais*.[168] Even though this is itself quite a monadological proposition, a more general version of the monadological Cogito would go one step further: *je suis donc je sais*.[169]

Harmonia post-estabilita

These features enable very different monadologies from the one espoused by Leibniz. In particular, several varieties of process philosophy (see Chapter 1 above, especially *Three speculative accounts of contingency*), mainly those of Tarde, Whitehead and Latour, can be read as monadologies. The main contrast between these monadologies and Leibniz's is that Leibniz makes an appeal to the world as a previously existing entity in a pre-established harmony. There is a general concert between the monads, a previously arranged diplomacy – a kind of agreed-upon *pax* – that is guaranteed by the unity of the world and by God's choice of this world. God chose this world – a choice which was contingent on this world happening to be the best of all possible ones – in a non-necessary move. Leibniz has a separate argument for God's freedom in this choice, but his monadology ensures that monads respond to the world and don't act by blind necessity. However, he adds that the world is a unity because monads interact in a previously concerted manner, in a pre-established harmony.

While Leibniz can be read as a philosopher of design – he endeavored to show how design can be implemented by assigning small areas of jurisdiction to governing entities – he paved the way for a diaspora of agency. He conceived of design in terms of governing entities acting over their jurisdictions. Process philosophy monadologies – such as those I just mentioned – tend to do away with design while keeping the diaspora of agency by giving something like a blank check to these governing entities. As a consequence, there is no articulated whole formed by the ensemble of all existents, no pre-established harmony.[170] Latour speaks instead of a post-established harmony,[171] and of aggregation as a pileup.[172] There is no concerted articulation of monads; diplomacy among them must be done on the ground and step by step. There is no global instance that can provide a harmony among the parts, no global *pax*, no pre-established clockmaker.

Deleuze compares Leibniz's metaphysics with Whitehead's by contrasting *closure* – the closure of predicates in the interior of a monad – and *capture* – where actual entities are, so to speak, in the wilderness of the world capturing others for some sort of engagement (what Whitehead calls "nexus").[173] A *closure monadology* has the institution of a jurisdiction pre-established in the interior of a monad while its exercise is dependent on a purely inert matter. Whitehead remarks that Leibniz starts out with a generalization of a Lockean account of mental operations, and pays little attention to the bodies that appear simply as what is governed. He then contrasts his philosophy of organism with Leibniz's government of monads and says that he intends to "hold the balance more evenly."[174] The idea that monads are governing actors can be disentangled from any assumption about a purely governed material. By contrast, a *capture monadology* is one where a world of existents is the ultimate actuality and each of them is up for grabs through associations, nexus, or networks. There are still a mental and a physical pole, but the former has to do with instituting an authority and the latter with exercising it.

Whitehead's philosophy of organism revolves around these two poles that are already present in Leibniz. He starts out with four basic notions: actual entities, prehensions (perceptions and perceptions of absences), nexus, and his ontological principle. The principle amounts to feature 3 above. Actual entities are not substances, and as such do not subsist on their own in time – they are also worldly, as they have no substrata (feature 5). These actual entities are always affecting and being affected through prehensions, and efficient causation is itself a way an entity affects others in a way that the effect is perceived. Whitehead would have it that to be is both to be perceived and to perceive. These entities prehend other entities forming nexus to such an extent that they are responsible for everything else that exists – no account of things can be presented without an appeal to the actual entities, according to his ontological principle. Actual entities are involved in the concrescence of things (which pertains to prehensions) and find themselves in space and time (which has to do with a theory of extensions). The first, genetic dimension of the actual entity's life is where the scope of an area of influence is negotiated; it is the dimension of (a) instituting the nexus that would enable the entity to affect the concrete. The second, morphological dimension of its life, is where the concrete is already formed and the authority of the actual entity is (b) exercised. The two poles are not associated with a governing spirit and a governed body, but rather to a concrescent nexus of actual entities and a concrete entity that is thereby formed. Eternal objects such as "red," "triangular," or "silent" are not actualities; instead, they take part of the prehensions of actual objects, and therefore they are qualities in perception that makes a difference in concrescence. They are potentialities that are only brought in by actual entities in their endeavor to perceive.

Whitehead's philosophy of organism has all the elements of a monadology and I read him as turning Leibniz's system upside down. In fact, he replaces most of Leibniz's further assumptions by what can be understood as their contraries. So, harmony is post-established, the world is an open entity subject to the concrescence driven by the actual existents, and God's (derivative) nature is written by what is created by the actual entities. The actual entities become genuine protagonists, and even inscribe the ever enlarging nature of God. The movement rehearsed in Leibniz with his conception of agency dispersed in the world is dissociated from ideas concerning design and ultimate authority. As a consequence, actual entities are subject to capture and are genuinely at the mercy of (or in *communitas* with) other subjects in the world that co-exist. It is a capture monadology, or a process one where nothing precedes the sovereign agency of the actual entities in whom no event is written but who bring about everything that becomes concrete.

Tarde and Latour also put forward process monadologies. Tarde talks about associations on the smallest scale, occupied by monads; they themselves host associations. Monads are also understood as being like infinitesimals, infinitely small, none of them governing the smallest possible feud. For Latour they are indefinite in number: it is the processes of association and dissociation themselves that determine how many they are. Monads don't pre-exist interaction – monads themselves are not pre-established. Similarly, Whitehead's current actual entities are a product of concrescence – of the coming together of different actual entities. An actual entity's capacity to engender other actual entities reveals its constitution – "[...] how an actual entity becomes constitutes what that actual entity is,"[175] says Whitehead's principle of process. In all cases, processes are more central than any material. In Whitehead's ontology, subjective forms and prehensions are general and apply to a variety of materials, while for Tarde, associations are general processes fairly independent of the materials that implement them. Tarde envisages sociology as a study of associations, which goes hand in hand with a monadology – the former looks at the structure of the social ties, while the latter deals in the various populations that are available for social interaction. In all these cases, monads – or actual entities – are units of processes and units of experiences.

In process monadologies, the rejection of substance is complete: nothing fully hosts its being. Neither monads nor associations nor networks are sufficient in themselves; actual entities are understood as agents in a process. Latour's actants are heavily connected to their networks and they cannot subsist without an association that lays the basis for their existence. Distributed being is close to the idea that existence requires sponsors – nothing is maintained by itself, and everything requires sustainability from somewhere (features 3 and 4 above). For Latour all events are trials (of strength, of weakness) – things are tested against their surroundings all the time. Everything could be involved in anything, producing anything else. Latour writes:

> "Can you doubt the link that joins B to C?" "No, I can't, unless I am ready to lose my health, my credit, or my wallet". "Can you loosen the bonds that tie D to E?" "Yes, but only with the power of gold, patience, and anger." The necessary and the contingent (1.1.5), the possible and the impossible, the hard and the soft (1.1.6), the real and the unreal (1.15.2)- they all grow in this way.[176]

A grain of sugar dissolves in water only if the rest of the world provides adequate conditions (see chapter 1, *Communitas and immunization*).

In process monadologies, alliances are made on the ground. Latour claims actants are not by nature in agreement or disagreement, commensurable or incommensurable, and so they must negotiate.[177] Latour and Tarde explore the authority of each monad to enable them to craft alliances, arrange pacts and negotiate coalitions. The governing character of the monad – a monadology can be read as an ontology of governing bodies – is made to work and becomes crucial to the process of forming and dismantling networks and associations (or nexus and concrescences). These alliances are biased by perspectives. Tarde ascribes beliefs (and desires) to his monads, while Whitehead understands all his actual entities to have the equivalent of knowledge and action through prehensions. Nothing, however, can avoid the distortion provoked by its social milieu or the concrete surrounding environment. No process monad can reach a position to see the whole scheme of alliances from above – each diplomatic act is based on the information on the ground that each monad is in a position to obtain. It is because process monadologies make no appeal to a regulating whole that they provide an explicit account of what is up for grabs.[178] There is no top-level element that can make entities less available to their co-existing ones. Instead of a concert, a process world is a jam where every existent is in the Open and can be captured at any moment. In fact, process monadologies can be understood as a way to exorcise any immunity.

Holisms

Monadologies provide a strategy for thinking about contingency in terms of infinite (or worldly) dependence. It is a holistic move: it assumes everything is connected. The idea of a general dependence – and that of open bridges between any two items – provides a framework to think about openness (or vulnerability or lack of security). Holism has a family resemblance to lack of immunity; it makes a necessary connection between two items impossible – no two items relate to each other irrespective of whatever else. Global compossibility entails that no two things can be connected in an immune way. Hence, sugar dissolving in water depends on all sorts of conditions that we take for granted only because we do our best to make them present. From a monadological point of view, we needn't appeal to anything exclusively internal to a grain of sugar to explain that it dissolves in water –

if it happens more often than not, it is because there are regularities in the setting, some of which we sponsor. We can say that sugar is soluble in water, but this is no more than shorthand for an interaction of many external elements, some of which we deem (or make) stable; without them, the sugar would not dissolve.

Analyses of dispositional predicates in terms of internal features – such as powers[179], physical intentionality[180] or natural essences[181] – have to appeal to a plethora of external conditions and circumstances that act as antidotes[182] for the still-active internal feature. A monadological approach makes no appeal to any exclusively internal feature. An interaction – such as the dissolving of sugar in water – is due to a conjunction of external elements of different sorts. Hume is sometimes criticized for providing too little to replace necessary connections. If this criticism is fair, it could be, from a monadological point of view, less due to Hume's actualism – the thesis that the real is the actual – than to his atomism – the denial of the holist thesis that things are interconnected.

Because no interaction between two items is indifferent to the rest of the world, the monadological account can be described as a form of secular occasionalism[183]: there is always an intermediary producing the interaction of any two items. In this case, the intermediary can be extended to everything else. This is a fair way of describing the holism in a monadological approach – although I prefer to put things in terms of compossibility.

Now, is the connection between everything necessary? Leibniz took global compossibility to have a top-level limit, which is the world. This is why Arnauld had the impression that there was no room for contingency in Leibniz's system. There is a point of view that considers everything, for there is a world that aggregates every monad and makes them all globally immune. Other possible worlds are outside the scope of this world's global compossibility. This view follows a holism with an upper bound – not junky, but still not a priority monism. Leibniz's holism posits a whole; there is such thing as everything. In fact, each possible world is a whole in this sense. A monadology without this top level would entail a holism without a whole. Compossibility would know no limits and, therefore, allows no global immunity. A holism without immunity brings compossibility to a further degree – a junky degree. A junky-and-gunky monadology ushers in a holism where each monad has every other at its disposal while being in the hands of every other. It follows that there is nothing safe from the next round of negotiations. To be sure, some things are harder to renegotiate than others, but there is no ultimate priority of the whole. To exist is to co-exist, and to be is to be engaged in diplomacy. To coin a phrase in French: être *est entente*.

Schaffer has explored the ties between priority monism – that the whole is prior to its parts – and the relatedness of all things.[184] He argues that a commitment to relatedness of all things entails priority monism, and therefore, that a form of holism implies a form of monism. To be sure, a holism that entails priority monism has to posit a whole, and thus not all varieties of monadological holism would qualify; some varieties are not under the spell of Schaffer's argument. But there is a more interesting reason why at least some monadologies don't fall within Schaffer's scope: the argument holds specifically that an internal relatedness of all things – a holism of internal relations – entails priority monism. I believe the bite of his argument is that a holism of internal relations has to posit a whole – and, it follows, such a whole is prior.

By "internal relatedness of all things," Schaffer means that every concrete thing is in at least one internal relation with all the others (and not that all relations are internal). Aware of how vague the terminology of "internal" and "external" is, Schaffer spends some time elucidating what he means by an internal relation, and ends up defining it in terms of modal constraints.[185] Certainly, there are senses in which Leibniz's monads are in internal relation to each other – they are not modally free from each other, but rather they are compossible. In contrast, process monadological holisms – which are junky – have no room for internal relations in any reasonable sense, for monads, or actual entities, are modally free. This means that they could be associated with others, but the need for such association depends on the setting they are in; they associate because their surroundings engage with them. All relations are sponsored, and in that sense they are all external. As in all monadologies, no event is prompted either by *automaton* or by *physis*, but in this case it is a monadology where no whole regulates coexistence. It entails the external relatedness of all things.

Interestingly, non-metaphysical forms of holisms also satisfy most of the features of monadologies in general (at least 1, 3, 4, and 5). Consider epistemic or semantic holisms – theses that knowledge, confirmation or meaning cannot be ascribed to individual units but only to critical masses. Although there are a great variety of these holisms, arising mostly from the work of Quine and Davidson, they tend to have some common elements.[186] Knowledge, confirmation, or meaning is conceived as being distributed. That is, one cannot know a single thing; nothing is confirmed or disconfirmed without further assumptions, or no word or expression means anything on its own (features 4 and 5). The counterpart of feature 4 is that to know, confirm, or mean something is only possible if other things are known, confirmed, or meant. Semantic and epistemic properties are ascribed to networks, and here again, there need not be a whole, need not be a top level in the form of well-demarcated bodies of knowledge (everything one knows), or well-articulated classes of theoretical claims (single theories distinct from their background assumptions), or language (in the sense of a set of sentences coming out of a generative procedure).

Davidson's holism[187] is a clear expression of the connection between thought and knowledge.[188] His externalism concerning mental content ties thought intrinsically to truth and therefore to some knowledge. Once I cannot know about myself without knowing something about the rest of the world, there is no (Cartesian) ignorant thought that accesses no more than my own states and events.[189] His argument leads to the idea that in order to interpret my own beliefs – or know what my words mean – I have to share things about the world with others. The interpreter and the interpreted have to share some content, otherwise there can be no detection of thought. This shared content, which can be impossible to pinpoint, cannot constitute less than knowledge of the external world, if there is any sense at all in which to conceive an external world. Otherwise, the argument goes, there would be no sense to assessing my beliefs against anything that could make them true. The world is reached by thought through its coherence, which means that it has to start out with some knowledge.[190]

Independently of the merits of Davidson's argument, it is interesting to point out some of its monadological elements. Thought is not isolated; it is impossible without accessing something of the world, for there is no self-standing realm of thought – or meaning. Knowledge of something (or belief about something) is already knowledge or belief about something else – there are no atoms of knowledge. Instead, knowledge has to come in some sort of critical mass. The revealing exercise of interpretation – in a radical scenario or not – is a process of gauging with compossibles. Everybody has some knowledge, but to the extent that they have different beliefs, they know different things.[191] Any of my beliefs can be kept or changed, but only at a cost to be paid in adjusting my other beliefs. It would be worth exploring to what extent Davidson's doctrines show the power of monadology to enlighten holisms and vice-versa, even though in his case, holisms seem far from his central metaphysical assumption. I'll return to some elements of his doctrines below. In this chapter, however, I concentrate on metaphysical (monadological) holisms.

Partial monadologies

Monadological features associated with the idea of a post-established harmony can help us understand how items that exist are responsive to each other. Monadologies combine the emphasis on individuals and an account of their interconnectedness. Graham Harman has championed an object-oriented ontology whereby the ultimate components of what exists are objects that, although of different natures, share a similar quadruple structure.[192] Objects are attached to their qualities, which can be either sensual or real. The former are qualities impressed on other objects – the shapelessness of snow when melting in a river or the sweetness of an apple appreciated by a trained Alpine resident – while the latter are qualities of the object proper and not of the object as the content of an impression. Real qualities are lasting ones, the ones that resist changes of perspective, like the height of a mountain viewed from different locations. Objects themselves are also sensual and real – for instance there is a real melon and a sensual one, a real otter and a sensual one.

Objects, qualities, reality and sensuality (or appearances, or affordances) are points that articulate the two axes of Harman's quadruple structure: real objects, sensual objects, real qualities, sensual qualities. Real objects interact with each other only indirectly, through sensual objects – it is the sensual melon that is devoured by a mouth, the sensual otter that is touched by another otter. It is, Harman stresses, a form of occasionalism, for something else has to interfere in order for two real objects to be in contact with each other. Harman conceives of object-oriented ontology as a general scheme to explore the plot brought about by any kind of object. Several authors have recently shown how fruitful this approach is – among them Tim Morton, Sara Ahmed, Tristan Garcia and Levi Bryant. Morton draws on Harman's quadruple structure to introduce the idea of hyperobjects: enormous structures like the planet or its atmosphere that intersect with each other in space and time.[193]

An object-oriented ontology is not a monadology, but satisfies some of its features. Harman insists that objects compose other objects and there is no primacy in this *matryoshka*. Object-oriented ontologies are flat. Harman has criticized both the overmining and the undermining of objects in the history of philosophy: not considering objects but their aggregations or their components as central elements. Objects are not to be over-arched by anything else and objects enjoy an ontological democracy. Objects are understood as having both a real and a sensual component.

They are perceived and perceiving, which redeems feature 2. Also, objects contrast with matter. As Morton's hyperobjects make explicit, objects can be found in all sorts of material stuff and are to be neatly distinguished from their materiality, which furnishes only some of their qualities, both real and sensual. Indeed, Harman understands his ontology to display the advantage of avoiding materialism.[194] As for connectedness, sensuality is conceived through other objects – it is only because other objects have sense that there are sensual objects and qualities. Feature 3 is also obviously satisfied because everything is to be explained in terms of objects.

On the other hand, objects are partially autonomous. They have secret lives; they survive, when withdrawn from their public appearance, in a reality that is independent of any other object. Such independence makes an object less worldly; it keeps its identity in other worlds, for all it needs is that there are other objects to provide sensuality. Still, objects are not substances in the sense of self-standing units that can be taken apart from anything else. There is a sense in which objects are governing entities. They have a space-time associated with them and they relate solely with other objects – not with their material territories as such. Also, there is no global object that can apperceive all the others – that would amount to a sensual object that encompasses all other objects. Perspectives (in terms of sensual objects and sensual qualities) always lack an element of reality, the one that is withdrawn from sensual access. This withdrawn element is something like a substratum. Further, it is not clear that objects cannot be vacuous actualities. It is not clear, therefore, that features 5 and 6 are satisfied.

Object-oriented ontology postulates partially autonomous objects, and that makes the resultant partially monadological. This partial autonomy results from the idea that the tension between objects and relations is to be resolved inside the objects themselves.[195] Harman posits that objects have a withdrawn dimension, the counterpart to their availability to be sensed. The real part of an object is what resists any qualitative relation and any sensual integration. In line with the spirit of Leibniz's monadology, there is a blind spot to every perspective while to be entails to know. As a consequence, the noumenal is not a feature of what escapes our knowledge but rather an inherent feature of any object, the part of it that is withdrawn. However, this withdrawn feature stems from objects being partially autonomous and therefore self-standing in their realities. As a consequence, objects are not worldly, and something distinguishes their identities and their indiscernibilities. Objects, unlike monads, can be (at least partially) detached from their relations with the rest of the world. If so detached, they enjoy at least some independence from other objects. Object-oriented ontology, as a deviant or partial monadology, is therefore farther from contingentism than a standard monadology.

Leibniz's monads were substances without substrata; other monadologies made monads something other than substance (actants, actual entities). Monadologies indeed appear in several forms, and some of them are interestingly deviant. Another case I would like to mention briefly is Simondon's process of individuation, which seems to point toward a monadless monadology. In fact, Simondon's process philosophy (see Chapter 1 for some of its tenets) can be viewed as an attempt to focus philosophical attention on operations rather than on operating modules – metaphysics, he suggests, should be more allagmatic and less obsessed with the *dramatis personae* of the world. It is interesting to conjecture that perhaps

Simondon espouses a partial monadology that is the mirror image of object-oriented ontology. In any case, it satisfies precisely features 4 and 5, which are absent in object-oriented ontology.

Allagmatics, the theory of operations that Simondon brings to the forefront, deals not with how a piece of matter acquires its shape but with how shaping the piece of matter involves all sorts of twists and vicissitudes.[196] *Allagma* is the cost of an operation – for example, the cost of a process of individuation. Individuals appear as no more than by-products of a class of intertwined operations. Feature 4 is therefore present as any individual is concresced by a process of individuation and is part of further allagmatic operations. Something other than the individual always comes also out of an individuation process – procedures of composition, gestures of ontogenesis, dynamics of making something singular – and more than the individual is always present in its formation – forces, movements of aggregation, transfers of information. Individuals are not the main characters; they are nothing but the provisional end points of ontogenetic processes of individuation, in which relations are more prominent than any relata.

Indeed, Simondon thinks individuals are little more than useful resting places, for their gestation cannot be explained solely in terms of their achievements. Water and earth together compose mud, one would say, but only if they are placed in the same place, at the same time and in a certain manner. Without the operation, one gets no mud out of water and earth. Similarly, the operations connecting things are far more crucial to how things are – which has to do with a continuous ontogenesis, for Simondon – than their components. It is a Lewis Carroll-like move of making explicit the infinite postulates needed in order to draw a conclusion from a *modus ponens* argument without a rule of inference – Simondon would insist that premises aggregated together lead nowhere without the performance of the right operation. It is through the relations between the many terms involved in a thing's production – terms internal and external to it – that it ends up being the way it is. Further, there is no final endpoint to ontogenesis. Simondon shifts the attention from substances and terms to relations and operations. Instead of looking at what stays put, he looks at what precedes and constitutes individuation. To be is to operate. This has a monadological feel to it, but the resulting monadology is only partial, since feature 3 is clearly absent (and arguably, 2 cannot therefore be present).

Still, Simondon seems to be close to the spirit of a monadology in which he takes his emphasis on relations to the extreme of rendering *relata* irrelevant. If substances in a monadology are hardly any special harbor for being, Simondon makes them even less privileged. Although it makes no room for monads – apart from the dim place given to those transitory and ontologically squalid ready individuals – Simondon's ontogenesis can be viewed as monadological, since everything is to be explained in terms of its constitutive operations. The difference is that these operations are not performed ultimately by operators, by individual actualities. In fact, no self-standing individual can be detached from the relations that make it what it is. Neither is there room for pre-individual atoms, of the sort Harman[197] dismisses, for processes of individuation – which are necessarily pre-individual – cannot be taken as individuals without appeal to whatever individualizes them. Allagmatics is structurally gunky. Being lies in the way individuals are constituted. Feature 5 follows suit: no substances and no substrata. No individual, and no operation, carries any potentiality that is independent of everything else in its world – no modalities independent of the vicissitudes that make ontogenetic operations co-exist. Also, there is hardly any room for any modality other than compossibility.

If we take Simondon's partial monadology as the mirror image of object-oriented ontology, it is clear that the emphasis on feature 4 in the former and on feature 3 in the latter points towards the split between priority monism and priority pluralism. While a monadology is neither, object-oriented ontology leans towards pluralism and Simondon's partial monadology shies away from the postulation of any individual. However, Simondon seems to have little room for an image of the whole process without a blind spot. Indeed, his appeal to transduction provides a continuum between the information-processing capacities of physical beings and those of human subjects theorizing about the world from their own standpoint. Transduction is both a theory about how to be is to know something – to be is to proceed by analogy with what the being finds around itself – and a doctrine about the status of such a theory – we produce the theory by making an analogy with what we find around ourselves. Simondon writes:

> [...] it should be assumed that science will never be accomplished, for it involves beings with the same degree of organization: a material system and a living being organized trying to think through this system through science. [...] the relation between thought and reality becomes the relation between two organized realities that could be analogically related through their internal structure .[198]

Thinking is always situated and perception is always engaged in a perspective. Simondon's focus on situated operations is in line with the monadological taste for interconnectedness as much as object-oriented ontology is in line with the monadological stress on the basic character of the individual existents. They are partial monadologies, though. A complete monadology accommodates both the taste and the stress and revolves around interconnected individual existents.

Fragments, compositions, composers

The sort of process monadology I believe to be a revealing ontoscopy of what is up for grabs starts out with the notion of fragments. The point of departure is to consider fragments on their own and not as pieces of something hidden or broken. Attention to fragments looks at parts focusing neither on wholes nor on ultimate components. They compose a world in which every part also has a proper part: junky and gunky. So, fragments are composed of further fragments, and a world of fragments can be described in terms of Heraclitus's fragment 207 (see Anarcheology 2/207*), "[...] like a jigsaw puzzle that cannot be completed and yet is never in pieces." Fragments can be thought of as traces, but not of vestiges of anything else – rather, as uninterpreted pieces. We can treat them as elements of the world, more like shards than like atoms. Although they can be further fragmented, they appear as units. We can take them as ready-mades. Yet they are also elements for further arrangements. They can be compared with actants in Latour, because they are units to the extent that they are treated as units.[199] They are not units *per se*. They are also like Souriau's phenomena, because they display a generosity, the generosity of an ingredient which is incomplete, and yet on offer.[200] They offer themselves as building blocks. They display what Souriau labels the *inachevé* character of whatever exists – the uncompleted character.[201] They are like blank checks, or like existential promissory notes. I understand fragments to be like anything that can be found, either lying on the floor or during, say, a process of translation. These are found not as anything complete but rather as units of availability, units up for grabs.

Fragments are like process monads, like actants, like actual entities. They compose the basis of a capture monadology if they are seen as having multiple modes of existence (see Chapter 1). Souriau's existential pluralism has it that a single thing can exist in more than one mode; hence, the proposition that there are several modes of existence can fit together with an ontological monism. Likewise, fragments also exist as compositions – they are composed of other fragments, assembled from other compositions. In short, monads exist as fragments but also as compositions. They are up for future compositions but carry the vestiges of their previous ones in them.

Just like objects made of other objects, fragments are composed of other fragments. They also display an important dimension of Harman's objects: they have a secret life, a withdrawn dimension to them. Also, they often belong to more than one composition and therefore appear as characters in more than one plot. This is why I conceive of them as also existing in a third mode: they are also composers. Composers assemble other fragments – they are sponsors who turn fragments into compositions. Composition has a role similar to that of prehension in Whitehead's scheme: composers enroll existing fragments for their products. Composers are agents that produce concrescence. Here, each fragment is a fragment-for-a-composer rather than a fragment-in-itself; there are no actual entities that are not at the same time compositions-for-a-composer. There are no free-floating fragments; they have all been composed previously and are therefore compositions, and parts of compositions. Composers find the building blocks for their compositions in existing fragments; no composition is done from scratch. A composer is never entirely its own composition; typically, a composer brings about something else. Holism follows from the interconnectedness of all composers. A composer finds ingredients in fragments that appear in its field of apperception. They are sponsors, but they cannot sponsor on their own. Nothing composes on its own, because there is no non-composed fragment – like building a cathedral out of stones that were carved for the Inca buildings in the Qusqo area of Peru.[202] Indeed, in the monadology of fragments, there is no separation between those that sponsor and those that are sponsored – between subjects that act and believe and their objects, which are passive and mere contents of beliefs. Composers can be seen as more on the subjective side; they harbor perspectives.

This completes the elements of our triune existential monadology: monads exist as fragments, as compositions, and as composers. They interact in these three different modes with other monads. As composers, they have areas of jurisdiction in which they co-govern. The act of composing involves (a) instituting a scope and (b) exercising governance. As compositions, they are areas of jurisdiction co-governed by their composers – and to an extent they can even be, in part, the composers of themselves. Monads relate to each other through composition while always being themselves fragments in further compositions. All monads put together also bring about a composition, but surely such a composition is also a fragment (as everything is a proper part) and a composer assembling together what is around it. In the monadology of fragments, there is no concerted composition, for the movement of each composer has to be negotiated on the ground with all the others. Each composer is a fragment and composes out of fragments. This triple existential character means that fragments are monads of an ever-incomplete other fragment. Such a monadology, as the next section makes clear, brings home how the articulation of monads can elucidate the process of a gunky and junky assemblage.

Fragments, compositions and composers: A monadology

The monadology of fragments is a flat ontology: nothing has a privileged ontological status over anything else. Everything shares a common plane. There is no overwhelming upper hand initiating or maintaining anything. Fragments are forged within the shared space of all other fragments, which is a space where every composition lies out in the open. This openness shows the *communitas* of each fragment. Fragments can be very different: they surely can be objects, but they can also be ethical calls, machines, invitations, crises, plays, scenes, slogans, books, languages, expeditions, conversations, mood changes or the arrival at the edge of a lake. Further, they can be movements of thought, beliefs, fears, gestures, leaps of faith, perceptions of color, perplexities or ingredients in the proof of a theorem within a formal system. In other words, monadology spreads through what we normally think of as mental. Fragments are composed of aggregates of different materials and they can be pieces of events.

Each fragment has an internal composition that is ontologically no different from its surroundings: further fragments. This is a dimension of the flat-ontology character of this monadology: there is no ontological distinction between what is internal and what is external. There is no structurally different interior. Also, fragments can overlap in areas of jurisdiction, like Morton's hyperobjects. The borders between conversations and mood changes, for example, can be intrinsically fuzzy in a way that imbricates their areas of jurisdiction. Further, not only can fragments overlap with each other, but they can also be spatially discontinuous.
My writing of these lines here in the *Zócalo* of the port of Veracruz is a fragment of this book but also a fragment of an assemblage of people doing different things while waiting for Petrona Martinez to start her gig on the stage in front of us. The public waiting for Petrona is itself a composition and a fragment of the attendance at her venues during her Mexican tour. Petrona's tour is also a fragment dispersed in time among different locations. Compositions – as fragments – can display all sorts of spatial and temporal forms in their areas of jurisdiction. They can be scattered in space and time – their unity, indeed, is always in the eye of a composer.

In fact, the monadology of fragments develops the idea that there is no mundane view from nowhere. Fragments are always fragments-for-a-composer and cannot be identified as fragments if viewed from nowhere. In fact, the monadology can be described in different terms according to monads' three modes of existence: in terms of scattered fragments for any composer, in terms of how monads are brought together by different composers and in terms of what they do as composers. Monads can therefore be described as items in an inventory for compositions, as complete compositions out of other composition, and as composers sponsored by further composers. This last description can be considered transcendental, for it presents monads in terms of their conditions of possibility: what has made it possible for a fragment to be there, or which composer has brought it about.

Fragments have a transcendental nature; they constitute other fragments by means of their composition process. Composition is never achieved from nothing and is never the work of a single composer – the raw materials for a composition are simultaneously its co-composers. This transcendental description of the ontoscopy makes clear that there is no room for elements that are fully subjected to something else's action. Every fragment is a transcendental subject. Perhaps the monadology of fragments provides a sociology – in Tarde's sense – of transcendental subjects: they must compose together, for there is no extra-social raw material available. It is as if phenomena were themselves transcendental subjects with which a subject has to negotiate in order to attain a worldview. These transcendental subjects make the alliances that sponsor the monads with which they associate. A transcendental description provides a picture of the chains of sponsorships that connect the monads together.

Comparing the transcendental dimension of the monadology of fragments with composition within a language can prove fruitful. To write or say something is to engage in a co-production with all the bits and pieces that language users have left in the fabric of sentences. Composing in a language is always co-sponsored by the resources the language offers – its expressive biases, its grammatical constructions (associated with a descriptive metaphysics), its tenses. For example, when Michel Callon crafted his powerful motto "no economics, no economies," he appealed to English words and their capacities. Hardly any other language can convey the same message – translations of the sentence make it longer and more convoluted. The English words *economics* and *economy* are themselves compositions made of other fragments, but they act as co-composers of the motto. Language composition displays several elements of the monadology of fragments: words are fragments and compositions, and they have a composing force that provides decisive biases. Language composition especially exhibits features of this monadology if we accept meaning holism, with its rejection of singular words or phrases as bearing semantic atoms. Language, as Quine wrote in the opening of his *Word and Object*,[203] is a social art. And social art is what the monadology of fragments is: fragments are associated to produce compositions, each of them carrying a driving force that affects further compositions.[204] Here, as in Tarde's monadology, monads are always associated, and the intensity of their social ties hints at their influence in each composition. Just as with language compositions, no composition has a single or an ultimate origin. The difference, of course, is that in the monadology of fragments there are external composers that are not themselves words or sentences. This is the limit of the analogy: there are no composers that are not themselves up for further composition.

Composition is also concrescence. Different spaces and different times are composed together by capturing other fragments. Spatially extended monads could be tables and chairs but also colonial powers and universities. As long as it is seen as an individual available for compositions, the fragment holds up – but solely for those who see it as such. Hence, universities are not fragments for ticks or for winds, but it is a fragment – or rather a stable composition – for its administration. From this point of view, the university is a point in a space – a space of faculty ranks, a space of commercial interchange, a space of legal interaction. Spaces are themselves fragments up for grabs in compositions in the eye of a composer. Spaces are concresced for those who manage to perceive them as such. Something similar takes place with times. A new composition can enroll fragments from previous times. Latour claims that, after 1864, aerial germs had existed all along.[205] In terms of the monadology of fragments, aerial germs are compositions – composed by Pasteur, among others.[206] Their existence is not placed in an already-given time, independent of any composer, but rather can take place in a past that needs several sponsors. Pasteur's merit would then have been to negotiate with co-composers of all kinds to make sure that aerial germs were robust in their eyes – robust enough to be part of their compositions concerning the past previous to his composition. Scientific discoveries establish compositions that are thought of as having been there all along. They are compositions crafted with fragments of the past. There is no ultimate temporality (or overarching spatiality), as there is no ultimate composer – and no general, all-encompassing view.

The monadology of fragments has many features in common with other process monadologies, and the stress on concrescence is central to

Whitehead's philosophy of organism. In fact, Latour's appeal to networks reinstating times of the past, like the era of Pasteur, can be traced back to Whitehead's denial of a pre-existing order of time – no concreteness without actual entities engaged in concrescence. The monadology of fragments, however, can go one step further than Whitehead. For him a raw material for prehension – and hence for concrescence and composition – is a class of eternal objects. But these are not actual ingredients for composition, and as such they are already there. They are Platonic components that are available for use by actual entities – so that tomatoes can be red for us and universities can be competent for an assessing board.[207] Those objects are ready to be taken by actual entities and are not themselves decomposable. They cannot be described as both eternal objects and as fragments, compositions and composers. Whitehead claims that these elements for predication are not actual and therefore don't have to be subject to his ontological principle (no actual entity, no reason). The monadology of fragments considers the material for predication as consisting of monads more than anything else. The predicate "red" can be explained in terms of a network of actualities involving concepts, sensory devices, pigments, lights and so on. A predication is itself a composition – and in order for S to be P, an entente has to be found between the two poles. The appeal to eternal objects is replaced in the monadology of fragments by a composition that is clearly a composition-for-some-composers. No appeal to mere potentials is required.

Fragmentalism and the secret life of fragments

Kit Fine considers the relation between reality and perspectives from the point of view of the problems in the philosophy of time brought up by J.M.E. McTaggart, who introduced the distinction between A-series and B-series for time.[208] The A-series is indexed by terms like *past*, *present* and *future* (or *yesterday*, *today* and *tomorrow*, etc.). The B-series presents moments in time like pictures in an exhibition that can be seen in any order and at any pace; it is time viewed from nowhere. The A-series, like the arm of a clock, is what introduces change into B states. McTaggart's argument is that there is no change and no genuine passing of time without the A-series and therefore without the vocabulary of past, present and future.

To understand the passing of time, we need to be able to locate ourselves in a present tense. McTaggart then despaired of the reality of time, because time introduces tense – and perspectives – into the world. His conclusion is grounded on three assumptions concerning the nature of reality: it is neutral – no perspective is privileged over the others; it is absolute – not relative to a perspective; and it is coherent. McTaggart's A-ism (the thesis that time requires an A-series apart from the B-series) is based on these three assumptions and therefore must reject the reality of time.

Fine explores the alternatives to a realist A-ism. One can reject the first assumption about reality and embrace, for example, the idea that only the present is real. It is a popular idea – Fine dubs it "standard realism" – in the philosophy of time.[209] It can be extended to grant privilege to any perspective – the human take on things, the actual world as opposed to all other possible worlds, or the first-person perspective of self-knowledge. One can also reject at least one of the two other assumptions and posit that there is no such thing as a reality independent of tenses or perspectives, and therefore that it is not absolute or that reality is not coherent.[210] In order to explore this last option, which unifies all perspectives on reality, Fine crafts the concept of an über-reality which is the (incoherent) aggregation of all perspectives. True, one cannot be in über-reality, and therefore either "I am sitting" or "I am standing up" ought to be false in the present (and maybe true in the future or the past). There is an assemblage of all perspectives, but nothing can move in this assemblage without being in a particular perspective.

Fine favors this last position – that reality is incoherent – and labels it *fragmentalism*. A fragmentalist conception of perspectives brought together in an incoherent aggregate is akin to the monadology of fragments. For Fine, each perspective is a fragment of the über-reality formed by the superposition of all perspectives. In monadological terms, perspectives are compositions that fragments bring about, and they are never single-authored. In both cases, perspectives interact with each other without cohering. The overall image is one like Latour's in which we cannot count how many monads there are until we consider each monad's perspective. The overall image that the monadology of fragments provides is not that of a landscape that can be achieved by a viewer, but actually no more than a juxtaposition of perspectives, affording no worldview.²¹¹ Fragments cannot be fully displayed on a world-map. Each fragment composes its own map that, as a composition, is itself a fragment. Unlike Leibniz's monads, fragments are governing and governed bodies. In a monadology of fragments there is no jurisdiction assigned to a of a fragment, but rather a fragment is a self-standing unit that can be decomposed and recomposed at any time. They affect other compositions while not being immune to other composers. Fragments are more like countries than like objects. They have flexible borders (like Leibniz's monads) and disputed jurisdictions and must appeal to diplomacy to make a composition.²¹² They are, nonetheless, not only countries but also states, provinces, municipalities and so on. They achieve jurisdiction by internal and external diplomacy, for they come in *matryoshka* format. They form a gunky and junky *matryoshka* of world maps growing in all directions.

Fragments are not atoms. Like Leibniz's territories associated to monads, they can be always divisible and this vulnerability is the basis of their ontology. It is important to notice, however, that they are not simply governing bodies because no piece of matter is theirs by entitlement. As in other post-established harmony monadologies, there is no distinction between a monad and its legitimate area of jurisdiction. There is no innate distinction between the governing entities and the governed ones. Governments are themselves areas of jurisdiction. The distinction between bodies and spirits that motivated the (speculative) generalization of the Leibnizian monadology – there are relations like the one between body and spirit everywhere – is replaced by a generalized focus on government. Unlike Leibniz's monads, fragments can themselves be fragmented, and they are incorrigibly incomplete. They are not self-standing governments, but are pieces of authority that can be decomposed and made part of different compositions. Rather than as infinitesimals, they can be understood as indefinitesimal pieces of authority.

I would like to close this section with a note on the internal structure of a fragment. As I have said, there is no need to posit an internal composition that is different from what is outside. If we compare fragments with Harman's objects and their quadruple structure, we can consider how to make room for the ontological withdrawal. Harman conceives of objects as having secret lives, withdrawn not only from us but also from any other object. Reality for an object is to resist, to escape, and to withdraw. Objects supersede, they transcend. Harman talks about the fission and the fusion that together create something new from the tensions involving objects and their qualities.[213] An object goes through fission into several sensual or real qualities. Interestingly, such fission is not in embryo in the object, which is always estranged from its qualities. These qualities then go through a fusion that establishes them and maintains them as objects. Fusion and fission express the internal contrast between real and sensual objects on the one hand and their qualities on the other. They are similar to fragmentation and composition in my monadology, except that in the latter, because there is no ultimately different internal structure, nothing is ultimately fragment (quality) or composition (object). Harman makes clear that it is tensions that bring together the four dimensions of an object – they are neither internal relations nor separations with incidental connections. He names them time, space, eidos, and essence. The first is the tension between sensual objects and sensual qualities, the second between real objects and sensual qualities, the third between sensual objects and real qualities and the last between real objects and real qualities. They all have to do with a dynamic of unveiling and withdrawing.

This dynamic also appears in the articulations between the three existential poles of the monadology of fragments. The tension between fragment and composition is deployed in time; a composition is the fusion of several fragments – the tension is expressed in the duration of the process of composition. The tension between composition and composer requires a distance in space, for just like the withdrawn real object, the composer is not disclosed by the forthcoming composition. The composer as such is not revealed in the composition – like Berkeley's concept of the spirit, which doesn't appear in the ideas available for perception, the composer is separated from the appearing composition. Finally, the tension between fragments and composers can be understood as something akin to Harman's eidos. The composer makes the fragment as it is, but this again is not expressed in any fragment. The last tension in Harman's quadruple structure, the one of essence, finds no immediate equivalent in the monadology of fragments. This is because there is no internal structure to the monads; they exist in three modes and are composed of further (existentially threefold) monads. To be sure, Harman himself asserts that the real object doesn't possess its real qualities, for they are as external to it as are its sensual qualities.[214] In the monadology of fragments, there is no essence of a fragment, because there is no ultimate substratum to distinguish identity from indiscernibility.

Monads are worldly things, though there is some transcendence, because no monad in the world fully captures what a monad is – none can see beyond its field of vision, so to speak. Withdrawal, therefore, has to be worldly as well – what is withdrawn about a monad from any other monad is the compositional associations it has with all the others. Each perspective opens up a blind spot. Because there is no view from nowhere, each monad always has something withdrawn from each of the others, but doesn't hide the same secret from all of them. Its secret life comes not from inside, but rather from the (baroque) vastness of the intertwined connections. In a sense, the inner reclusion that takes place is not from the intimate chambers; it is instead from far away. This is an interesting displacement: withdrawal does not have to be thought of in terms of what is too hidden to be exposed, but can simply be what is too distant to be brought into focus.

The monadology of fragments has other points of convergence with an object-oriented ontology. In particular, the dynamics between real and sensual objects – and the impossibility of a real object touching another real object without the mediation of a sensible object – can be at least roughly captured by existential triunism. Composers don't touch other composers; they touch fragments (or compositions). Those fragments, like sensual objects, don't touch anything; only composers can touch other fragments in return. While it is not clear that the ten possible links between the four poles of the quadruple structure can be mimicked by the six possible links between the poles of the existential triunist monadology, the comparison makes explicit the resources of such monadology to cope with the ontological trickeries of withdrawal.

Ceteris Paribus devices

The monadology of fragments is an ontoscopy that presents the world as a board for compositions. As is often the case when processes are involved, it has a Darwinian ring to it. All ingredients can affect what is composed, just like the elements in the environment can affect a living form, given the right conditions. There are no fixed species, no fixed evolution environments, no fixed fitness functions. Similarly, the history of fragments is a history of accidents built on top of other accidents. Surely, history itself is not a one-track process – as there are no world-maps for fragments, there is no unique chronology for the processes of composition. However, it is historical in the *Naturphilosophie* sense of not following necessary laws (see Chapter 1). No fragment is immune to anything; no process of composition is safeguarded or secured. Still, as in Darwinian scenarios, some fragments and compositions are immunized – not by anything transcendent, but rather immanently. Some fragments are meta-stable and, as such, rely on other composition processes to be resilient. Resilience is not a mark of anything but constancy and permanence among sponsors.

Immunization is always an achievement, and not something that transcends all events on the ground. Species in biological evolution are again a good example. The process that produces genetic variation often takes place in terms of a phylogenetic tree where species trace their ancestors down to a common root. Biologists like Carl Woese have challenged the universality of this tree structure.[215] He claims that under some conditions of horizontal genetic transfer, it is no longer reasonable to try to map genetic variation in terms of a species tree. The consequences for the notion of species are far reaching: Woese coined the term *Darwinian interlude* to describe the period of time in which evolution through species and tree-based genetic transfer was prevalent (and immunized). He conjectures that many factors contribute to a species ceasing to be meta-stable and for horizontal genetic transfer to become prevalent. His analysis shows how species, as the engine of most evolution of life in the planet, are ultimately vulnerable, albeit kept meta-stable. Their disturbances are kept at bay by their sponsors, which continuously compose things with them.

The Simondonian lesson indeed applies to the monadology of fragments: permanence of sponsorship must be explained, for permanence doesn't unveil a substantial mechanism underlying compositions. Permanence must be explained instead of hypostasized as necessity. One of the resources available for such explanation is repetition: it generates an expectation in the eye of the composer. This expectation, sponsored by the repeated gestures of composition, can be enough to mark out an area of meta-stability. The monadology of fragments posits that there is no immunity without (immanent) immunization. And yet there are many real-world enclosures sponsored by the joint interaction of composers, and they afford a basis for other stable compositions. The monadology of fragments is not an ontoscopy of instability; it is a provision to explain stability rather than positing it as a starting point.

These circumstantially immunized fragments and compositions are like laboratory models, which in the strict sense are valid only when the circumstances are controlled. These lab-like models are crucial for describing things in terms of regularities – because regularities are often detected through lab-like devices, laws of physics do (strictly speaking) systematically lie, to use the strong phrase introduced by Nancy Cartwright.[216] Labs attempt to immunize processes from all sorts of real-world disturbances and to mimic what is thought to be immunized (albeit less thoroughly so) outside. So the curve of a body in freefall is said to approximate that of a law observed in lab-like conditions. The law describes an attractor that is satisfied if and only if the rest of the world doesn't interfere. The attractor is never actualized, but it is virtual (see Chapter 1). Labs intend to mimic not the real-world composition, but the attractor: if the setup were immunized from the many influences, it would behave according to the model.[217] Attractors express what would be the case if a process were immunized from anything else.

Labs are controlled environments where slower processes – typically the degeneration of lab equipment – maintain some variables under control. In general, slower processes maintain variables sufficiently fixed for faster ones. So the vertical gene-transfer process is maintained to the extent that the barriers sponsored by species are in place. The slower process of the planets distancing themselves from their gravitational center maintains the regularity of movement of the stars within the solar system. What is immunized can be understood as a kind of conditional necessity; p is necessary given that q. This can maybe be understood in conjunction with the idea of compossibility (feature 4); this pair forms perhaps the crucial modalities for dealing with the sensible. An important element of modeling is mimicking stability by immunizing processes. The resulting models are *ceteris paribus*: stability in, stability out. Or, in other terms, meta-stability is achieved through *ceteris paribus* devices that maintain processes immunized from most of the rest of the world. These devices can be found in the lab and in the world at large. Lab modeling is a complicated reckoning about how two sorts of immunizing devices can run in parallel. From the point of view of an ontology of contingency, these devices are in need of explanation. Indeed, in many circumstances, compositions are made to be robust, resilient; but there is a cost to (meta-) stability.

Being up for grabs

Attention to relative necessity makes clear how contingency is a matter of scope. A closed space can be fully immunized. *Ceteris paribus* devices are enclosing devices and, as such, they provide monadological immunization: a local limitation on holism. When we find ways to isolate proper parts of the sensible, we disconnect some fragments from the wide horizon of indefinitesimals. The scope of contingency, in a monadology, is the scope of *communitas*, of what lies in the open and is not protected from anything else. Contingency connects to virtuality; a monad is up for grabs by any other monad, it has no intrinsic stability and its relations depend on all the other relations. Immunizing cuts off the lines of dependence.

The monadology of fragments shows contingency to be an issue of interference – that which moves something out of its (*ceteris paribus*) attractor. Interference here is neither from a random element – like Epicurean *clinamina* – nor from a transcendent source – like a miracle or a ruling from a principle of facticity. Rather, it is the interference that follows from co-existence; nothing exists in a self-standing space. In the monadology of fragments, there is no transcendentally immune composition for a class of all monads, let alone for a proper part of such a class. Every composer sees its composition as co-existing with others: to be is to be in a shared space of fragments where everything is up for composing. The sensible is the realm where everything is contingent on something else. Nothing is necessary once and for all – as nothing hangs loose once and for all (compare with ANARCHEOLOGY 2/196). The monadology of fragments presents contingency as a matter of aggregation; the assemblage of things is what makes them up for grabs. The realm of fragments – the sensible – appears as an open board for indefinite compositions; because there is no whole to contemplate, there is no spot ultimately free of accidents.

The monadology of fragments is a form of priority nihilism. As I have said, it pictures a world that is gunky and junky. In fact, the main thesis that *symbebeka proton to onton* entails the rejection of both the priority of the whole and the priority of the parts. It follows a holism entailing neither a monism where a cosmos encompasses all things nor an atomism where ultimate components make up anything. Priority nihilism also means that nothing is reduced to anything else: to map the composition of a monad, one would need to map all monads. A map of scale 1 allows no reduction. A map is possible if some elements are rendered ineffective by some kind of *ceteris paribus* device that would provide for a local immunization; otherwise, the sheer interference of the other monads is enough to make sure that fragments are up for grabs. Because they all equally share a space of availability, they all co-exist.

Even though there is no cosmos – no whole hosting everything else – there is a common space where every fragment is at risk. Call it a *plane of immanence* or a *plane of equality*.[218] Contingency takes place in such a space. Each monad is hostage to all the others; no necessity survives without an immunization process. Compossibility is a consequence of the mutual hosting of all monads: there is no independent, solely intrinsic, *causa sui* potentiality. The distribution of being entails that nothing is itself potentially anything, not even itself: a fragment is always a fragment in a composition. Dispositional language expresses no more than what would happen if everything else remained as it is; sugar is dissolved in water if the conditions of temperature, pressure, etc., remain as expected, a seed will grow into a tree if given the expected circumstances, a running white billiard ball will make a red one move provided that everything else inside and outside the billiard balls behaves as expected. Dispositional judgments are judgments about expectations: about what conditions are required for some events to be expected. The relation between a composer and a fragment is a relation between two composers – like Simondon's relation between two organized realities. As such, it is a relation between two matrices of sensitivities. The sensible is up for grabs because it is open to interference. We recover here the original (holistic) Leibnizian intuition about contingency: the sensible is up for grabs because it depends on everything else that is sensible. It is on this dependence that something can be *mise en jeu* by placing itself at the limit of death, of nothingness.[219]

Aphro-doubt   Gisel Carriconde Azevedo, Digital photography, 2009

Chapter 4
Doubts

Indeterminacy and insufficiency

Amin Maalouf expresses the worry that an era of questions and problems is to be followed by an era of solutions.[220] He fears solutions, seeing them as dispelling an element of opening, a game that questions display. Questions are eroding devices that he recommends cherishing. They leave things up in the air. They deal with starting points, with the unsettled, with what is not determined. They have something to do with beginnings, with what escapes declarative language. Deleuze cites Lautman, who lists three aspects of a problem: it differs from a solution, it transcends the solution that it prompts, and it is immanent in any solution that would purport to make it less visible.[221] In a similar vein, Jabès writes, "we cannot interrogate but power, non-power is the question itself."[222] The question, and the questioning, opens up a space in terms of solutions – it suggests their insufficiency. Solutions, expressed in declarative language, are determinations: things are determinately thus and so. The accidental, often invoked when there is the possibility of a question, spells a non-power, an an-*arché*.

This is because the accidental is up in the air, for it is not (fully) *determined*. As we saw above, this has something to do with *automaton*, which Aristotle contrasted with *physis* and *techné*. The contrast is between what is determined to be so and what has happened without anything else determining it to take place – neither (its) nature, nor an agent. There is a silence to the undetermined: not enough pull to go either way. Not enough reason to choose any solution to the problem. There is an under-determination. And yet we think of what comes out of this absence of a governing drive as a random, brute, contingent fact. This is why the an-*arché* is linked with facticity: it indicates under-determined facts that are regulated or shaped by nothing apart from themselves. This link between contingency and the underdetermined – and with matters of fact – will take us, in this chapter, to doubts and their ontological status. We will start considering how both facticity and indetermination bring in luck.

Facts have the structure of determinations – things are determinately thus and so. However, when we say that the snow is in fact white, we are claiming that it is determinately so, although by no reason other than facts themselves. What is merely a matter of fact has no weight, as it is a determination with no non-factual determiners; it could have been determined otherwise. If we bear in mind that contingency is settled in the space of governments – including in their absence – we see that it speaks the language of determination – and its insufficiency. The determined is somehow immune to any other interference; the undetermined is exposed to the elements, for there is no ready-made fate for it. What is fully determined is therefore immune to anything else. An *incomplete* determination, on the other hand, is just sufficient for things to be, as a matter of fact, thus and so. Determinations can be seen as rulings, but they may be ungrounded rulings that are blowing in the wind and up for grabs. They carry the force of necessity, but it can be insufficient – facticity points at determinations that carry only enough of this force to be mere facts.

Determinations are also common to facts and thoughts. People entertain determinations when they hold beliefs (or related states like fears, imaginings, certainties or convictions). There is, nonetheless, a continuity between the thoughts "it seems to me that *p*," "I'm convinced that *p*," and "it is a fact that *p*," on the one hand, and the fact itself that *p* on the other. Beliefs and facts have the same determined content. (This is what makes an identity account of truth possible; according to such an account, a belief is true if it is identical to a fact – the thought "spring has arrived" is true if it has the same content as the fact that "spring has arrived.")[223] When I believe something, I believe that things are thus and so; I believe in a determination. Beliefs are about the stuff that facts are made of; beliefs can therefore reach the world, if the world is made of facts. Beliefs can also be determinations that are insufficiently determined – beliefs, like theories or world-views, are sometimes under-determined.

If undetermined *facts* point to contingency, undetermined *beliefs* point to what is called epistemic luck.[224] There is epistemic luck when a belief happens to be true, but only because the world has done us a favor, to use the apt phrase by McDowell.[225] It is only a matter of luck that our belief is true – it could be false, as nothing determines our belief toward truth. Typically, the issue of epistemic luck appears in two contexts of epistemological discussions. The first is in the discussions about what links justification of a belief on one hand and truth on the other. This is what is at stake in the famous cases brought to attention by Edmond Gettier.[226] In these cases, a belief happens to be justified and also happens to be true, but it is often considered to be less than knowledge because somehow its truth is due to epistemic luck. The belief could have been equally justified and yet false. The second context of discussion in which epistemic luck appears is skepticism. Skeptical challenges are often about the insufficiency of justification. We may think there are enough grounds for a belief and yet have skeptical doubts showing us that things could be otherwise, and in such a circumstance, what has determined us to hold that belief is insufficient. In both cases, beliefs are only true if we are (epistemically) lucky. Similarly, when a determination is not a belief but a fact, it is contingent if it is insufficiently determined.

Facts and beliefs, therefore, dwell in determinations. Contingent facts and unjustified or unknown beliefs are determinations that could have been otherwise. Determinations contrast with indeterminacies. Beliefs contrast with doubts – beliefs are commitments, for I hold my beliefs to be true.[227] When I doubt something, I don't hold a determination to be true (about the matter in question). If I have doubts about *p*, I don't believe *p*. We can look at this in terms of propositional attitudes: one can have different attitudes toward *p*, that of believing and that of doubting among them. I consider it better to take the content of a belief to be the attitude associated with the proposition, rather than the proposition itself. So while a belief has the content of a determination – say, that seawater is salty – a doubt has the content of indeterminacy – say, that seawater is salty or not salty, or that maybe seawater is salty. When I say that facts and beliefs have similar contents, I mean that both deal in determinations. Doubts, on the other hand, don't. When I doubt it is as if I entertain two opposite thoughts simultaneously – that there both is and is not a dagger in front of me, say. Now, if doubts and beliefs are thought-states, do they have equivalents in the world?

Unjustified or unknown beliefs can be compared with insufficiently determined facts – with what is contingent. Further, contingency points toward what is undermined by doubt; they have a family resemblance. If the world has indeterminacies, doubts are (eventually) cognitively more virtuous than beliefs, for they access something that beliefs miss. This is the case when we acknowledge unredeemable indeterminations: if one is in doubt about whether Schrödinger's cat is alive or not, one is arguably in a virtuous cognitive position. A world made of facts – and therefore of determinations – contrasts with a world with room for irreducible indeterminations. Perhaps the state of uncertainty and the attitude of doubting are the best clues for depicting a world of indeterminations. Doubts make what is up for grabs visible.

When facticity is tied to an-*arché*, the under-determination grounding determined facts comes into focus. In other words, we can see the indeterminacy surrounding the factual. This is what is captured by the state of doubting. Facticity and doubts are, in turn, sometimes understood in terms of sufficient reason. There is enough reason for a fact to take place but not enough to determine it to take place. The non-necessary has something to do with sufficiency: it is not necessarily hot in May in Granada, but the winds and the lack of rain are enough to make it so. The principle of sufficient reason holds that there is enough reason for things to be one way or another. It is possible for a belief based on sufficient reason to be true – and maybe the world makes it so, as a favor – but there is not enough reason to make it necessarily so.

We reveal the insufficiency of such a belief to constitute knowledge by unveiling the epistemic luck involved in it. Skeptical doubts purport to disclose such luck. They deal in insufficiency. Thus, in a world of contingencies, skeptical steps are full of knowledge. Skeptical challenges not only uncover our lack of knowledge but also provide knowledge of the insufficiencies. If contingency has elements of insufficiency, doubts reveal them, for being up for grabs puts things in a state of *epokhé*, of suspension of judgment. Reversing the traditional image, certainty would then be a failure to see the hesitation of the world, while claiming that things are thus and so would be missing the point that they stand in a constant state of indeterminacy, which doubts themselves can best capture.

Doubting

Doubting contrasts with believing. While believing engages with determinations – holding that their determinate contents are true – doubting seeks to erode the content of beliefs and replace them with uncertainty. The attitude of doubting is one of showing how insufficient the pulls toward believing a determination are. Sextus Empiricus established a neo-Pyrrhonist path according to which the exercise of doubting is a reliable guide to life, in particular telling us what we should refrain from believing.[228] To a great extent, these lessons concerned how to deal with epistemic luck – and therefore, with cognitive contingency. Dismantling dogmatic arguments by showing that they are not impermeable to doubt makes the Pyrrhonist skeptic confident that reaching a stable class of beliefs can bring no tranquility.

Doubting – and the subsequent recommended suspension of belief – reveals the impossibility (and ultimately the undesirability) of dogmatic positions. The neo-Pyrrhonist uses prevalent doubt to tell us something about our beliefs: in at least most cases, we are not entitled to assert that things are thus and so. Doubts can, however, reveal things of quite a different nature. Descartes took our ability to doubt as disclosing something about our own nature – and in fact about a substance that composes the world. He took doubting as a clue about how things are: there is something (in us) capable of doubt. Doubts are not only obstacles to seeing things through – because they erode determinations – but also clear revelations of something else: an ingredient of the world that makes doubting possible. Hume extracted some (positive) knowledge from the occurrence of doubt with his conception of a second creation unveiling our psychology and our habits, and also, in a sense, with the transcendental conclusions he drew in part from our ability to doubt our access to things in themselves. His strategy was to make doubts reveal something about the doubter, and eventually about some special realm that ought to be part of our image of the world – like a *res cogitans* – or part of our overall explanation of knowledge and action – like Humean instincts and habits, or like Kant's transcendental sphere. In any case, doubts reveal something about how things are, by revealing something about how doubters are. Their message is not only one of impossibility, but their presence tells us something about how things are – and at least in the case of Descartes, their presence provides us with at least one determination: there is a *res cogitans*.

Now, these two kinds of lesson drawn from the occurrence of doubt, the attempt to extract impossibilities from it and the attempt to learn something positive from it, share the assumption that things are under some determination. Either we grasp these determinations as to how things are, or they escape us. The skeptical challenges can teach us to doubt beliefs while holding that there are determinations in the world. In particular, neo-Pyrrhonists and most skeptics under their influence tend to concentrate their ammunition against determined beliefs, not determined facts. The common assumption between the two kinds of lessons drawn from the occurrence of doubts is ontological: in the world, there are determinations. Things are thus and so in the world.

When considering being above or below the Earth – and above or below our antipode – Wittgenstein, in the *Philosophical Investigations*, invokes those situations where we feel compelled to expect a determination either to hold or not. He considers the presence of "7777" in the expansion of π:

> "God sees – but we don't know." But what does that mean? – We use a picture; the picture of a visible series which one person sees the whole of and another not. The law of excluded middle says here: It must either look like this, or like that. So it really – and this is a truism – says nothing at all, but gives us a picture. And the problem ought now to be: does reality accord with the picture or not? And this picture seems to determine what we have to do, what to look for, and how [...][229]

The guiding picture yields that whenever there is a doubt – say, about whether "7777" appears in the expansion – there is a determination, although it is seen by one person but not by another. So we can say that either the sequence appears in the expansion or not. The experience of doubt is then hostage to the idea of ignorance – local or global – according to which there is something further to be known, but it is unreachable. Doubts, in this picture, point at a lack. A determination is there, but we cannot grasp it – skeptical challenges show the obstacles to accessing it. The picture holds us hostage: for each doubt – if we can individuate them – there is a corresponding determination; either "7777" appears in the expansion of π or it doesn't. Wittgenstein continues diagnosing our allegiance to the picture:

> [...] Here saying "There is no third possibility" or "But there can't be a third possibility!"– expresses our inability to turn our eyes away from this picture: a picture which looks as if it must already contain both the problem and its solution, while all the time we feel that it is not so.

The picture – that a determination exists, but if we have genuine doubts we fail to reach it – compels us either to exorcise doubts or to accept limits on the scope or the content of what we can know. In the latter case, the neo-Pyrrhonist can then aid us with her path to tranquility among suspended beliefs.

Neo-Pyrrhonism falls within the realm of Wittgenstein's picture. In other words, skepticism barely aims at the knowledge it tries to attain. It is about beliefs and not about facts – although, as is clear, it provides means to erode several sorts of determinations. The picture makes doubt an obstacle for ontoscopy – the skeptic is often keen to point out how doomed the enterprise is. It also sketches a divide between the subject of knowledge and its object: the subject hosts doubts, while the object is already determined. This is how Sextus Empiricus reads the modes of Aenesidemus and Agrippa and the repository of arguments in the Pyrrhonist tradition. The first five modes of Aenesidemus appeal to the differences in subjects – wine is sweet for me now, but not in another circumstance, not for other people, not for other animals. The subjects are variable – their species, their backgrounds, their ages, their habits – while the object – the determinations concerning the wine – remain the same, or so Sextus concludes. The modes are condensed in Agrippa's mode of relativity: relativity of impressions and opinions makes us doubt each impression and opinion – why would any of them be better than the others?

The standard anti-skeptical reply to these arguments today is to appeal to response-dependence property realism.[230] Response-dependence properties require the right response to be perceived – the wine is in fact sweet, because well-trained wine drinkers in appropriate circumstances have the perceptual and conceptual apparatus rightly tuned, and they detect that it is sweet. Such response, to be sure, depends on one response among all others being deemed right. In other words, as there is a determination in the world, we ought to make sure we are equipped to grasp it. Sextus, on the other hand, engages the arguments to show how we should suspend judgment. Other modes of Agrippa appeal to the insufficiency of a determination's justification: what determines a determination is a recursive question that admits no acceptable answer. There are no sufficient reasons to posit an undetermined determiner, and if we don't, we can only appeal to determined determiners. Sextus reads these modes as being about belief; there is no justification if there is no unjustified justifier, for otherwise nothing would sustain a belief but deference to other (unjustified) beliefs. Further, Agrippa's mode of *diaphonia* – the plurality of disagreeing voices – is understood as support for the thesis that subjects are irreconcilably different and the best we can do is to refrain from belief. In all these cases, Sextus understands arguments as targeting belief in some sorts of determinations. He uses each challenge to reinforce his recommendation of an attitude weaker than believing whenever we contemplate a determination.

Heraclitus and Aenesidemus

The skeptical endeavor, as launched by Sextus, is to use doubting to show that beliefs are insufficiently legitimate. The move is to argue against the solidity of determinations as epistemological arguments, that is, as arguments that sponsor a rift between knowledge and belief. The lessons from the repository of possible doubts are about justification, and being about justification's prevalent insufficiency, the lessons are about human humility. We should refrain from committing to determinations, because we are plagued with doubts; to ignore them and enlist behind a body of determinations about the world is to adopt a dogma. Sextus instead recommends equal distance from all dogmas – his aim is to cure people of conviction. To do so, he works to systematically exorcise what makes people commit to determinations. He engages with the arguments – his own reasonings and what he draws from Aenesidemus's and Agrippa's skeptical modes – as if they are about our take on how things are. While concentrating on the safety of our access to determinations, he doesn't let the arguments hit determinations themselves. Neo-Pyrrhonism is like dressing determinations in armor so that doubts hit nothing but our beliefs about them. Sextus then makes sense of the idea that this is the only thing we can do to avoid recoiling into one form or another of dogma.

In fact, Sextus complains about Aenesidemus's late conversion to the Heraclitean doctrine of the *polemos*.[231] His charge was that in doing so, Aenesidemus chose to read his modes (and all the arguments in the Pyrrhic tradition) as arguments establishing that things in the world are themselves in *diaphonia*.[232] That is, Aenesidemus held that the plurality of voices – the indeterminacy – spans beyond beliefs and toward the world itself. Such a claim about how things are, according to Sextus, is no more than recoiling into dogma. Aenesidemus would be recommending and adopting the belief that things are, say, indeterminate. By doing so, he would be using skeptical arguments to pave the way towards a dogma. Aenesidemus, however, could have been taking doubts to challenge whatever is considered to be determined.

Some say that Sextus indeed introduced something new in the Pyrrhonist tradition (his own neo-Pyrrhonism) by confining the skeptical arguments to the realm of beliefs.[233] In fact, Aristocles tells us that Timon, one of the followers of Pyrrhus, claims that for Pyrrhus things are indifferent, unstable and indeterminate and, as a consequence, no belief can be true.[234] If this is so, beliefs are doomed not because they are themselves unjustified, but rather because their objects are untamable. Indeterminacy is primary in the world. It is hard to find out exactly what Pyrrhus was aiming at with his critical doctrines – the determinacy of things or merely the justification of beliefs – as he didn't write anything. Conche believes that Pyrrhus was against the thesis that things are thus and so. Conche grounds her thesis on a text by Aenesidemus in which he attempts to restore the core of Pyrrhus's views against what he saw as a distorted view them. In the text, Aenesidemus claims that the Pyrrhonist doesn't determine anything – not even that nothing can be determined.[235] The text opposes *dogmaticoi* to *aporeticoi* – the assertive to the problematic – ascribing the latter only to the Pyrrhonists; the emerging image is that of a doctrine according to which the world is itself made of problems. Conche argues, against interpreters like Diels or Natorp, that there is indeed no contradiction between Pyrrhus's ways and a Heraclitean view of reality and, as Aenesidemus reportedly held, the latter followed from the former. Conche's claim is that the Pyrrhonists' main tenet was universal instability and insubstantiality. The recommendation that one should refrain from believing follows as a consequence.

By taking the Pyrrhonist path to arrive at something close to Heraclitus's doctrines, Aenesidemus took doubt to reveal something about the indeterminacy of reality. Doubts reveal, therefore, their own reality: the indeterminacy that they carry is somehow out there. Thus, Aenesidemus embraced what I call an *ontology of doubts* – the thesis, to be developed below, that doubts point at something real. This realism about doubts admits of different forms, as we will see; it is, in all forms, a powerful ontoscopy of what is up for grabs. It claims that doubts plague not the space of beliefs but the space of facts, for they erode determinations themselves. Such an ontology attempts to engage the Pyrrhonist arguments – and skeptic challenges overall – to target determinations in general, including facts in the world. The question that Sextus raised is: is such an ontology a form of dogmatism?

As an ontologist of doubts, Aenesidemus would take his modes, for example, as strategies to show that (some) things were not determined. The wine is not (determinately) sweet, for I have different perceptions of it at different times and other people and other animals don't feel, say, its sweetness. Then maybe the wine is not sweet (nor non-sweet). Aenesidemus can be a realist about the properties of the wine – that they are indeterminate – without taking these properties to be response-dependent. The modes exorcise the picture Wittgenstein denounced. Determinations themselves – in either the form of predications or of statements of what exists – are under suspicion. An ontology of doubts would therefore directly counter the picture where the world is made of determinations (either "7777" appears in the expansion of π or it does not),²³⁶ as it claims that the world does hold doubts; things are not fixed and established although some see them and others don't. Reversing the traditional image, certainty is a failure to see the hesitation of the world – to say that things are thus and so is to fail to see that they stand in a constant state of doubt, where nothing is established once and for all and independently of anything else. As we will see below, to be certain can mean to be out of touch with a world of doubts, while to suspend judgment is to attain a direct perception of things that do not follow a ready, determined judgment but rather hover in between multiple determinations, up in the air about which to follow. In a world of doubts, to hesitate can be precisely to be in tune with how things are. Not only can indeterminacies model what is up for grabs – up to be determined – but skeptical doubts reveal why no determination is resistant enough to be real.

The idea that the world is itself polemic – hosting a polyphony of determinations where none of them always conducts the orchestra – is a way to understand the importance Heraclitus gave to the *polemos*. Things, for him, were not alien to disputes. He thought nature was neither a fixed layer where a ground holds everything else – laws or principles or basic components – nor a ready order that could be unveiled once and for all. Nature has a tendency (or a liking) to hide itself, says fragment 123. This can mean that it is never fully revealed if we aim at portraying it in terms of determinations. *Polemos*, on the other hand, is behind everything: gods and mortals, slaves and masters, says fragment 53, nothing is indifferent to its force. The force is that of tension, the force of what stands against, of what is disrupting (see also Anarcheology 2/141* and 145). Heidegger's translation of *polemos* as *Auseinandersetzung* calls attention to the German word for dispute: set things aside in a different position.²³⁷ *Polemos* would occupy the place we commonly ascribe to determinations. Things are not (all) determined; they can go one way or another, and they only seem to satisfy determinations. When Aenesidemus went Heraclitus's way, he may have put his modes at the service of the ontology of doubts. For Sextus, this was a recoil into dogmatism. Aenesidemus could have replied, as we will see, that he had actually broadened the scope of skeptical arguments.

Formulating ontologies of doubts

An initial way to formulate the ontology of doubt is to say that nothing is determinate. This amounts to the same thing as the original Pyrrhonist doctrine: reality is itself indeterminate. In this general form, the idea is to say that doubting is a better path to cognitive virtue than believing. Such a first formulation would amount to a global skeptical attitude: nothing is safe from doubting, doubts spread everywhere and no determinations are safe from proper, well-formulated attack. This first formulation conceives of contingency as spreading everywhere. The picture is therefore one in which the world is entirely indeterminate, no room for facts.

The claim can be compared with Meillassoux's principle of facticity, according to which everything is necessarily contingent.[238] On the positive side, the comparison is relevant because here, too, is a (Pyrrhonist) principle of indetermination immune to anything that could take place in the world. Contingency appears here as transcendent. On the negative side, however, the comparison enables us to appreciate how doubts provide a finer image of what is up for grabs than do mere (ungrounded) facts: doubts point at insufficiency and remind us of the revealing family similarity between accident and epistemic luck. In any case, this first formulation combines a firm realism about doubts with antirealism about determinations. Such antirealism can take different forms. One might, for example, be an instrumentalist and hold that some determinations can be required in the exercise of doubting, but they don't need to be real to be useful. We can use beliefs to proliferate doubts, but it is only doubts that have any chance of being cognitively virtuous.

The idea that doubting makes use of determinations has been used to argue against (global) skepticism – and often to defend the notion that some beliefs ought to be accepted, or even held true. The point is that we cannot engage in doubting without grounds, without determined points of departure. Suppose we formulate an argument for global skepticism as follows (let's call it GS for short):

(Premise) I can doubt anything

(Conclusion) I can doubt everything (at once)

One could argue against GS either by showing that the premise is false – that there are things that cannot be doubted – or that the inference is invalid and, although anything can be doubted, it doesn't follow that everything can be put in doubt at once. This would be because one cannot doubt anything without the aid of at least one determination.

Two important twentieth-century variations of this argument against GS are those put forward by Wittgenstein and Davidson.[239] Davidson purported to show that doubting itself is not possible if some beliefs are not true. This version of the argument holds that in order for doubts to make sense, they have to be placed on a background of commonly held beliefs – and ultimately of true beliefs. Davidson argues that doubting all of one's beliefs simultaneously would make doubt unintelligible, as there would be no way to understand what the doubts were about. This argument, which depends on the Quinean dissolution of any rationale for a dualism between beliefs and meanings, supposes that in a web of beliefs most of them have to be true (or not false) in order for any of them to make sense. I can doubt your beliefs about the water temperature on the coast of the Chilean Pacific, but only if I don't doubt your beliefs about water, about the Pacific coast or about Chile. Otherwise I won't be able to understand what is at stake in the doubt. Doubts have to be non-global, or they are unintelligible. In other words, it is only in an environment of truths that doubts make sense; the exercise of doubting does not stand alone but requires roots in a ground of determinations.

The special flavor of Davidson's version of the argument has it that the roots or grounds of a doubt must themselves be grounded or rooted in true beliefs and not only provisional assumptions, because again it makes no sense to claim that all provisional assumptions are doubtful. The appeal to a critical mass of background beliefs is reiterated up to the point where a good deal of them ought to be true (and the argument can establish neither which ones are true nor whether there is a common body of true beliefs to any disagreement). Intelligibility, the argument goes, is related to truth – not in individual cases but in critical masses. If doubts depend on true determinations, the ontology of doubts in the first formulation cannot stand. If the argument works, it challenges not only global skepticism but also realism about doubts, if coupled with antirealism about determinations. If the argument establishes that there are no doubts anywhere without truth grounding them, realism about doubts must then espouse realism about determinations – that idea that some beliefs may be as cognitively virtuous as doubts.

An ontology of doubts in the first formulation, however, is compatible with milder versions of the argument against GS that require determinations without positing their truth. Such a version can be found as concerns Wittgenstein's notion of hinge propositions, the propositions that ground doubts. They have to be taken temporarily as certain in order to provide a framework in which doubts are intelligible. The game of doubting needs hinges from which doubts can hang in particular circumstances. In *On Certainty,* Wittgenstein mentions hinges in three sections:[240]

> 341. That is to say, the questions that we raise and our doubts depend on the fact that some propositions are exempt from doubt, are as it were like hinges on which those turn.
>
> 343. But it isn't that the situation is like this: We just can't investigate everything, and for that reason we are forced to rest content with assumptions. If I want the door to turn, the hinges must stay put.
>
> 655. The mathematical proposition has, as it were officially, been given the stamp of incontestability. I.e.: "Dispute about other things; this is immovable – it is a hinge on which your dispute can turn." there is indeed something there to be known.

Hinges are propositions that are provisionally exempt from doubt. One cannot intelligibly doubt everything at once, but piecemeal doubting can rely on changing hinges. A hinge is examined from within the game of doubting; that is, its status as truthful, conventional, arbitrary or contextually acceptable is not primarily at stake. Rather, they follow from the remark that doubts are not spinning in the void and therefore they require some fixed points to get off the ground. Wittgenstein considers the act of doubting and how it displaces certainty to show that hinges are not

fixed points that fail when doubts appear, but rather that doubts and hinges interrelate as players in a game. Hinges are not necessarily prior to doubts, but they can displace doubts – just as doubts displace determinations.
A proposition can dispel doubts, like a mathematical proposition that is safeguarded from dispute by sending doubts off to other areas. Here there is a divide between what is determined and what is doubted, but it is not between what can be known and what is in itself elusive or open to hesitation. It is a divide that emerges from the process of doubting itself; hinges are part of the economy of a working door.

Wittgenstein's image of the interdependence between doubts and hinges relies on an image of knowledge placed in the game of doubting. Hinges cannot be subtracted from the logical space of reasons that emerges from the scope of doubt. Such space is where reasons are used, both to challenge assertions and to defend them – but also to motivate doubts and to dispel them. The argument that doubts require hinges is transcendental: the conditions of possibility for the game of doubting – a game in which we engage whenever we are in the space of reasons – require determinations. There is a divide between doubts and determinations, but it is one that moves with the flow (of doubting). On the other hand, there is a game of holding fast to something, keeping it come what may – the biting the bullet that forces us to doubt something else in order to preserve what we want to preserve. It is another transcendental move, but in the other direction: the conditions of possibility for the game of holding fast to something – a game in which we engage often enough in the space of reasons – involve doubting something else. Wittgenstein admits that things can be kept come what may, but in order for a determination to be preserved at all costs, it has to meet all these costs. These are moves that can take place in the space – the space of reasons, which we can also call the space of sufficient reasons – shaped by indeterminacies and beliefs. If we read Wittgenstein's contextual hinges as places in this space, what emerges is a board of doubts and hinges. It is like a chessboard, with white and black squares, except that new doubts reveal unknown corners of the board. This board is a model of inquiry – beliefs are challenged by doubts, but doubts themselves must be grounded on supporting beliefs.

The image is akin to that emerging from Quine's lessons concerning the continuity of theory and meaning. Quine holds that it is a matter of *our* sovereignty to decide what we place in the center of the sphere where the periphery is what is less immune to revision. We decide to protect logic and mathematics, say, against the turbulence of experience, since no such turbulence is target at a specific belief or a particular determination taken for granted. The turbulence – revision through experience – is itself up for grabs, and thus teaches the rejection of the second dogma. Quine's rejection of it convinced him that only if we hold some things to be fixed can we enable experience to make an impact on us such that we change our minds – so that we can draw verdicts from experience. The periphery of the sphere changes in contact with experience, while the center – where we place what we hold fixed – stays put. If nothing is held fixed, no message from experience can be heard – it forces us to revise, but we can detect no specific message, and therefore anything can be revised (or everything can). In Quine's view, the world – supposedly made of fixed determinations – affects the system, this sphere where the most protected bits are in the center, only by provoking those turbulences through our sensorial input.

What matters here for an ontology of doubt is the image of sovereignty, which is a strategy in the game of doubting: protect some determinations (hold them fast) come what may, and you make it too costly for doubts to challenge them. (An opposite but, for our purposes, equally revealing strategy would be to decide to doubt some things come what may – for instance, some people decide to doubt some religious assertions at any cost and make it very expensive to subscribe to those assertions.) In any case, the image is that determinations and doubts somehow give rise to each other – they belong somewhere together. They are on a checkered board. The ontology of doubt in its first formation accommodates this second argument for the need for determinations better than the first argument does. In particular, one can be an instrumentalist about hinges – they are ladders to be used in the doubting exercise, doubts that can be thrown away afterwards. Sextus himself seemed to have favored accepting some commonsense opinions, not as full-blown beliefs but as accepted contents that would allegedly ease life with other people.[241] Apart from this pragmatic reason for acceptance, a skeptic could also accept some hinges in order to generate further doubts. Perhaps the skeptic, as the ontologist of doubts, is ready to pay the price of accepting some determinations, because such acceptance favors the proliferation of doubts. The ontologist of doubts may see such a proliferation as helping her stand in a better cognitive position. In any case, antirealism about determinations is not compulsory for the ontologist of doubts.

The argument against GS – especially in its first version – can compel a different formulation of the ontology of doubts, which would run like this: there are determinations and indeterminacies in the world. That is, there is a real board of doubts and hinges, and a doubt can be as cognitively virtuous as a belief. Doubting is no mark of ignorance, but believing is no sign of mistake either. There may be two boards of doubts and hinges: one formed by our doubts and our (provisional) certainties, and another formed by indeterminacies and determinations in the world. In this formulation, the ontology of doubts is a thesis about the furniture of the universe being composed both of states of affairs and of indeterminacies.

It is interesting to compare the ontology of doubts with neo-Pyrrhonism. I will come back to this friction below, but some brief comparative remarks are now in order. The skeptic conceives of the board as within the confines of our thinking. The game of doubting and holding fast, and by extension its board, is what we do with the input of the world – it is not something impressed on us by the world itself, but rather something established within the scope of our jurisdiction. The second formulation of the ontology of doubts rejects such confinement and embraces realism about the board. The contrast between doubts and determinations is not one in which doubts are solely our contribution while determinations are what we attain from the world, if we're lucky. Rather, doubting knows no boundaries; the interplay of certainties and hesitations is external to us and is not a product of our ignorance in a world of facts. In both formulations, doubts are out there, and hence the practice of eroding beliefs with doubts is a strategy of inquiry. The first formulation shares with the neo-Pyrrhonist the aim of avoiding beliefs: the neo-Pyrrhonist to achieve the skeptic *ataraxia* – a non-dogmatic sense of tranquility – and the first formulation to obtain knowledge. The second formulation shares with the urban skeptic the adherence to some determinations: the skeptic because some determinations are to be accepted

– albeit not believed – and the second formulation due to a realism about the whole board.

The epistemology of doubts

Realism about the whole board brings us to a different epistemological setup. The ordinary epistemological scenario, like the neo-Pyrrhonist, assumes a realism about determinations combined with an antirealism about doubts. If we're realists about the board, somehow our cognitive hesitations are not a mark of our deficiency or limitation, but rather a good strategy to cope with an environment full of indeterminacies. Hesitation becomes a cognitive tool. This new epistemological setup can inspire several positions, and I only aim to mention one or two of them.

In its second formulation, the ontology of doubt can inspire a direct realism about the board whereby we can directly access it. When we fiddle with problems concerning how things are, we can be in direct contact with the embroidery of determinations and doubts. If we have the correct beliefs and the appropriate doubts, we reach the real board – if not, we don't reach anything. Thus, direct realism can be coupled to a disjunctivist approach[242] according to which there is no common content between appropriate and inappropriate doubts – or between correct or incorrect beliefs. In one case, we reach all the way to the real board, while in the other, we are not on a board at all. Perceptual disjunctivism[243] holds that we can either perceive objects – a dagger in front of us when there is a dagger in front of us – or have a very different experience altogether – when there is no dagger and we hallucinate – and there is no common factor between the two cases, the veridical and the non-veridical. Analogously, for a disjunctivist direct realist about the board, the case in which we access the real doubts and real determinations is different from the non-veridical case. In the second case, there is no represented board at all; something of a completely different nature is taking place. We access the real board when our thought touches the interfaces between hinges and doubts out there, and we merely have an impression of being on a board when our thinking is off the mark. When we are on the real board, our hesitations and our convictions are under the direct influence of the indeterminacies in the world.

Here we can also bring in the idea put forward by François Laruelle's non-philosophy that the external world, rather than our sovereign distinctions and articulations, ultimately determines its own real cognition in the last instance. Laruelle holds that objects in the world impose the way they are to be thought (and cognized); thought is less an exercise of sovereignty on our part and more an incorporation of our ideas by the world. [244] It is philosophy alone that tries to control thought by distancing it from the nuances imposed on it by its objects. The rejection of the philosophical attitude, for Laruelle, is the release of our authority over thought and cognition – those are incorporations of their objects. Laruelle takes the known object to determine cognition in the last instance. He invokes a foreclosure of the real to knowledge.

Laruelle's determination in the last instance is an acccunt of knowledge according to which its objects impose themselves on us. As such, it can mesh with a direct-realist view of the board. It is not a claim that knowledge is possible because we receive ready-made realities, but rather that cognition is under the determining influence of what it ends up attaining. It ascertains the sovereignty of what is attained over its own cognition. What interests us concerning the ontology of doubts in Laruelle's inversion of authorities is that it makes room for the board to impose itself on us. As much as determinations can impose themselves on our convictions, doubts impose themselves on our hesitation. (Or, in the disjunctivist picture, something completely different takes place.) The board of doubts is therefore (sometimes) forced on us when we think. It is not that anything is imposed on us as a determination free of doubts, but rather that the board ultimately encompasses our thinking. We participate in the game of doubting – it is not something we concoct but something we find ourselves playing along with the world.

Direct realism concerning the board and imposition of the game of doubting in the last instance can be compared with the role Meillassoux ascribes to the facticity of the correlation. His speculative account contrasts with several forms of metaphysics of subjectivity – which, for him, includes all forms of process philosophy – in that it takes off not from the correlation between a subject and its object but rather from the facticity of such correlation. There is nothing, he insists, that determines a correlation to be the way it is. Its contingency reveals a principle of insufficient reason. It is a mere matter of fact that anything is locked into a particular correlation; there is nothing absolute in this. However, an absolute can be unveiled when we realize that facticity rules. In an account of contingency as resembling epistemic luck and akin more to doubts than to (insufficiently determinate) facts, the speculative step toward the reality of contingency is somehow different. Our experience of the contingency of correlation comes from our doubt concerning the objects of our knowledge. We doubt its content – a determination. Skeptical arguments make us suspect not only that a correlation is shadowing any contact we may have with any absolute, but also that it is contingent that we are stuck in a particular correlation, and indeed in any correlation at all. It is enough to consider Aenesidemus's first modes (or Agrippa's relativity mode). We can experience the same wine as bitter or sweet, and further, it is contingent that we experience things the way we do and that different subjects experience otherwise. The exercise of doubt, as the skeptical arguments make clear, uncovers the contingent correlations in which we find ourselves. The ontology of doubts, nevertheless, claims that what is revealed is not only that facticity is widespread and a principle of insufficient reason transcends all, but that the world is constituted by indeterminacies, even if they have to be backed up by determinations. Doubting shows a world in which nothing determines some things to be one way or another, and therefore the indeterminacies can be genuine.

Doubts in the open field

The idea of an ontology of doubt brings up a contrast between ways of facing suspension of judgment: the contrast rehearsed when Sextus reproaches Aenesidemus. It is, of course, possible to put the ontology of doubts itself in doubt. It could be, as Sextus argued, a form of dogmatism: things are such that there are doubts in the world. It sounds like a substantive thesis about the world, a claim about its furniture – a dogmatism about doubts. The accusation of dogmatism, however, can be reversed. The ontologist of doubt can accuse the neo-Pyrrhonist of being dogmatic about an ontology of determinations. This shows that an ungrounded assumption has been made when alternatives were possible. It then becomes a matter of contrasting the two dogmas, the realist and the antirealist, about doubts. Aenesidemus could have replied to Sextus that he was taking the skeptical arguments to the issue of whether there are only determinations in the world. Replying in that way, he would have been denouncing unsuspected dogmatism. To be sure, the skeptic can then reply that she does no more than use passing determinations to proliferate doubts. In any case, the contrast can be portrayed as a metaphysical dispute as to what doubts teach us and how far they reach. Presented this way, the friction inaugurated by Sextus's critique of Aenesidemus is no more than a battle of accusations.

It is, nevertheless, an intriguing friction. It can be placed not in trench warfare but in open-field combat. The skeptic can, then, retreat to a less fraught situation and take her commitments to be no more than passing. The ontologist of doubt, by contrast, would have to leave his entrenched position that the board of doubts and determinations is part of the world. The open-field alternative would be for them to actually play on the board in order to decide whether the board is in the world or somewhere else. Once their claims are put aside as dogmatisms, both the skeptic and the ontologist recognize that nothing beyond the board determines its reality. The issue must be decided within the board, playing by the rules of the game of doubting.

The game proceeds in the usual Pyrrhonist manner: an attempt to suspend judgment as to whether doubts are in the world or in our heads. The two positions would then arguably converge: the ontologist of doubt would no longer hold onto a realist claim about doubts, while the skeptic would revise her previously unsuspected attachment to the reality of determinations (and the unreality of doubts). The efforts on both sides would dwell in absences of determination – not with the presence of incertitude among beliefs or of doubts among facts. On the one hand, the effort may undermine the dogma of eroding all conviction (about determination or doubt). On the other hand, the same effort may erode determinations of all kinds (in beliefs and in states of affairs). In other words, friction between the ontology of doubts and skepticism is such that the former erodes determinations while the latter erodes conviction. The techniques put forward by the Pyrrhonists, which proliferate doubts, apply either way.

The two can therefore converge. Skepticism has always been an incursion into the realms of contingency – even when confined to a doxastic arena. Ontology of doubts is an attempt to make sure doubts have a broader impact. In both cases, doubts are central: they are sought and kept. Tension between the two positions arises when we think of one as asserting what the other is tacitly denying. Sextus apparently suspected that Aenesidemus took the attention to doubts prescribed in the Pyrrhonist recipe as an intermediary stage on the way to a more consolidated position, such as a Heraclitean ontology of the *polemos*. Sextus was unhappy with anyone who took Pyrrhonic doubt as a step toward what he can only see as dogmatism. The ontologist of doubts, however, doesn't have to accept this diagnosis. She can insist that Aenesidemus wasn't moving toward dogma at all. What Aenesidemus could have been after, according to the ontologist of doubt, was a way to go forward by considering that nothing in the world can, even in principle, resolve or exorcize doubts. The ontology of doubt would be improving on Sextus's neo-Pyrrhonism by insisting that not even in principle is any attitude more recommendable than an *epokhé*. Suspension of judgment is not the second best but the very best attitude one can have toward some or all content.

We can find a way to reconcile the insights and the blind spots of both positions. The ontology of doubt holds that doubts are everywhere – and therefore they can also be found within our knowledge and within our doubts – as *polemos* can also be found in our knowledge of *polemos*.[245] If this is so, then the ontology of doubts cannot be taken to assert that we are convinced of the existence of external doubts – or that they are immune to doubt themselves. The interplay between doubts and determinations recognizes no fixed territories. The ontology of doubts is a therapy to the neo-Pyrrhonist tendency to locate doubt within the realm of our thought. We do find doubts through the Pyrrhonist modes, but they don't come with tags bearing their permanent addresses.

The techniques of suspending judgment could point not to the relativity of dogmatic beliefs, but rather to the truth of relativity itself. The skeptic, after her ontology of doubt therapy, on the other hand, claims that the relativity brought up by the activity of doubting does not require asserting any truth beyond the suspension of judgment. The ontologist of doubt would then complement this by saying that doubt can be anywhere – it has no fixed territories, as there are no fixed territories for determination. We can now present a third and last formulation of the ontology of doubt, which holds that doubts are not confined and determinations are not endemic. According to such a position, doubts can be known, but knowledge of them is also full of doubts. This third and perhaps deflated ontology claims that there is no safe haven immune to doubt. It is not about contemplating doubts from the outside, from a position that is immune to doubting. There is no dogma, not even about doubts themselves. This ontology of doubt is no more than a reminder that suspension of judgment can be both the method and its result. It is therefore an exercise in looking at contingency. Or rather, it is an ontoscopy.

Being up for grabs

The open field shows how doubts reveal what is up for grabs. Contingency is widespread – it is not everything, it is not an ultimate component, but it is *proton to onton* in the sense of chapter 1. The sort of insufficiency that doubts are made of is central in that it affects everything else sensible. Doubts elucidate how things are – not because everything is indeterminate, but because indeterminacies give shape to what is around them through the board of doubts and determinations. There is a sense in which doubts impose themselves on us, in which indeterminacies produce our hesitations. In the open field image, the board is the environment in which we move. We cannot find access to the world – to anything absolute – on a hesitation-free path. More than revealing a game in our thought or even revealing the world with its indeterminacies, doubts place us amid the workings of contingency.

We have looked at three different formations of the ontology of doubt. The last simply refrains from any commitment to a world of facts. The first, and maybe the strongest, is committed to a world of indeterminacies – beliefs are, by their own nature, cognitively inadequate, as they have determinations as their content. The second makes room for some determinations in the world, within the context of the board of the game of doubting. The board itself is an agent in the game – it constrains and entitles moves within the course of play. The emerging picture in the second formulation is of a flexible board where determinations are not fixed but depend on the indeterminacy that is spotted. The formulation posits that some determinations exist, though not which ones nor even how many. It is a consequence of the argument against GS presented by Davidson that some unspecified determinations are true. A belief, as Davidson sometimes puts it, has a presumption of truth in its favor. I see this as suggesting what I call the *metaphysics of some*: there are determinations, but nothing determines once and for all which they are.[246] In the world described by this metaphysics, there are always some facts, but they are contingent on how we approach things, on what problems drive us. They depend on the perspective from which they are seen. It is as if our provisional acceptance of some determinations has been extended to the world, making it no longer a world of facts in general but a world of some facts that emerge from the board. Facts themselves are under the influence of indeterminacies and depend on the perspective from which they are approached. Such perspective is itself dependent on doubt – a doubt targets a determination while being grounded in some truths, according to Davidson's image. Doubts exhibit contingency while they unveil facts that ground them – no more than some facts, and those are undetermined.

Shown from the point of view of doubt, what is up for grabs doesn't appear primarily as open to interference. Rather, it presents itself as insufficiently determined. This contrasts with how it appears in a monadology of fragments. There, we understood lightness of being in terms of openness and *communitas*, whereas here it is an issue of *automaton* and under-determination. Also, in the three formulations of the ontology of doubts, the board appears not to be up for grabs itself. Contingency is transcendent. In the monadology of fragments, we witness immanent immunization forces, while here, the board is not itself an object of doubt. Insufficiency is a structural feature of the sensible, something that we can compare with Meillassoux's principle of facticity. But the board, in the latter two formulations of the ontology of doubt, leaves room for the non-contingent within its quarters. In these two formulations at least, indeterminacy is widespread and crucial to understanding the sensible, but it is not the sensible's ultimate principle. To be sensible is to be meshed with what is up in the air.

Doubting brings contingencies to the fore – this is what makes the ontology of doubts an ontoscopy. Doubting can be a way to access what is up for grabs, what is undecided, and therefore cannot command assent to any determination. The ontologies of doubt are like the doctrine of the *polemos* in that they conceive doubts as not only (possibly) both in the world and in our thinking but also in our thinking (possibly) because they are in the world.[247] Doubts expose insufficiency. The sensible contrasts with a realm of determinacy, where there may be room for investigations capable of drawing conclusions without margins for doubt because everything is in itself sufficiently determined – and therefore necessary.

Not a quaver   Gisel Carriconde Azevedo, Collage on paper, 2011

Chapter 5
Rhythms

Rhythm-oriented ontologies

Zbigniev Karkowski, as part of his endeavor to broaden the set of musical instruments to oblivion, aimed to expand music to the point that nothing else could be recognized.[248] In the closing lines of his essay on the topic, he claims that

> [...] all the forms existing in the universe: plants, trees, minerals, animals, even our bodies have their shape created by resonating to some specific frequencies in nature. In a very real sense then, at the core of our physical existence we are composed of sound and all manifestations of forms in the universe are nothing else but sounds that have taken on a visible form. [...] There is no doubt that the body metabolism functions primarily via a combination of electrical frequencies, pulse rates and biochemical hormones. [...] There is nothing else but sound, all that exists is vibration.

Karkowski suspects that everything resonates with what surrounds it. He talks about sound composing everything through frequency and vibration – nothing can be indifferent to that which resonates around it. Karkowski is hinting at the idea that our auditory experience is revealing concerning how things interfere with each other. He conceives of interference like a contagion through proximity. Transmission through contact points toward an image of what exists not as substantially closed but rather as intrinsically open to what is around it.

Resonance appears not only among organic systems but also, suggestively, among sedimentary rocks. It is interesting to look at a particular form of sedimentary rock that is very common where I come from – the ancient soil of Brasilia. Many of the rocks in the region are rhythmites. A rhythmite is composed of layers of sediment laid down with a periodicity. They register rhythms of the local events, rhythms that can be seasonal, of shorter-term processes such as tides or of longer-term processes like regular floods. The rhythmites around Brasilia register patters reminiscent of sea tides and, as such, they reveal that the area may have been home to a prehistoric sea. The sea, which might have been here millions of years ago, left its vestiges on the ground because it had rhythms. The geology of rhythmites is the study of the periodicity of past events. It studies how what takes place around rocks marks them. Sedimentation is rhythm-oriented. It takes place at the pace of what is in the vicinity – and provides a condensed register of its neighborhood as its layers keep track of what has happened there.

Sedimentary rhythmites are philosophically interesting. They are, perhaps, philosophers' stones, for they overtly illustrate what it is to be oriented by rhythms. In fact, as sedimentary rocks, they are clear registers of the pace of past sedimentation. They explicitly solidify the rhythms around them – their shapes register the periodicity of what is happening. They are also speculatively interesting: they are constituted in a way that is perhaps not *sui generis*. Maybe rhythmites and their paced sedimentation are not unique; maybe they represent a more widespread vulnerability to surrounding rhythms. Things are shaped and composed by patterns around them. Rhythmites receive repetitions that form beats surrounded by intervals. These rhythms shape sedimentation, which registers the surrounding events as beats; they contract the repetitions in a materiality that stores the patterns of the events taking place around them. Sedimentation is indeed an antenna.[249] It captures the beats it is capable of capturing – these sedimentary rocks have a pace that is up for grabs for the events around it. But sedimentation is also a broadcaster. Rhythmites both capture and transmit.

Sedimentation is the speculative takeoff lane for a more general rhythm-oriented ontology. To be sure, there are several possible varieties of such ontologies: rhythm-orientation can be vindicated in different ways. Rhythms can be understood, for example, as having units that are themselves abstract and systematically instantiated by concrete things. In this case, there would be pure rhythms separate from things following repetitive patterns. The rhythm-oriented ontology that I will develop here, however, makes no appeal to pure rhythms. It is rather an ontology of events in which, in a certain sense, events determine the pulse of everything else. There are no original rhythms. The pace of events, and the intervals between them, can be changed. This openness in pace makes whatever is constituted by events susceptible to change by rhythms. As in all possible forms of rhythm-oriented ontology I can imagine, repetition is a crucial ingredient.

Repetition and entrainment

Deleuze explores Hume's thesis that repetition doesn't change anything in what repeats but does change something in what contemplates the repetition. [250] His endeavor is to replace the philosophical focus on substances and their representation with an attention to the processes of repetition. Repetition carries a force, not through necessary connections but through parts of the actual world shaping others. Deleuze thinks of repetition as both spatial and temporal – repeated shapes and repeated paces. Instead of a universal guided by underlying necessities, repetition can set the same pattern in different concrete things by contagion. Repetition is the grammar of the universal: local patterns in concrete things affect what is around them, and universality then grows from contact. The Humean lesson is that the marks of repetition are not left in what is repeated, but rather in what the repetition affects. Patterns are themselves sculptors of whatever media are open to them – they are not abstract interferences, but can be transmitted from one concrete thing to another. One such medium is human expectation: we are engraved with a habit of expecting something if we are sensible to what is repeated.

Repetition is a blueprint for universality without appeal to instantiations – it is not that the shape of the chair instantiates a chair shape, but rather that it repeats the shape of another chair. But anything can repeat anything – a bug can model a leaf, an armchair can model a valley, work-management software can model a desk, ontogeny can recapitulate phylogeny. It is a form of generalized-recapitulation ontology.[251] That is to say that there are no pre-established limits to repetition – anything can repeat anything. Here, Deleuze makes an important distinction: repetition can be *naked* – exact, independent of the medium that repeats it – or *dressed* – mediated, affected by what repeats. An armchair repeating a valley is dressed; it depends on what the armchair "wears," for it is a medium very different from a valley. Similarly, each chair repeats the patterns of other chairs, but imperfectly. We can find naked repetition between two instances in a sequence of numbers – but Deleuze holds that even this depends on a dressed repetition, for instance that of a sequence of signs on a paper. A naked repetition requires a supporting dressed repetition – there are no self-standing naked repetitions among the concreta. Expectations created from perceived patterns are dressed repetitions – they take a very different shape from the original patterns, but, still, they repeat.

Because the medium changes from iteration to iteration, repetition gives rise to difference. Deleuze seems ready to propose an ontological game of Chinese whispers, in which a message transmitted repeatedly produces something else. It is an insinuation of the Epicurean idea that swerving from an orbit creates something new.[252] Repetitions happen in time: for the shape of a chair to model another, one must precede the other. This enables Deleuze to understand the past, the present and the future in terms of repetitions. The past is always what has prepared the current moment; the *répétition* is both what has been repeated and what has been rehearsed. The past is the current form of the rock – or of the chair, the leaf or the embryo. The present is what repeats. It is shaped by the past. The present is the resonating moment; it is when expectations are put to work and when past repetitions give pace to what is to come. The present is the repeater: what brings what was rehearsed to act. Finally, the future is the repeated – what can be foreseen is what has been present in past repetitions. The future appears as what is repeated, what is scheduled by habit, what is induced.

There is no future without induction. It is in this sense that Blanchot says that the disaster has no future: it has no place on the calendar.[253] The unpredictable cannot be placed in the future. The calendar is, in fact, a way to predict the future, based on very entrenched expectations like our certainty that there will not be more than one Monday next week. The calendar is itself based on repetitions, and all it can say about the future is what is going to repeat.

It is because the present repeats and the future is the repeated that the pace of past repetitions resonates through time. This is what brings rhythm into the picture. Delanda understands rhythms as intensive time.[254] Intensities are distinct from qualities in that they can affect their surroundings, just as a colored paint transmits its color to the surfaces it touches. If something metallic is placed close to a piece of wood, its qualities will not transmit by simple proximity – its shape, its size, its volume – but its temperature will. Temperature is an intensity: closeness to something cold is enough to make something else colder. Some properties become intensities under particular conditions – the flavor of spices, for example, affects whatever is cooked with them. Intensity is about contamination without a specific transmission agent; it is broadcasting and reception without a dedicated antenna. Delanda portrays rhythm as an intensity. So the rhythms of one's body affect each other – locomotion influences digestion, breathing affects the heartbeat, hormone cycles interfere in sexual peaks. Similarly, the surrounding rhythms have an impact on the internal rhythm of a body. Rhythms impact other things by the force of resonation. A rhythm from the streets resonates in my body, makes my feet move, changes my breathing, alters my digestion. Rhythms interfere in the timing of things. They affect time – and this is why DeLanda appropriately understands them as intensive time. We will see later that from a rhythm-oriented perspective, there is no time beyond timing: the aggregation of rhythms alone constitutes time. Rhythms set the clock.

DeLanda calls the process by means of which a rhythm resonates in other things *entrainment*. The pace of one cycle entrains others. The rhythms in the street entrain my pace of working, music entrains dancers. Entrainment, to be sure, is always dressed, as opposed to naked. It happens through mediations. Different people are entrained differently by the same music, depending, for instance, on the different marks left in their bodies by the rhythms they have been entrained to in the past. Yet on the dance floor, they synchronize. A common rhythm is in fact what makes a dance floor what it is – different responses to a common entrainment. People on a dance floor can be compared to organisms acting together through nothing but a common rhythm. DeLanda writes:

> The phenomenon of entrainment allows many independent sequences of oscillations to act in unison, to become in effect a single parallel process. The most dramatic and well-studied example of this phenomenon is perhaps the slime mold Dictyostelium. The lifecycle of this creature involves a phase where the organisms act as individual amoebae, the behavior of each constituting an independent sequential process. At a critical low point of availability of nutrients, however, we witness the spontaneous aggregation of an entire population of these amoebae into a single field of parallel oscillators, eventually leading to their fusing together into a single organism with differentiated parts.[255]

Because rhythms entrain, there is little sense in talking about intrinsic rhythms. Circadian cycles are entrained by the rotation of the Earth, sea tides are entrained by the moon, a woman's menstrual rhythm is entrained by other women's cycles. Entrainment displays characteristics of an intensive process; it is a process of contagion indifferent to agents. It is what makes rhythms intensive time: they entrain what is around them in different ways, depending on the media where the repetition will take place. To be entrainable is to be subject to rhythm, and entrainable are the vibrating components of laser light, chemical reactions, geological formations and organic cycles.

Entrainment points toward a common surface of a lack of immunity to rhythms. This common lack of immunity sets things up for entrainment – an ontological dance floor. To be sure, the rhythms that entrain are the ones that can be heard – it is only some sounds that make it all the way through my window. The passers-by in the lobby of the library where I am situated entrain me only through their steps close to me. As intensive time, rhythms are transmitted through proximity. Also, there are immunizing mechanisms that stop entrainment. The rhythm of the stars is less entrained by life on the surface of the earth than vice-versa. If a woman is on the pill, she is less easily entrained by other menstrual cycles. Again, the dance floor is a useful metaphor: Differences in the way people dance have to do with folds in their bodies that register past rhythms. They can also decide to move some parts of their bodies but not others by deflecting the passing rhythms away from some movements. Still, some cycles of their bodies are affected by the closeness of the rhythm. Mere proximity makes entrainment possible. A rhythm-oriented ontology is like this dance floor: entraining rhythms go a long way.

Events

Given that rhythms are all-encompassing, it is difficult to start describing a rhythm-oriented ontology. Its main claim is that rhythms are a crucial element in what there is: rhythm transmission illuminates how concrete things acquire their shape. Yet because only perceived rhythms entrain, it is not straightforward how rhythms manage so much. A plausible starting point for a rhythm-oriented ontology is the beat. The beat is like a point in audible space – as elusive, seemingly dimensionless and ubiquitous as a point. Yet if we take rhythms to be present in every episode of resonance, we would find beats in the shapes of rocks, in the folds of our bodies, in the stains on the wall. We can understand rhythms in terms of beats and time or in terms of paces and intervals. This doesn't mean that beats have a priority over rhythm; as we will see, maybe the best is to take them to mutually depend on each other. A rhythm requires time to unfold – as perhaps time requires beats that tick the clock. In any case, if we start with beats, we ask what it is that beats. We ask what, in ontology, is the correlate of my knockings on the table.

A candidate understanding of the beat is the event – anything that happens. We say that events take place – they occupy a space that was already busy with other events that have themselves taken place. An event is also said to be something that brings a change; perhaps the event is itself a change. The Aristotelian account of change in the *Physics*[256] involves three ingredients: that which undergoes change, that in which it changes, and that which is actually changed. If this is so, and we take an event to be a change

– as a beat divides between two intervals of time – the event has to act on a change-bearer, something that receives the change. It is not always simple to identify the change-bearer of an event. Sometimes an event gives rise to too many dispersed changes: the outbreak of a plague changes many bodies, the inauguration of a president brings difference to several institutions, the start of the spring alters a number of organisms. This is why the individuation of events is puzzling: what makes an event one – as opposed to many? The issue provides insight into the sense in which beats are separate from each other and how they act on rhythms.

The problem of the individuation of events reveals some dimensions of rhythms. To begin with, if events resonate in beats, what separates those beats? Davidson attempted to individuate them through causes and effects, seeing them as points in a causal chain.[257] The problem, as Quine quickly pointed out, is that the space of causes and effects is itself made of events, and therefore events can only be individuated by an appeal to other individuated events, can only be identified with respect to other events that have already been identified. In other words, only in a space of events, where things take place, can something take place. An event affects a change-bearer that is arguably constituted by other events – if, in fact, we can say that the change-bearer in this account is the causal chain. Similarly, the beat is a distinguishable beat only given an underlying rhythm over which it comes in.

Davidson's account of the individuation of events is often rejected on the grounds of circularity. Something, however, can be said in favor of biting this bullet and embracing the claim that an individuated event can only make sense against a background of other events. This can look plausible if we consider that time cannot be eventless. If there cannot be time without change, something like an event has to bring about that change. So circularity may be enlightening in this case. Further, the entanglement between rhythms and beats is not one that can be easily unraveled. Two poles emerge that, in a nutshell, mimic those of priority monism and priority pluralism: a beat depends on the underlying rhythm, or the composed rhythm is built on the aggregation of beats. Though a way out through an appeal to circularity may seem attractive here, it would simply mean espousing the equivalent of priority nihilism. It would entail that an individuated beat can only appear in a rhythmic context – the change-bearer of the beat event must be the overall rhythmic environment surrounding it, as rhythms and beats mutually depend on each other.

Still, other accounts of the individuation of events manage to avoid circularity. The most discussed of these is Edward Lemmon's, developed as a response to Davidson's original approach. Lemmon identified an event with a spatio-temporal position.[258] The event is individuated by its spatio-temporal location. Here, the change-bearer is irrelevant, once events are no longer considered as changes. They are simply things that take place. It is a way to avoid obvious circularity – but if time itself cannot be understood without appeal to events, the threat of circularity may return, for a position in space-time will be a position among other events. There are other apparent drawbacks to the approach. Different events often happen simultaneously. The ringing of the phone and its slight shaking can be different events with the same space-temporal location. A supporter of Lemmon's account can therefore feel compelled to take any two or more events that occur at the same space and time to be actually the same. This is a heavy burden, for it goes against ordinary ideas about different events.

Lemmon's account can nevertheless be defended on a different basis, and this can shed light on how best to handle events as beats. One can say that the events are actually different because they are positions in different – albeit connected – space-time areas. That is, we can try to place the ringing of the phone and its shaking in different overall areas. This path is even more evidently subject to the circularity objection, for these space-time areas look dangerously like causal chains in Davidson's account. The circularity of individuation strikes again, for without individuated events, it may be difficult to individuate these space-time areas. This could be an ultimate drawback to an approach that tries to individuate events without appealing to already individuated events. This may then stimulate Lemmon's followers to accept that what seem like different events are actually the same after all. However, the alternative of different space-time areas deserves some pause.

If we can legitimately postulate space-time areas, we are entitled to talk about separate-yet-simultaneous rhythms of events. Perhaps a beat can only be heard against the background of another rhythm of which the beat is not a part. The beat of a train departing – the event: the train is set in movement – is individuated against the tick of the clock – the event: it is now 11:19.

The counting of time is taken to be unaffected by most other rhythms. If we set the chronometer for the journey, its rhythm is also indifferent to the clock rhythm, as would be the rhythm of turn taking in a chess match. The fact that time can be detached from further time is what makes room for the possibility of time travel: a timeship, travelling in time, would make a journey of one hour toward the next millennium.[259] Considering two different chains of events that are indifferent to each other is, therefore, something we do ordinarily. If we consider these separate areas, we can separate events that happen simultaneously but in these different areas; my dancing affects the others dancing around me, but also my heartbeats and my dancing are two separate rhythms. My banging the surface beneath me is common to both separate areas, but it translates into my heart cycle as one beat and onto the dance floor as another beat. If beats are events, we can see each of these as separate events.

Another alternative to Davidson's causal-chain-based account of the individuation of events is Jaegwon Kim's.[260] His main idea is that events are instances of properties in objects. Here, clearly, the change-bearer is the object that subsists through the many events – through the changes of state it undergoes. So setting a train in motion is an event, for it makes the train instantiate the property of being in movement. Kim's account relies on an ontology of objects and properties; if there were no objects, there would be no events. Further, an event cannot be individuated without objects (or without aggregates of objects). If an ontology of objects is assumed – according to which everything happens to objects – this could be a good account. But events are not thought to depend on objects and properties, so taking them as instantiations of properties of objects doesn't help. Kim's account, nonetheless, is a clear example of how events depend on change-bearers – they operate a change on objects. If we take events as beats, we have them making changes within a rhythmic soundscape. A rhythm-oriented ontology that would have the beat – or the event – as some sort of *arché* would have to assume a background of silence – or nothingness – against which the beat has taken place. It would then be this beatless rhythmic soundscape that would be changed into something else.

Carol Cleland has defended an alternative account of the individuation of events that, while having clear change-holders that are not quite like rhythm soundscapes, can help elucidating the connections between beats and rhythms.[261] She holds that an event is a change of state in a determinable property. A determinable property – which she calls a *phase* – is a quality that admits of many states. So having a color is a phase; it admits of states like red or blue. Red also can be a determinable property, admitting of many shades. So an event is a change within a space of states bounded by a phase – like a change of state in the space of colors. Because the distinction between states and phases can be relative – red is a state of color but also a phase admitting shades – she appeals to a trope-like[262] entity that she calls *concrete phases*. These are tropes of phases that she takes as basic individuals whose individualization is always already given. A particular colored patch (the concrete phase) may turn from white to brown (the change of state). An event is a concrete change that acts on a concrete phase – something that happens to the phase that makes it change states. She continues to say that objects and space-time locations can be construed in terms of these basic individuals – concrete phases and events are changes in these individuals – they are the change-bearers.

Cleland's approach, relying on concrete phases as things that are changed by events, provides arguably no more than a partial account of the individuation of events. This is because she assumes that concrete phases are themselves already individuated. If we are convinced that the issue of individuation ought to be pursued further, we must consider that concrete phases seem to be individuated only by means of further events. This is precisely because the distinction between phases and states is relative. So if ringing is a state of the phase of being a working telephone, and if a particular working telephone is a concrete phase, then to be a working telephone is also a state of another phase – and arguably another concrete phase – like the phase of being a telephone, working or not. What makes a telephone – concrete phase – start working is an event that changes its state. If this is so, phases also result from events that are changes in other concrete phases – concrete meta-phases, we can call them. If we don't take concrete phases as primitives, we have to individuate them through other events, and ultimately, we return to issues of circularity.

It is again an interesting circularity: events can only be identified in terms of other events unless we break the circle with primitives – be they objects or concrete phases. Cleland believes objects can themselves be understood in terms of events (and concrete phases). Now, concrete phases themselves can be unpacked in terms of events, for if we take them to change states in a phase – inaugurating new states – and if states are themselves determinable properties, an event also inaugurates a phase. States and phases are bordered by events. Events are both what bring about a state and what end a state – and a phase. When we postulate primitives like concrete phases or objects, we don't focus on their borders. The difficulties with the individuation of events can suggest that we should instead postulate events as basic entities. The borders, and not what they border, are the constituents (of objects, concrete phases or whatever else). Look at the covers, says such an event-oriented ontology, not at what is inside. Events are what separate states and phases. If we take them to be basic, we may wish to take them to be individuated. But if events are changes, then it is not convincing that they can be individuated independently of what they change.

The alternative is to consider that they change the products of other events – objects, phases, states that need separators. Ultimately, events act on what other events have acted on. They are like folds in that which is already folded; indeed, maybe embryogenesis is the best model for what events concoct. They stand against a recursive soundscape: they change what has been changed before. If we understand beats as events, we can take whatever is inaugurated by an event – a state, a phase, etc. – as the interval between one beat and the next. The intervals are part of the rhythmic soundscape against which a beat is distinguishable. It is hard to conceive of a first beat – a creation *ex-nihilo* – for a beat can only be identified against a background of other rhythms, and a silence with no beginning is not a standard interval, for those are made by a starting beat and an ending beat – by changes. Beats are constituents of intervals as events are constituents of what they change. What endures, therefore, endures in a rhythm. Instead of looking for substances, we look for what puts an end to subsisting. Instead of looking at the sensible as the realm of degeneration and decay, we look toward change itself. Considering events as beats and as the recursive building blocks of the grammar of the sensible is an open door for a rhythm-oriented ontology that assumes everything can only exist against a rhythmic background. An event is mainly a change in a rhythm soundscape.

This primacy of the surface over what it covers lets us understand the sensible as what pulses, like a dance floor. A rhythm-oriented ontology brings equality to all events: they all take place on the same rhythmic surface. Arguably, the more obvious auditory features of rhythms help with appreciating this equality. Indeed, the categories related to the auditory – such as propagation, diffusion and silence – are better suited to dealing with nonhierarchical mutual interference than the visual. While vision privileges distinctions between the figure and its ground or between what is revealed and what is concealed, audition privileges a flat appreciation, something like Garcia's *plane of equality*.[263] In rhythmic terms, the intervals not only lack intrinsic depth but are also dependent on the beats that demarcate them. Events, seen as beats, are prior in the sense that in this rhythm-oriented ontology nothing is seen as independent of its starting and ending points. Beats are only relatively *archés*. Yet no event's pace is determined by anything other than the pace of other events – beats take place in a wider space of beats.

The rhythm soundscape is made of rhythms on top of other rhythms; the preceding ones, nonetheless, enjoy no primacy for coming earlier. There is no *arché* in rhythms – new rhythms can prevail by entrainment as much as old ones. No ancestral rhythm entrains all the others. In fact, it is always the overall emerging rhythm that affects something. As in a monadology of fragments, in this rhythm-oriented ontology nothing is inherently protected from the other things that co-exist with it. Here, too, there is no *arché*, for beats – and events – are themselves recursive and ultimately gunky. Not only are concrete phases (or objects) made of events, but events themselves are made of further changes. In other words, a rhythmic soundscape is required to identify a beat against an interval, but also a beat itself is made of other beats. The event of making a telephone work is composed of many other events – adjusting parts, replacing cards, connecting cables, etc.

A beat is perceived as such given a specific soundscape – an event is an individual with respect to the change it promotes. Beats have a *matryoshka* nature: as rhythms are embedded in each other, beats are made of other beats. As events can be decomposed into other events, and a beat is always identified against a rhythmic background, the beat of an event is recursively constituted by other events.

If an event is made of other events, so is time. Time is understood in terms of timings – a rhythm is a product of an entrainment that times events, like a clock times activities in a day. Time is no more than a collection of timings, and therefore a collection of rhythms and entrainments. Moreover, an A-series of past, present and future is needed for an event to make sense – this A-series indicates where we are in the B-series.[264] The A-series is made of events. It is also what makes time possible, if there cannot be time without change, nor without a present as ticked by a clock. Present time – the current tick, the repeater – is itself a *matryoshka*: it comprises many events, and therefore many beats made of rhythms in an embedded clock. The beat is composed of intervals and other beats.[265] In order for me to start dancing – an event – many other events had to happen; I had to start moving my arm, for example, which in turn consists of many other, smaller events. The now of the stars is made of an indefinite number of nows of the ants; the tick of a clock requires a pandemonium of rhythms inside its machinery. This embeddedness of rhythms is their basic an-*arché*, for there is no original beat that is not itself an assemblage of simultaneous rhythms.

Rhythmic transduction

I write these lines at Aharon Amir's place in Brighton. He is an artist interested in the rhythms of search, and we have been discussing entrainment and how rhythms get entangled. In his room, we sit on the floor facing the window and set equipment to record the pace of our conversation. On one of the walls is a radiator. Surrounding it is a pattern of squares formed by the change in the wall's temperature when the heater is on. The activity of the radiator is registered on the paint of the wall. The many squares around the device echo the rhythm of the many times the event of switching the heater on and off has taken place. Such events were informed by all sorts of climatic, emotional and economic factors: the coming of the winter, the presence of more people in the house, the price of gas heating. The cycles become entangled in a composite rhythm that makes its marks on the wall. This composite rhythm entrains the gradual failures in the paint. To be sure, the radiator also entrains the wall, along with other rhythms associated with climate, density of the paint, and overall humidity.

The an-*arché* of the beat shows up in the inextricably composite character of all rhythms. Not only is the beat itself made of composite rhythms – the rhythms present each time the radiator is put to work – but also no rhythm entrains on its own. There is always a relevant rhythmic soundscape mixing with it. Rhythms are always in entanglement.

The passing of a rhythm from one setup to the next is a matter of transmission. The composite rhythm is broadcast and entrenches where it can. When it does, we see how the wall parodies the heater and the heater parodies the cycles at the house – to isolate the marks of one rhythm on the wall, we would need to filter what has been broadcasted. We can understand rhythm transmission in terms of transduction, in Simondon's understanding.[266] Information flows from one rhythmic device to the next. Transduction explains how objects are compressed rhythms – they are intervals between two events filled with other events that change the objects' phases and their states. Objects are crystallized rhythms (and the rhythmite is the paradigm). Simondon claims that transduction is everywhere – it is the stuff individuations are made of. If we understand this information flow in terms of rhythmic entrainment, we see how it is only in an ocean of moving rhythms that we can find individuals: objects, concrete phases, and states, but also the event itself, formed by the composition of rhythms that provoke it. Information – like rhythms – is always being lost and regained, always aggregating and separating again. Transduction in a rhythm-oriented scenario is what binds together independent concrete things – they are exposed to the rhythms of information flow.

Transduction is also what produces expectations. Simondon held that not only does transduction provide an account of the world but it also helps us understand in what terms the world is accessed. Transduction explains our inductive contact with the world, both through the inductions we make to construct theories and through all our bodily responses to our surroundings. The pervasive character of induction shows how we, as inhabitants of the world in which we have acquired our habits, dwell constantly in expectations – a result of our entrainment by what we have found around ourselves. Induction itself is a form of entrainment. We can only think about the whereabouts of the sun tomorrow if we have a sense of rhythm – enough to be sure of when tomorrow is. It is inductively that we acquire a sense of tomorrow – we expect the clock to tick, the rooster to crow, the hours to pass. The future makes sense only if there is a clock, a cycle or an expected rhythm to which we are tied: the repeated. The acquisition of an inductive hypothesis through our expectations is a rhythmic response to experience. It is, of course, dressed entrainment, as the medium of habits and instincts is very different from the one of the billiard table. Still, the movements of the billiard balls entrain our expectations. We filter and modulate what the balls broadcast. Like anything else, we modulate the rhythm around us through our particular medium. Because modulation and filters act whenever entrainment takes place, experience is never pure receptivity – experience cannot be captured in the form of naked repetition. There is always a measure of spontaneity involved, if we understand spontaneity in terms of mediation – going through a medium. Naked repetition, in contrast, is the given, the immediate. In order to hear the signal, we must resonate with it.

In fact, in a world of modulated signals and rhythmic broadcasting, there is a general version of Kant's formula against the given that intuitions without concepts are blind:[267] signals without modulations are insufficient. They are insufficient both because unmediated signals lack presence among concrete things to entrain anything and because modulations make some things heard by throwing others into indifference. Without modulations, everything is heard; this is a sort of wind deafness. Signals without modulation are white blind – they see too much. McDowell's version of the formula – that intuitions without concepts are mute[268] – can illuminate how signals have to be entrained: signals don't say anything to those who are not ready to resonate them by modulation. In other words, one has to understand the signal, and in rhythmic terms, this means being capable to retransmit it – a dressed repetition. Modulation – the mediation that makes it possible to hear a signal – is what makes a rhythm capable of entraining. Rhythms that don't resonate among concrete things don't entrain. Modulation is the staple of transduction and therefore is part of how we acquire inductive access to the world.

Rhythmic transduction can also explain how we acquire concepts and respond to norms. Wittgenstein, at around section 185 of the *Philosophical Investigations*[269], makes some remarks about the difficulties involved in learning to follow a rule – and therefore to follow the established use of a conceptual norm. To learn to follow a rule (say, +2) is to be able to follow a sequence after seeing some examples. Wittgenstein's famous case is a pupil learning the +2 rule from examples up to 1,000; continue the sequence that begins 0, 2, 4, …, 994, 996, 998, 1,000. The issue is in which sense the pupil makes a mistake if he reckons that 1,004 comes next. Now, to learn a rule from examples is to be entrained by a rhythm. This is explicit with the rule of +2. The pupil who reckons that 1,004 comes next has been entrained by the sequence, but not quite in the way meant by the tutor. The examples entrained her in a different way. To learn a rule is to find a way to engage one's resources into being entrained by a rhythm that is sufficiently similar – enough to satisfy those who are teaching it. It is an exercise in undressing repetition – in capturing a signal that is sufficiently independent of its medium to be a shared content.[270]

In order to learn a public language – and any conceptual norm – one uses one's own rhythms to produce a suitable repetition of another, external rhythm. This can be compared with learning a dance step: we engage our own articulations, shapes and abilities, which were themselves once entrained by something else, to repeat the public movements. The resources can be said to be private – albeit acquired through entrainment – while the overall movement is synchronized with other, public movements. The rhythms of the pupil are among the resources engaged in learning. We cannot learn to follow a rule, learn a concept or a dance step, if we cannot associate its rhythm with others that are already available to us. This is entraining. It acts always on other rhythms. There must be something in the pupil that prepares him for the learning – and this has to do with the pupil's body cycles. When the pupil of section 185 of the *Investigations* captures the wrong rhythm, there is nothing to be done but to entrain her further, having in mind that the pupil's receptors may be resistant to some rhythms. If the tutor is successful, the learned rhythm will have in itself the marks of the resources the pupil engaged to learn it. A rhythm is made of beats, and although a learned rule may be public, like a language, it will be executed with a private accent.[271]

There is much to be explored concerning induction, norms and cognition within the framework of a rhythm-oriented transduction. Such a framework can shed light onto issues like the need for recognition, the content of experience or the role of inference in following norms. My purpose here is no more than to present the outline of a rhythm-oriented perspective on our access to the world. Access is thoroughly rhythmic, and there is much more to be explored in a rhythm-oriented ontology than what I have sketched here. Among its precursors, it is interesting to mention Lucio Pinheiro dos Santos and his *rhythmanalysis*, in which he explored the role of vibration and pulse in issues concerning human health to develop a therapeutic method that contrasts with the focus on thought and speech espoused by psychoanalysis.[272] Pinheiro dos Santos held that rhythms, as the ultimate ingredients of human bodies, provide a crucial therapeutic clue. Rhythm-oriented ontology, where rhythmanalysis belongs, looks at ontological issues with an eye to how the propagation of rhythms leaves its marks in the concreta. We turn now to how this picture of rhythms, transmission and entrainment provides insight about what is up for grabs.

Depthless rhythms

Rhythm-oriented ontology presents the world as an ontological dance floor. I invoke the dance floor to present the idea that entangled rhythms coincide on a single surface. Auditory experience is not primarily an experience of figure and ground, but rather of simultaneous beats. The surface where rhythms appear is an assemblage of several layers of entrainment – like the surface of the painted wall around the radiator. The various processes of entrainment meet in a common surface, leaving their marks there and shaping it to receive the signals of further rhythms. Just as in an anarcheological procedure, however, rhythms don't become fully invisible in hidden layers; they ripple out onto the floor all the way to the imperceptible. This is not a matter of layers, but rather of what occupies the horizontal space. On this floor, the non-hidden leaves its marks – not deep marks, but folds in the surface. The whole dance floor is entrained by the music, but each section is also entrained by all the rhythms of the ways people dance on it. It is a floor: a common surface that is built by whatever steps on it. Floors are registration devices.

Floors contrast with grounds – they are more like skins than *archés*. They are related to flat surfaces, to planes, to meeting places, to platforms where things take place – the floor of a parliament. The floor is the superficial thing that we build everyday by throwing things on it, by moving it around, it is made of the leftovers of what is above it. The floor has the solidity we need to step on it and yet is never fully stable. A floor is always dispensable, because there is always something beneath it. It is superfluous apart from being superficial. It is thoroughly replaceable – and yet it cannot be fully replaced at once. The floor is a sedimentation surface of incidences, as it is the space where events are registered; the floor is the common territory of all events. In that sense, it is rhythmic. It is the common space of the effects – the *plan d'immanence*. It is a space of concomitance, not of roots – rhizomes and not trees. It is a space of interference, not of foundations – its geology is horizontal. Floors are perhaps to anarcheology – as the study of what is irrespective of any origin – as grounds are to archeology.

The artist Ai Weiwei's work often engages with floors and surfaces. His *Stool* installation builds a floor out of an enormous number of stools brought from different dynasties and republican periods in northern China.[273] The artificial floor, a surface connecting the seats of each stool, brings in elements of different ages of China and makes clear that all floors are mosaics. He also inserts rocks carved into contemporary shapes in the floor – in an inarcheological[274] manner – and paints commercial logos on ancient vases. In *Han Dynasty Vases with Auto Paint*, he paints millennia-old vases with metallic paint used in cars. The surface of interaction of these vases – the floor of what is visible of them – look like cars, while their interiors preserve the ancient shape and color. The painted visible surface entirely changes the appearance of the objects – they now resonate with the streets of another time. Floors, like surfaces, have two sides, what is below and what is above, and both sides compose them. Yet for a floor, what matters is what it registers. It is a skin entrained by the rest of the body, yet having a single layer. The layer is a crossroads of everything – of all the different stools. It is where everything meets.

Floors are also like appearances – for an appearance, nothing that is hidden matters, only the perceivable, the superficiality of what does not go beyond the skin. Wittgenstein makes explicit the difference between the surface of appearances and the supposedly grounding connection between layers when a foundation is sought. In his *Remarks on the Foundation of*

Mathematics he mocks alleged foundations as no more foundations than a painted rock is the support of a painted tower.[275] On the painted surface of a canvas, a rock and the tower it grounds are on the same layer; depth is achieved in the surface, but in the painting the tower needs no support from the rock.

A speculative dermatology

Commenting in an interview about Paul Valéry's famous dictum that the skin is the deepest, Deleuze defines philosophy as the art of surfaces, or, rather, as a general dermatology.[276] It is an invitation to look at membranes and to resist the temptation of the interior. The membrane of appearances is a recurrent image of the unsubstantial. Deleuze's interest in planes, surfaces, rhizomes, smoothness and differences of degree is a shift from the ontological interest in the internal, implicit, and intrinsic. Instead of asking what each thing is, one asks what separates them. Look at the skin, says the injunction. Look how it is revealing: it repeats the other surfaces – it is a medium. The skin, like appearances, is a border that reflects all the national tensions. National borders echo what takes place on other surfaces – like a beat is entrained by other beats. Deleuze suspects that if we have enough articulated surfaces, we needn't look inside them. Appearances are rich enough, because they're multiple and entangled – appearance upon appearance. Skin on top of skin: dermatology. It is speculative that we can project the injunction of looking at the skin everywhere – membranes exorcise the hidden. Everything has an appearance; skins are unavoidable. Dermatology replaces archeology: there is nothing to excavate; things are just knitted together. Speculative dermatology is an endeavor in flat ontology: to exorcise the seemingly underlying depths.

We can begin presenting speculative dermatology in terms akin to Hume's attack on necessary connections. Hume limited the content of what is directly sensed, holding the empiricist belief that there are unmediated deliverances of the senses and we should avoid going unnecessarily beyond them. He started with the remark that while distinct things can be perceived by our senses, the connection between them is always unclear and seemingly unavailable to unaided sensible intuition. He intended to exorcise obscure relations by showing how it is not possible to sense more than actual objects distinct one from another. Connections beyond those of simultaneity, succession and contiguity are no more than projections of something that cannot be recognized by the senses alone (nor by the senses aided by reason, for reason cannot go into these matters of fact). The emerging actualist ontology is one of distinct objects in a mosaic, unrelated and yet concomitant, assembled and yet disconnected. No relations beyond those that make each object distinct from the others.

One can follow this Humean line to further restrict the content of unaided sensibility and argue that we do not, in fact, perceive distinct objects, for we conceive them only if we postulate permanence in time and continuity in space to be enough for an object to be distinct from others. What we actually perceive is no more than the distinctions themselves. We sense the border between the fence and the grass, the street and the pavement, the sea and the sky, but we don't sense the objects that they distinguish. The fence may be in fact many different objects, and the pavement and the street may be parts of a single object – say, the road. In other words, we perceive the distinctness in things – neither their interconnection nor their standing unity. The distinctness tell us where joints are, not what the joints actually do; the content of what is between the divides is itself a projection on the perceived divisions. Senses give us the joints – not the things that joints separate. They give us distinctness. These joints, of course, can be either borders between things or articulations of parts of these things. It is like drawing the world map – we just draw the borders. We can further detail the map by drawing the borders between U.S. states, French departments, English counties, and so forth. We increase precision by adding more divisions, more separators and more joints. Adopting Hume's empiricist assumption for the sake of this presentation of speculative dermatology, distinctness is what is directly sensed, not objects and not parts of objects. Just the divides.

These divides can be the starting point for a speculative ontology of articulations. The speculative step posits that distinctions ought to be everywhere. Instead of substances (or objects, or things, or individuals) we should look at the divides between them. The divide – the skin – is what ends up producing everything by selective permeability. The thesis can be put in terms of priority: skins are ontologically prior to what they cover.

Things are made of a skin that divides them from the rest of the world. Different things have different skins. No interior is needed. Speculative dermatology holds that nothing is substantial, but everything is made of skins, membranes, and surfaces – nothing between them. Skins and empty spaces. If we look at Harman's scheme of quadruple objects, we have to take real objects and real qualities – but not sensual objects or sensual properties – to be undermined (or rather overmined)[277] by their dermatological constituents. They are membranes and more membranes, articulated. In a membrane-oriented ontology, nothing but articulations matter. This approach brings the empiricist concern with what is available to the senses to an ontological level. It does so not by confining reality to the surface of appearance, but by considering reality in terms of the surface of appearance. It is not about reality being restricted to appearances, but rather about our conceiving that appearance is not false because it is depthless – or unsubstantial.

Nietzsche saw in the Greeks the courage to live on the surface, on the skin of things, and therefore to embrace the Olympus of appearance.[278] It is as if the interfaces between things – the distinctions – are actually what articulates their appearance, for the joints are what originates sensation. To encounter the interior of matter, claimed Schelling, is to find the surfaces of the bodies.[279] No matter how many times matter is divided, the divisions themselves are what hit the senses. To be sensed – or to interact with anything else – is to have a surface. At least in the sensible, to exist is to be findable – through surface contact. The sensible is made of things that can be sensed. The interior is therefore made of further skins. Just as we excavate the floor only to find further floor, there is nothing but covers, borders, distinctions under the skin.

If dermatology is general, it should look at the different skins, the skin of the ear versus the skin of the tongue – and how the eye does not affect whenever is entraining it, while the hands do. Differences in surfaces allow differences in what they contain, as interiors are demarcated spaces. Additionally, a general ontology focuses on the difference between the skin of a rock and the skin of a tree. They differ in texture, in permeability, in what affects them, but also they are different in the skins inside them. Some are compact and tight, while others harbor space. A poem by Szymborska features a conversation with a stone.[280] The stone replies to the interlocutor who wants to get in and visit the empty spaces inside it: you cannot get in; you can break me into sand, and still no grain will let you in; you cannot get in because I don't have doors. If the rhythmite is the philosophical stone of a rhythm-oriented ontology, Szymborska's doorless stone is the equivalent for a speculative dermatology. The absence of doors is not impermeability, but absence of an interior that can be other than what is demarcated by surfaces. The stone warns its interlocutor that discovery is not about going beyond the skin. There is nothing but other surfaces hidden inside anything. There is no discovery beyond the skins. Attributed to Heraclitus (*frag.*, fr. 123) is the thesis that *physis* loves to hide. Fragment 277b (see Anarcheology 2/277b) holds that nobody will unveil it once and for all.

The surfaces that cover bodies are therefore what can be used in a speculative flight toward a general dermatology. It is an empiricist flight, for it understands the sensible in terms of what can be captured in the experience of touching. Galatzia says his skin – and in fact his whole body – is a touchscreen.[281] It responds to contact. Skins are touchscreen membranes: by covering what exists, they make them sensible. There is no discovery in the sensible that is not a touchscreen. Yet the surfaces are different. Speculative dermatology can be tactile, emphasizing skins, like I have been. It can also be auditory, or it can be visual and focus on the skin of the eye and on the surfaces of visual experience. It is in the framework of an appearance-driven speculative dermatology that we can place a rhythm-oriented ontology like the one I rehearsed above. Rhythms are apparent and they are made of a surface of beats, interacting and entangled.

A rhythm-oriented speculative dermatology brings together the interaction of skins and composition through rhythms. Beats are like membranes that define intervals. They are like rhythmic skins: there is nothing to rhythms but a distribution of joints. What has skins evokes the depthlessness of rhythms: beats are made of further beats – not interior beats, but entangled beats. Interaction between things involves transduction. Entrainment is, in fact, a model of interaction: movement, pace and vibration are passed through skins. Rhythms, combined with skins that are shaped, like rhythmites, by being entrained by their surroundings, leave no room for substantiality. Beats entrain skins. The combination of rhythms and skins – and their dynamic interaction – makes any appeal to what is hidden under the surfaces ultimately dispensable.

If we press the connection between surfaces and appearances, the superposition of surfaces becomes an interposition of appearances. If *archés* are the opposite of appearances, dermatology is an anarcheology. It is an ontology of the concrete strictly as sensible. As such, things are what they seem to be; to be is to appear. To appear as something is, in a sense, to be up for grabs, though not because skins can appear one way or another – nor because they have an intrinsic potentiality that is itself unapparent – because that would ultimately rely on how skins substantially are. The surface is merely a result of the confluence of entrainments; it reflects what coincides on it. Here, contingency lies in concomitance, in the accumulation of skins and the entanglement of rhythms. What ends up entrained is a result of the assemblage of what takes place. A rhythm-oriented ontology inspires the broader perspective of general dermatology. Skins are the perceptual events – the distinctness that can be the content of unmediated sensibility. In both cases, there is nothing but the unbearable superficiality of events.

Sublunar

An ancient way to refer to the contingencies of the concrete – placing them in contrast with the necessity that would rule the movement of the stars – is to associate then to a sublunary sphere. Below the moon, everything is more exposed to accidents because there is less fixity and arguably substantiality is harder to grasp; the sublunar was the address of the sensible. The dismissal of geocentrism as an image of outer space made the interest in the specificities of the sublunar subside. The Earth, after all, was no more than an instance of something broader that is to be understood by a general physics. The more recent appearance of geology, and of studies of the history of life on Earth, reintroduced some interest in the specificities of "geos" and did so while introducing the idea of a natural history. The history of accumulated accidents emerged, as we saw, as an approach to making sense of the contingencies of the sublunar. However, it was only with the work of Lovelock that the specificities of what he called once more *Gaia* came to the fore.[282] Lovelock has shown that the atmosphere of the Earth can only be as different as it is from its neighboring planets because of its history of hosting various interconnected forms of life. The sublunar – in its atmosphere and in its geology – is infected with life and this makes an important difference with respect to the outer stars. Further, Lovelock has emphasized how what is outside a living organism – or a plethora of them – is somehow part of its cybernetic system through air interchanges, temperature control and maintenance of functioning systems. What is outside the skin of a living organism provides its meta-stability. The skin itself is what is crucial for the organism to be what it is. The presence of an environment for life emerges as part of life itself – and is a distinctive feature of the sublunar.

Deleuze and Guattari have focused on the geology of morals to show how a general dermatology could provide a general account of the sublunar.[283] They present an image around the surface where the interior and the exterior are both part of a stratum – and this for both the organic and the non-organic.[284] Organisms as much as geotic structures have an environment associated to them that cannot be taken less as less than a part of them that is articulated around the stratum – the surface, the floor, the skin. This is why the environment that hosts life is itself living for the skin is not a device of separation as much as it is of contagion, of asserting a proximity – and a capacity to entrain.[285] It is as if the dermic is what is somehow peculiar to the sublunar – or at least it is what can be considered central to our image of what exists in our terrestrial surroundings. Deleuze and Guattari argue that there is a dermic common structure to what takes place around the surface of the Earth. They provide a general metaphysical scheme for what is under the influence of a floor. Unsurprisingly, this general scheme is also a scheme for what takes place in the passing of time through a sequence of events. The main element of this scheme is the notion of double articulation. Two operations are not only simultaneous but also provide materials for each other. The first is sedimentation where stuff thrown on the floor gives shape to the surface – it is the process by which stones are formed from what is around them and the surface of the Earth is covered by the debris of what has taken place here. Sedimentation is a form of entrainment because it informs the floor; the past is coded by the traces it leaves for the future in the common plane where both happen. This first articulation is understood as chiefly molecular as it aggregates all kinds of dust that fall in the floor and does no more than pile them up. There is a sense in which sedimentation creates a surface for it provides the elements with which it is composed – it provides a substance to the floor, a substance that shapes it. The second is that associated to the orogenesis, the folding that takes place when mountains are formed. They describe it as a folding that brings in a functionally stable structure which makes room for the sedimentation to take place. This second operation is one where the existing forms – products of sedimentation – consolidate into something substantial. The second articulation is what gives the Earth its topography that conditions what takes place next. It is an affair of sediments accommodating themselves, but it gives shape to further sedimentation. This is why the second articulation is molar; it provides structure for what comes next.

It is clear how the two articulations are intertwined. One provides the materials where the other indicates where these materials will be placed; one is matter and the other is form but matter itself produces form and form modifies matter. This geological double articulation is then speculatively extended to various sublunar issues. The two articulations take place around the stratum that is the skin of living organisms in the form of most exchanges of energy that sustain life – the skin is the basic bodily feature, but it has to be itself without organs. The articulations around a surface are common to what is living and what is not – it could be seen as a general dimension of animation that takes place in different speeds, in different paces, in different rhythms.[286] As such, it is the fine structure of intensity. Further, the interaction between an environment that sediments organisms and a genetic makeup that organizes these sediments on the basis of previous processes of sedimentation is thought in terms of the double articulation. Genotypes appear as a collection of folds that would shape the acquisition of behavior. They are shaped by the sedimentation history of the species where the environment left its traces. Genetic structure and environment contributions are therefore intertwined in a double articulation. But they exemplify a broader structure of interaction between earthly things and their surroundings – those things are formed within their surroundings and carry on in an interchange with it. Eventually some of this interchange is condensed in a molar form that will affect the incorporation of elements from the environment, elements that in turn will affect the molar structure. The surface of a stratum is therefore a regulation device – it makes the inner and the outer correlate.

This intertwined double articulation is rhythmic. Sedimentation provides a baseline of events that usher in some kind of orogenesis. Between the two, the surface – there is the movement from outside and the movement from inside and both couple because the outside and the inside merge where their effects beat. Deleuze and Guattari show how the double articulation is a model for recapitulation between living organisms and beyond as folds are entrained by other folds while a surface acquires its shape by what takes place in both of its sides. The ultimate recapitulation, however, is the double articulation itself that, like a rhythm, contaminates around the surface of the Earth. The presence of a floor – and not of a ground – is what makes earthly things what they are. Any surface that acts like a floor register the past events while conditioning the traces to come. At the same time, the double articulation exhibits the output of two coupled rhythms; a beat gets louder when, say, more and more people start clapping their hands to it but as more people join in, the beat itself changes. Any interaction of rhythms – and any interaction of double articulations – follow this pattern of co-existence: a rhythm incorporates others but not without eventually being affected by them. The double articulation spells out also the co-entrainment that spread through what is sublunar.

Being up for grabs

Rhythm-oriented ontologies make it possible to think of the up for grabs as related to events that just happen. The events assemble on a surface and relate to each other dermatologically: by transmission of intensity, by spreading, by infection, by contact. A key element in this transmission is transduction in the form of entrainment. The emphasis on appearance exorcises the appeals of substantiality – and therefore also deconstructs the contrast with accidents. Surfaces are up for grabs not because they are accidental but because they harbor no substance, nothing between the changes brought about by the events shaping them. They are nothing beyond the membranes, the beats, the changes themselves. Contingency appears here as mere distinctness, or as no more than concomitance. In a universe of rhythms, nothing but the perceived overall rhythmic soundscape affects the state of affairs, but the rhythmic soundscape is dynamic enough to be entrainable by any event that takes place close enough. Contingency shows its no-interior face: rhythms made by beats and generating intensive time, floors that are enough for things to spread on and skins that veil other skins, hosting the interior as an epiphenomenon. An-*arché* shows itself as depthlessness: events that aggregate and therefore give rise to a surface or a soundscape that frames everything else.

Rhythm-oriented ontologies reveal an aspect of contingency that is not explicit either in the monadology of fragments or in the ontologies of doubt. While the former builds on the centrality of contingency as exposure to composition, and the latter relates the contingent with the insufficient or the indeterminate, rhythm-oriented ontologies disclose how contact and contiguity entail contingency. Rhythms are a clear way to see this, for they tread in intensity and entrainment. An event-based rhythm-oriented ontology shows how any event that takes place can affect the pace of what exists – existence requires a timing, and therefore clock ticks are themselves events. Placed within a broader framework of speculative dermatology, rhythms appear as a surface where the effect of any contact is spread through a *matryoshka* of membranes without any interior. Speculative dermatology relates appearance to the unsubstantial – there is no ultimate redeeming of what appears by an underlying reality, and therefore to underlie is no more than a relation between surfaces. Contact and continuity are what give rise to appearances – appearances result from surfaces that touch, skins that affect each other. A dermatological ontology has a grip on how appearances are prone to deceive; there is no ultimate non-deceiving access, as any revelation is a revelation of the skin of things. There is no way to access what is underlying, but only a way of touching other surfaces.

Whilst the ontologies of doubt posit indeterminations as a (possible) constitutional ingredient of things – either on their own or along with facts – rhythm-oriented ontologies tend to view what is up for grabs as dependent on the isolation of a rhythmic soundscape. In the former, what is up for grabs is constitutionally so because insufficiency is itself constitutive of how things are and is therefore not dependent on how other things turn out. In rhythm-oriented ontologies, what is up for grabs depends on what takes place around it. In an anechoic environment, no outside sound gets in to entrain what is inside. Rhythmic soundscapes can be immunized from outside entrainment, which means that being up for grabs is not constitutional – things can be immunized and securely chained to the events in a rhythmic soundscape. Contingency, in rhythm-oriented ontologies, is immanent. In this sense, those ontologies resemble the monadology of fragments. In both cases, to be up for grabs is a product of how the rest of the world is arranged. Also in both cases, an immunization process that must be sustained, sponsored or protected can reduce vulnerability. Being up for grabs follows from the dependence of each thing on everything else; rhythm-oriented ontology yields a measure of holism where intensity can put things in contact and there is a cost to being locked apart. Fragments and rhythms show how contingency is about interdependence, and as such, contingency depends on being up for grabs.

There are important differences, though. Monadologies – but in an important sense not the partial monadology espoused by Simondon – are agent-based ontologies. The monadology of fragments posits three modes of existence of gunky units: they can exist as fragments, compositions and composers. Fragments are individual entities that act as composers and are available as compositions. Rhythm-oriented ontologies, by contrast, are closer to a Deleuzian variation on process philosophy that stresses the rhizome, intensive variables and composition. Deleuze conceives of a world of proliferating intensities rather than fixed forms, where events precede individuals and names designate forces rather than individual agents.[287] He takes proper names as designating effects, zigzags, like a difference of potential.[288] One difference between agent-based ontoscopies of contingency and intensity-based ones is that in the former, an-*arché* comes from plurarchy – the plurality of governments, as in a monadology – while in the latter, an-*arché* comes from a lack of genuine government.[289] Rhythm entrainment works through the ingredients of governability, in what makes it possible for something to influence and be followed. Governments need a distinct capacity to entrain in a sufficiently recognizable way. They must be able to transmit, to broadcast, to filter – rhythms are the building blocks of perspectives. An agent's view of the world is produced by what entrains it. Agents, as subjects, are constructed from rhythms. Rhythms are ingredients of subjectivity, larval, ecological and are not autonomous agents.

The contrast between a monadology of fragments and a rhythm-based ontoscopy can be also fruitfully compared with two of the four dispositions diagnosed by Descola.[290] While animism is based on an identity of interiority among different entities conjoined with differences in physicality, analogism is centred on differences both in interiority and physicality associated to analogies of form and structure across the board. While the former posits agents that have different interfaces with the others, the latter is compared to recapitulation and exemplified by the idea of a great chain of beings. Descola's dispositions are, among other things, different ways to understand what is up for grabs. While animism focuses on a structured interaction of a plurality of agents, analogism stresses how anything can be repeated elsewhere. Monadological thinking is like animism in many respects: monads are different but are all agents that are sensible to what takes place in other units of government – the relations between them has always an element of diplomacy. Similarly, a rhythm-oriented ontoscopy is like a multidimensional graph of beings where events produce a pace and a timing that interfere with events taking place elsewhere. While the former looks at alliance and negotiation, the latter privileges contagion and contact. The difference is between an agent-based interplay and the interaction afforded by the plasticity of events.

These differences points to what seems to be a salient feature of a rhythm-oriented ontoscopy of contingency. If we consider Meillassoux's cartography of correlationisms and their discontents, monadologies easily cluster with varieties of the metaphysics of subjectivity, while ontologies of doubt display several features shared with Meillassoux's speculative materialist thesis that facticity is itself absolute.[291] An orientation toward rhythms, instead of providing a variety of the metaphysics of subjectivity that makes correlation absolute, exploits the very constituents of a correlation. The absolute is sought in these constituents, that is, in entraining rhythms – in rhythmic landscapes. It is not that the correlation is itself absolute, but rather that correlations are revealed by what makes them possible. The speculative premise here is not a correlation but our rhythmic experience of entrainment and entanglement. From the facticity of correlation, Meillassoux's speculative step infers the absolute facticity of everything. The rhythm-oriented speculative step, by contrast, infers from the rhythmic ingredients of a correlation the rhythmic character of everything. As contingency is not transcendent, it is not an absolute but enjoys a primacy – a centrality. Being up for grabs is central in a world of rhythms – such a world is only intelligible if rhythms can find places to propagate.

Speculative dermatology thinks of what is up for grabs as what lacks substantiality, and therefore thinks it has nothing but further appearances contrasting with its first appearance. It doesn't stand alone; it has no interior that makes it anything in itself beyond its surface. We can also read doubts as skins, if we see indeterminations as borders between two facts. Ontologies of doubts make these distinctions – doubts – evident. To be sure, doubts appear in these ontologies as absolute, while a dermatological approach has skins as the contingent product of the contact between surfaces. The difference here, again, is one between the transcendence of ontologies of doubt and the immanence of rhythm-oriented ontology. In both cases, what is up for grabs appears near the borders. Both cases reveal how contingency is related to ambiguity – in terms of insufficiency or *diaphonia* in one case, and in terms of a division that makes more than one thing possible in the other. What is up for grabs is what can come to be in more than one way.

Poker chips construction   Gisel Carriconde Azevedo, Digital photography, 2009

Chapter 6
Contingency and its galaxies

The contingent and the up for grabs

Richard Rorty, in *Contingency, Irony, and Solidarity*, attempts to show how both the object out there and the subject that contemplates and acts upon it are products of a construction, and are sometimes intertwined. He claims that the world, as much as language, mental contents and intentional states, is a result of immanent forces where no upper hand is stable by itself. He brings in Freud, Nietzsche, Bloom, Wittgenstein and Davidson to show how words and thoughts, just like objects and events, exhibit a "sheer contingency", as he calls it.[292] Even though the thesis of an articulated construction of elements of both mind and world, sometimes mutually imbricated, is close to the metaphysical picture[293] emerging in this book, it should be clear now that contingency is rarely sheer contingency. To be sure, Rorty is also close to the endeavor of assembling equally relevant ontoscopies to deal with what is contingent when he insists that there is no ultimate, privileged vocabulary for describing anything. We are bound to have a plurality of vocabularies, none of them having inborn superiority.

This book, nevertheless, goes one step further and claims that what is contingent in the world, and not only our vocabularies, exhibits an irredeemable plurality. In this sense, it does to Rorty's democracy of vocabularies the same operation that Latour claims modes of existence perform on forms of ordinary relativism that, in his terms, don't traffic in hard cash;[294] it moves from the relativity of different images of the world to an image of the world that includes relativity. Hence, the multiplicity of vocabularies itself points toward a plurality in reality – a plurality related to what makes necessity absent. Contingency is never sheer, mainly because it is not the base level from which everything else is built up. It is not a primary raw material that constitutes structures and articulations and from which what is necessary, permanent or stable arise. This is the thrust of the Aristotelian flavor to the thesis that what is up for grabs is *prota ton onton* – not the ultimate constituent nor the universal explanans, but the central ingredient of the sensible. It is, so to speak, a mark or symptom of the sensible. This mark is not contingency itself – or non-necessity – but being up for grabs: the availability, the insufficiency and the superficiality that I have spelled out in terms of fragments, doubts and rhythms. It is not merely that there is no constitutive necessity to the sensible, but that being up for grabs is the gatekeeper of the sensible, and this porter regularly shifts his attire.

Indeed, what is up for grabs has many faces because it is about interstices. It has been presented in this book through a collection of ontosocopies that contrast with each other. As with the many modes of existence that followed from the parricide and the plurality in the kernel of being that arose from the fallen pile of muja (see ANARCHEOLOGY 1/J/N), what is up for grabs deals in transitions. Ontoscopies are not themselves modes of existence – they rather have to do with how things are presented – but what is up for grabs presents itself in several ways because it lies in borders that make plurality possible. As Selassie writes in his letter, there is no plurality without real, non-eliminable separators, and these separators have to be contingent. Separators are germane to what is up for grabs – disruption, as the second fragment of the Sahagún Colloquia above makes clear (see ANARCHEOLOGY 3/XVI-?-37-56), has a family resemblance with what is vulnerable. In the rest of this section, I will briefly explore a bit further this connection between what is up for grabs and what unchains – in terms of compositions from found fragments, of insufficiencies in determinations and of swerves on a prevalent rhythmic landscape.

That what is up for grabs is not a baseline for all the rest can be clearly appreciated in the monadology of fragments. It could seem that immunization comes from a baseline formed by the *communitas* of sensible things. However, what is up for grabs does not always precede immunized assemblages. As the monadology of fragments makes clear, there are no elementary particles that are in themselves up for grabs – fragments are up for grabs precisely because they are not atoms. They are compositions – any fragment is gunky. Immunized assemblages, as fragments, are objects of composition and therefore material for disruption. In a monadology of fragments, the frailty of any composition comes from the immanence of any immunization, but the meta-stability of an assemblage is equally immanent. There is no baseline in *communitas*, because there is no transcendent starting point. In a monadology of fragments, what is up for grabs inhabits the interstices of the three modes of existence – because an assemblage is a composition and a fragment (apart from being a composer). It is up for grabs either because its meta-stability as a composition depends on other fragments or because it is an available fragment. The difference in modes of existence between fragments and compositions is to a great extent subject to something like a Doppler effect (see Chapter 1 above, "Turning Ontologically Towards Contingency"). It is only because something else is a composition that a monad is a fragment – and only because something else is a fragment that a monad is a composition. The monadology of fragments is, in this sense, enlightening because it makes clear how what is up for grabs also depends on point of view.

Only to the extent that other monads are composers, compositions and fragments is any monad a fragment, a composition or a composer. A city is vulnerable to its inhabitants as much as to the ingredients of its soil. Like cities, monads are part of a regime of stability involving the regions under their governments as much as part of a regime of stability involving neighboring regions. What is up for grabs can come as an external attack or as civil unrest – monads are vulnerable because they are governing entities. Vulnerability, in its turn, reflects the weak points of the regime that maintains a government. Plots against it can come from many angles. Monads display this vulnerability – they are up for grabs because, as ingredients of the sensible, they have to be part of several plots. No government is like a substance – innately enduring – and no government has special dispensation to take care of its own stability. In this sense, being up for grabs invokes a diplomacy, a diplomacy of the multiple alliances that enable something sensible to carry on.

The monadology of fragments is one among a plurality of ontoscopies of what is up for grabs and one which takes contingency to be thoroughly immanent – its immanence comes to view. Viewed from an ontoscopy of doubts, there is a transcendent insufficiency to what is sensible – it is akin to indeterminations. To be sure, the multiple ontologies of doubt portray the board of doubts and determinations in different ways, but in all of them, under-determination is transcendently central to the sensible. In other words, doubts are prevalent and unavoidable and this is of the very nature of the sensible – it flows. A difference between the monadology of fragments and the ontology of doubts is that the second deals directly with determinations and establishes – through Pyrrhonist arguments – that they cannot be all that there is to the sensible. It makes use of transcendent, constitutive arguments to show that doubts must be present in what exists. Here again, this ontoscopy reveals the intimate link between contingency and plurality: insufficiency and under-determination point toward *diaphonia* – more than one possible discourse about how things are. Indeterminacies in the world, either along with determinations or not, erode the surrounding apparent substantiality or self-standing stability. It is clear from the discussion of the arguments against GS (in Chapter 4 above, "Formulating Ontologies of Doubt") that doubts cannot be appreciated without holding something as fixed. Doubting requires hinges, and it is only from a point of view of determinations that doubts appear (and, arguably, vice-versa). Here again, what is up for grabs is related to a Doppler effect: it only appears from a perspective with determinations afforded by doubts.

A third ontoscopy introduces plurality directly in terms of assemblage: specifically in terms of rhythmic soundscapes. The impact of a beat that comes out of the blue is dispersed by means of the common sonic surface where an event has to make an impact. The superficiality of the sensible makes clear how the interstices are precisely the gaps where what is up for grabs comes in. The sensible is explicitly presented as an agglomerate of surfaces conjoined in a dermatological way where events affect each other to the extent that they touch each other. A rhythmic soundscape is always superficial and therefore vulnerable to any event that disturbs it. The centrality of what is up for grabs is shown through the immanent superficiality of anything that has an impact on the sensible. Superficiality, in a sense, enjoys a certain transcendent character in the sensible. What is up for grabs, in its turn, arises from the absence of anything that, from an untouchable depth, maintains the surface as it is. But surfaces can just happen to be kept as they are; they can be left unaffected, although they themselves do not determine or cause this.

Contingent a priori

The distinction between the sensible and the non-sensible has played an important role throughout this book, for its main thesis is the centrality of what is up for grabs in the sensible. I have chosen to call it *sensible* to be close to the usual translation of Aristotle's *aistheta* as he explicitly focused on whether there is genuine substantiality within this realm. The *sensible* is also called the domain of concrete things, arguably because the articulation between concrete and abstract seems less dependent on human access than that between sensible and intelligible. The articulation is also close to the distinction Hume made between matters of fact and matters of reason (or relations of ideas). He took matters of fact as incorrigibly contingent – and in a uniform and non-structured way. Because matters of fact were all equally contingent, they were all to be known in an a posteriori manner: only experience could inform about them, and it enabled no justified belief concerning universals. In a Humean scheme, a priori knowledge was reserved for relations of ideas – or *abstracta*, if we want – while matters of fact could only be known empirically. (Additionally, matters of fact could only be objects of synthetic judgment.)

The distinction between matters of fact and relations of ideas – or between the sensible and the non-sensible, as far as their associations with the a priori/a posteriori distinction – has been challenged in different ways. Leibniz's principle of reason (see Chapters 1 and 3 above) explicitly rejects the idea of synthetic judgments and points to a continuity between the abstract and the sensible. Leibniz's monadology created the basis to consider all objects as mathematical – with infinite definitions. This makes the sensible no more than the realm of infinite predications. Monads have no substrata beyond their predicates – contingency is a consequence of their worldliness. As chapter 3 explored, Leibniz introduced a way to think of contingency as a structured feature and enabled the possibility of an a priori access to what is sensible – a *mathesis universalis*. An important upshot of the challenges to these families of distinctions is that the sensible is not all uniformly contingent, and therefore it can be accessed in a more structured manner.

A crucial development in this direction was Kripke's disentanglement of the necessary from the a priori. Kripke pointed out that reference-fixing descriptions can be known a priori while being contingent. That cats are animals, that Adam was the first man or that Venus is the first star to appear in the evening are reference-fixing descriptions that can prove false; cats, for example, could be shown to be robots, as in the example that Kripke borrows from Putnam. As Kripke writes:

> [O]ne should bear in mind the contrast between the a priori but perhaps contingent properties carried with a term, given by the way its reference was fixed, and the analytic (and hence necessary) properties a term may carry, given by its meaning.[295]

Kripke draws a distinction between what is known a priori and what is necessary – contingent things have to be known a priori for us to establish what we are talking about. Reference fixing must take place amid contingencies. If we discover that cats are in fact robots, we will still be talking about cats, even though we will have had false ideas about them.

To be sure, Kripke's contingent a priori comes as a pair with empirically discovered necessities. Eventually, he holds, we can discover the ultimate (essential) nature of cats – robots or animals – and that would mean that they are so necessarily. Kripke contrasts this discovery with the initial baptism of something, the exercise of individuating something about which we are talking:

> In an initial baptism it is typically fixed by an ostension or a description. [...] The same observations hold for such a general term as 'gold.' If we imagine a hypothetical (admittedly somewhat artificial) baptism of the substance, we must

> imagine it picked out as by some such 'definition' as, "Gold is the substance instantiated by the items over there, or at any rate, by almost all of them." [...] The definition does [...] express an a priori truth [...]. The 'almost all' qualification allows that some fool's gold may be present in the sample. If the original sample has a small number of deviant items, they will be rejected as not really gold. If, on the other hand, the supposition that there is one uniform substance or kind in the initial sample proves more radically in error, reactions can vary: sometimes we may declare that there are two kinds of gold, sometimes we may drop the term 'gold'.'[296]

The distinction between the initial baptism and the later discovery is what shows that we have to find ways to track things among matters of fact. But that we later come up with a necessary a posteriori description of gold is not relevant. If there are no necessities to be disclosed empirically, we still have to resort to reference-fixing procedures to predicate anything in the realm of the sensible.

The notion of a contingent a priori provides an answer to the issue of whether predication needs substantiality – and necessity. Predication requires no (primary) substance – or substratum – that acts as a subject. In the sentence "Socrates lost weight," no property is attached to a necessarily individuated subject; nothing needs to be assumed about Socrates apart from what contingently fixes its reference. To be sure, something has to be more stable than something else – Socrates changes more slowly than his weight. It is perhaps, once again, a Doppler-like effect: predication is a change with respect to a subject that is relatively fixed. If the fixed reference is investigated so that its necessary features are disclosed, these features will necessarily be predicated of it. But these features are not a priori attached to the fixed reference. Nothing but a stabilizing mechanism – a reference-fixing procedure – is needed for a subject to accommodate predications. Reference-fixing is not immunization: the subject of a predication can still be up for grabs.

Galaxies

In this book, in order to discuss issues related to substrata or to Kripke's account of modalities, I have eventually appealed to the notion of possible worlds. It is sometimes said that something is contingent if it happens in some but not in all possible worlds. The framework of a possible-worlds semantics allows for a meta-theoretical quantification over possible worlds so that we can say that something is the case in some or all possible worlds. The question then arises as to what established the space of all possible worlds. Possible worlds contrast with impossible ones - as Lewis makes clear in the opening pages of his *On the Plurality of Words*.[297] Lewis, together with many other philosophers, dismisses logically impossible worlds from any semantic or metaphysical consideration. But what are impossible worlds? Further, what makes a world possible? The answer to these questions is often quick and troublesome: logic. Impossible worlds are worlds ruled out by logic while possible worlds are allowed by logic. It is a quick answer, a ready one. But it is troublesome: why would we rely on *one* logic? Normally classical logic is taken for granted when this ready answer is given. This can be justified by claiming that classical logic is at least well entrenched. The issue that then arises is: is such entrenchment a matter of contingency? Indeed, the plurality of logics introduces a difficulty into the metaphysical use of the possible-worlds framework. Different logics evaluate modal claims differently. What is impossible in classical logic is not necessarily so in paraconsistent or intuitionist logics.

I have developed with Alexandre Costa-Leite a general framework to generate alternative logics.[298] Given any logic L understood as a set of formulas and a consequence relation – which can be classical or not – an antilogic is defined as entailing what L doesn't entail and not entailing what L entails. Additionally, a counterlogic for a logic L with negation is defined as entailing an L-negation of what L entails and not entailing an L-negation of what L does not entail (if L has more than one negation, it will have more than one counterlogic). Both are opposites of L, and it is shown that, on a suitable interpretation of the opposition relations, while the antilogic is contradictory to L, the counterlogic is contrary to it.[299] What is interesting about the several logics that are thus generated is that they enable very different results about what is logically possible – and what is (logically) contingent. A formula α that is not a theorem of L, for example, is not logically necessary in L but logically necessary in its antilogic. In other words, different logics imply different evaluations of what is contingent – because they correspond to different classes of possible worlds. In fact, it is not hard to see that a logic (or rather a consequence relation) is equivalent to a collection of possible worlds. These collections enable a study of their own as they present interesting relations between them. I have been working with some colleagues on these collections and how they inform about contingency in general. We call these collections of possible worlds associated with a logic *galaxies*.[300] The plurality of logics could pose little problem to metaphysics if the off-hand choice of one logic over all the others could be somehow motivated. It is hard to provide straightforward justifications, for they would have to be themselves based on a particular logic. Entrenchment considerations – which appeal to how much a logic is used – would favor classical first-order logic and its extensions. These could be a decisive factor, as one can point at classical mathematics – and empirical science, which makes use of it – as a place where classical logic is not only present but crucial. To be sure, such entrenchment would itself arguably be contingent. The advent of approaches like universal logic,[301] which attempt to provide an abstract analysis of the relation between logics, may have changed the landscape. It became possible to look at the plurality of logics not aiming to select one but rather to compare and contrast them. Plurality itself became a topic – the different ways in which logical systems relate to each other. It is no longer a challenge, but rather a starting point.

To look at galaxies is a way to bring this attention to logical plurality to collections of possible worlds. In other words, it is a way to consider plurality as a starting point for metaphysical consideration: in different logical systems, different things are contingent (or necessary, or impossible). There is, therefore, no contingency that spans all galaxies (as the case of any logic's antilogic makes clear) – that something is contingent must be indexed as necessary within a galaxy (true in all worlds within that galaxy). Hence, an atomic proposition p is contingent in the galaxy of classical logic, and this is necessary within the galaxy (assuming that at least some logical truths are necessary). However, considered from the point of view of the plurality of galaxies, it is only contingently contingent. Any local judgment of contingency is immanent to a galaxy: nothing is contingent with respect to anything else while anything is contingent in some galaxy. Still, there is something to be said about contingency in the framework of a topology of galaxies. Even though there can be no theorem in common between a logic and its antilogic, a galaxy of a logic and a galaxy of its antilogic can intersect – there can be worlds in common to two galaxies associated to contradictory logics. This intersection is itself a galaxy and has a logic associated with it. Even without developing this further here, it is easy to see how the interplay of relative contingencies can be illuminated by a focus on galaxies.

The negative lesson to be drawn from such focus is that the standard possible-world approach is insufficient to deal with contingency. It says nothing about the galaxy where the relevant possible worlds are placed – and nothing about the kaleidoscope of matrices of fixity and changeability that is attached to a particular logic. As an approach, it is guilty of attempting to shortcut metaphysical issues concerning contingency and necessity by an underlying appeal to a single logic – it makes a particular logic prior to all (modal) metaphysical considerations. While logical truth can provide no more than a local account of what is necessary, what is contingent within a galaxy reflects little about the interplay of different positions in the space of logics. It is in such space – the space of different logics that can be investigated through a topology of galaxies – that the contrast between what is contingent and what is not can be contemplated. To focus on a single galaxy is to take for granted, metaphysically, the import of a particular logic in determining how these differences articulate. Contingency is not only something that emerges from the plurality of worlds, but also something that can only be appreciated from the plurality of galaxies.

The framework of possible worlds without galaxy considerations is hostage to the idea that necessity draws the borders of what is up for grabs – and is in this sense prior. It is hard to overestimate the impact of the idea that the fixed comes first and provides the cartography for all the rest. The appeal to logical truth often comes with the assumption that logic is expected to offer the preliminary navigation map – and therefore is to be seen as prior to all experience. (Notice that something similar happens to the appeal to natural necessity, or even sufficient reason: what is law-like is expected to provide the general lines to be filled in by what can be one way or another.) This is how the borders of matters of fact are drawn – the sensible is demarcated by the primary colors of necessity. The focus on the plurality of galaxies, by contrast, makes explicit how the sensible – where accident is central – has many maps and is relative to what is held as locally fixed. There is no such thing as *the sensible* as a domain; rather, the term names something that is spread through different but topologically related galaxies. What is up for grabs is spread, with its many faces, throughout the interstices (and intersections) between those galaxies.

Contingent knowledge and the reality of the plural

The widespread occurrence of what is up for grabs – in what seems to be the sensible – points in many ways to plurality. It is possible to present this connection by seeing what is up for grabs as marks of the metaphysically plural. The furniture of the universe, if it makes sense to use such an expression, cannot be appreciated as a single landscape – it is rather like looking at many things at once, like in a Jastrow illusion, and this is why it requires multiple ontoscopies. What is up for grabs points toward the plural, toward a plot of separators. In a world of irreducible contingency, there should be more than one script, more than one order, more than one governing power. This is why the worlds in the intersection of galaxies can reveal something about the limits of necessity – about *an-arché*. Up for grabs and also, in a sense, up in the air and out of the blue. It lies wherever there is an irreconcilable *diaphonia*, an unredeemable variety of modes of existence, or a common space where there are genuine encounters with what comes from a different direction.

In order to deal with the plurality akin to contingency, I have introduced three ontoscopies. The idea in each case is to show that, because not everything is up for grabs and sumbebeka prota ton ontor, there is a structure around contingency either making it possible or following from it. Each ontoscopy is a way to view contingency – it can be described as point of view about what is up for grabs. It is interesting to pursue this line for a moment now that we are coming towards the close of the book. We can then find, at least, three points of view: that of the agents, that of the resulting action and a transversal point of view where the effects of agents on actions are considered in a pair with the effects of actions on agents. These three points of view correspond to the three ontoscopies: the monadology of fragments, the ontology of doubts and the rhythm-oriented metaphysics. It is clear that contingency is transcendent if we take the second point of view, but not the others – as the resulting action will involve indeterminacies no matter what the agents engage in doing. If we see the ontoscopies along these lines, we can associate them to the three different modes of existence that the monadology of fragments, the first ontoscopy, affords. The first point of view is that of composers – of agents performing their action. The second of compositions – the resulting doubtful output of all agents. The third of fragments as they are simultaneously available to composers and part in a composition. Modes of existence are not ontoscopies, yet each one arguably entail a point of view. If this is so, the first ontoscopy, postulating three modes of existence, prefigures the overall picture.

The book has argued for the centrality of contingency in the world. Before concluding, it is interesting to examine briefly where we stand concerning the Aristotelian predicament that there could be no knowledge of the accidental. Knowledge could seem to have a family resemblance with substantiality, and if so it would not thrive if what is up for grabs enjoys primacy. There are, however, a variety of other ways to think about knowledge that would make it situated and more akin to alliance building than to achieving a view from nowhere. To be sure, as I said in the beginning, science and philosophy of the last few centuries have developed resources to deal with what is not necessary where the paradigms ranges from historical approaches in biology and geology to the stochastic studies. This book proposes three ontoscopies where what is up for grabs is shown as central but not as the unique prior reality. In these three cases, something can be said about how knowledge can be gained.

In a monadology of fragments, knowledge of each monad and its composition process leads up to the contingency of the agglomeration: global contingency is appreciated by looking at the trajectories of each composition process. Knowledge itself comes in fragments, as we do when we focus on *Ceteris Paribus* devices. Contingency is built from the very assemblage of non-concerted monads, but some knowledge can be gained when we look at some of them and find ways to isolate them from the rest. But we also know that groupings of monads are not isolated, and that they are subject to interference. The plurality of fragments points toward the situated character of knowledge. In an ontology of doubt, we can get to know indeterminacies through the process of *epokhé*: through bringing conviction into question. It is a know-how – to know how to doubt – that is crucial in knowing contingencies, a know-how to which the sceptical tradition has largely contributed. Knowledge is, for instance, the application of the modes of Aenesidemus and Agrippa – the application of a technology to doubt, which means a strategy to discover indeterminacies and to spot *diaphonia*. Knowing doubts is to know the plurality of ways. Finally, in a rhythm-oriented ontology, and in its associated speculative dermatology, it is through rhythms that pass through us that we access the contingencies that entrain us. The acquired knowledge comes in the form of the entrainment that what goes on produces on us: habituation – the acquisition of a habit due to a rhythm of events that has been presented to us. In this last case, knowledge of the non-necessary is also not propositional knowledge, but rather it is like being tuned to a plurality of soundscapes that, like in the first case, erodes necessity by its very plurality. Knowledge is tuning in to a plurality. In all these cases, accidents can be thought through and, at least to some extent, they can be known.

Looking at what is up for grabs, we can also gain intuition about necessity and how it relates to contingency. We can understand that the relation is one where one is the plural of the other; namely, contingency is the plural of necessity. Or rather, contingency emerges from the plurality of necessities. Whenever there is genuinely more than one necessity – and not an ultimate overarching necessity ruling over all others – there is contingency. If we have, say, an irreducible physical necessity and an irreducible psychological necessity, there is a grey area of intersection between these necessities. Physical laws and psychological laws are such that they have to interact somewhere. Analogously, if there is more than one government, there is an an-*arché* area between them. The monadology of fragments sees contingency in the plurality of non-orchestrated composers. The ontology of doubts places it in the insufficiency of determination – a necessity that doesn't carry enough strength to rule. Rhythm-oriented ontology would find it in the multiple co-existing entrainments that events to which events are subject. The corridor, or the plane, where these different necessities intersect is out of the scope of any of them, it is under the scope of no necessity – before the commencement and before the command. Because it has to do with Rilke's Open, it has to do with the in-between – with an alley where things are unfixed. This is the space of what is *mise en jeu*, of what is up in the air – and up for grabs.

Notes

1. Cf. Met. E, 2. Book E revolves around the impossibility of a proper knowledge of the accidental. Aristotle claims that, for something to be knowable, it must be either universal or frequent. He remarks, however, that one should whenever possible explain why the accidental takes place (Met. E, 2, 1226b24-25).
2. Cf. Met M, 4.
3. Eudoro de Sousa (1975), among others, have claimed that the doctrine that everything flows was not quite in line with other theses of Heraclitus and was inappropriately attributed to him by Aristotle and Simplicius.
4. As it is clear in Met., books Z and H.
5. Cf. Heraclitus (Frag.). See also Bensusan et al. (2012) for an update on the doctrine of the polemos (cf. chapter 2).
6. Meillassoux's label (2008).
7. The term was coined by Derrida (1993) to denote what haunts as if it were present.
8. Cf. 1972.
9. See Martin & Heil 1999 for something like a manifesto.
10. Cf. Bryant, Srnicek and Harman 2011.
11. Recent trends in anthropology (see Descola 2005 and Viveiros de Castro 2009 but also Latour 2013 and work by Tim Ingold or Roy Wagner) are often close to the aims of recent speculative philosophy: anthropologists intend to take into consideration the density of the most recent years of ethnographical research to ground a search for something universal, albeit far more complex and subtle than previously thought. This can be compared with the effort of philosophers turning back to metaphysics after years of sophisticated research into texts, meanings and epistemic limitations.
12. See, for instance, Bennett 2010.
13. Cf. 1988, 2004, 2013.
14. Cf. 2013: chapter 6.
15. Cf. 2009.

16. Cf. 2013: 204.
17. Interestingly, other modes of existence also interact with these two, especially the mode of habits – which Latour understands as the mode of existence of the essences (2013: 263-4).
18. Blanché (1966) studies the modal oppositions in geometrical terms. In the original square of opposition between universal affirmative propositions (A), universal negative propositions (E), particular affirmative propositions (I) and particular negative propositions (O), we say that A and O are contradictories and E and I are contradictories, while A and E are contraries – I and O being sub-contraries. In a modal square, necessarily P is contradictory to possibly not-P (while necessarily not-P is contradictory to possibly P), and necessarily P and necessarily not-P are contraries. If we expand the square into a hexagon, the last two can be labeled non-contingent or absolute (the necessary and the impossible), while the contingent is formed by possibly P and possibly not-P.
19. This can be translated as once is never (or, more literally, one time is no time).
20. The particular is not necessarily contingent, as the necessary is not necessarily universal. Pace Hume, McDowell (1985), for example, argues that we can conceive and detect genuine non-universal necessities.
21. Here again, the temporal can be necessary. As with space, these are only symptoms; things that display variability likely have some lightness in being. Still, there are important similarities between what is temporary and what lacks necessity. Rini and Cresswell (2012), among others, have headed a project to detect similarities between tense and modality. See also Kit Fine's remarks about presentism and actualism (2005).
22. This is Aristotle's position about what makes something what it is in the Org. 1. There he distinguishes between primary and secondary substances. The former are what holds all predications – are the subject of all predication – and therefore are independent of any quality or relation.
23. Cf. Tre, Enq.
24. Cf. 1980.
25. Deleuze (1995), as I will explore later in the book, understands the future as that which is repeated. In fact, we can easily predict the repetitions of the calendar in the future; for instance, there will be no more than one Wednesday next week.
26. Cf. 2012: 30.
27. Cf. 1989.
28. Cf. 1997.
29. See Jankélevitch (1980).
30. Meillassoux (2008), whose position is close to this, as we will see in the next section, doesn't call it metaphysical but rather speculative (2008: chapter 2).
31. Cf. 2008.
32. Cf. Ellis (2002), Molnar (2003), Mumford (2004).
33. Cf. Ani., II.
34. Cf. Lewis (1997), Martin (2007), Bird (2007).

35. Nathan Englander's For the Relief of Unbearable Urges (2000) tells a story of Jewish man and a rabbi wondering whether an urge is genuine. To be sure, it is not always obvious to us whether or not something is an urge. A genuine urge, as opposed to a drive that can be contained without any consequence, is something that will have some effect. I further developed the idea of urges in a talk in Paris, called Quelques ingredients et quelques épices pour une ontologie et une politique des urgences, organized by the Universities of Paris 7 and 8 in April 2011.

36. Cf. 1985: 5.

37. Cf. 1985: 14.

38. See, in particular, Ford (1984), Debaise (2006) and Stengers (2002). It is interesting to notice that Process Studies, the publication of the Center for Process Studies issued since 1973, has been receiving increasing philosophical attention.

39. Cf. 2005.

40. Cf. 2009: 108.

41. Cf. 1988.

42. Cf. 2013: 62.

43. I believe "sponsorship" is an interesting translation for Souriau's word instauration. Souriau's word, much mentioned by Latour, has been compared by Harman (2009) with Heidegger's Gestiftet. I thank my friend and colleague Gerson Brea for his suggestion to understand Gestiftet in terms of sponsorship. I believe that the term is useful for understanding much of what is at stake in process philosophies.

44. Cf. 1943: I, chap. 2.

45. Cf. 1943: 91.

46. Cf. 1988.

47. Cf. 2008.

48. See excerpts in Meillassoux 2011.

49. Cf. 2006.

50. Cf. 2011: 67.

51. Cf., for instance, 1945.

52. Cf. 2008.

53. Cf. 1999. This is also the sense of "societies" in Whitehead's Process and Reality (1985: 89) where there are no order if there is no society. Societies are connections between actual entities and as such they are up for grabs.

54. Communitas can be taken as a network of connections where everything affects everything. Whitehead (1985) embraces a rejection of vacuous actuality, the idea that something can be actual while not affecting anything. The rejection of such idea amounts to the rejection of complete immunity. It is interesting to compare the notion of communitas with Whitehead's God. Whitehead conceives of God as depending on everything, as being under everything's influence. He isn't immune to the world but rather dependent on it. God is a principle of limitation because it is prehended – that is perceived. He provides the ways for actual entities (see Whitehead 1985: part V and Ford 1984: 113).

55. Cf. 1951.
56. Op. Cit.
57. Cf. Leibniz LAC.
58. Leibniz takes 2 to be contingent and, at least in the reading of Couturat (1901), which is mostly persuasive, he takes the sentence to be analytic. This would follow from a principle of reason according to which all truths are analytic. More about Leibniz, contingency and co-possibility follows in A monadology of fragments, chapter 3 below.
59. Cf. 1992 and 1995 respectively.
60. This is the outcome of considerable research in science studies and the reasoning can be found summarized in chapter 6 of Latour (2013). See also Cartwright (1983) for a clear statement of the lab effect. Cf., in chapter 3, section Ceteris Paribus devices.
61. Cf. 1972.
62. Cf. 1979.
63. Cf. 2005a.
64. I will explore below, in A monadology of fragments, how these two types of immunization can elucidate the elusive distinction between internal and external relations.
65. Cf. 1947.
66. 1977: 277.
67. In Hofstadter's (1971) translation of "[...] die Natur die Wesenüberlässt /Dem Wagnis ihrer dumpfen Lust und keins /Besonders schützt in Scholle und Geäst [...]".
68. Op. Cit.
69. Eternity and mortality are recurring themes of Hölderlin, the other central source of Heidegger's Verlassenheit. The images of his Schicksalslied evoke a water swirl where things get drowned, as opposed to eternal subsistence.
70. Whitehead considers the up in the air to be the salvation of reality. "[T]he salvation of reality," he claims, "is its obstinate, irreducible, matter-of-fact entities, which are limited to be no other than themselves... That which endures is limited, obstructive, intolerant, infecting its environment with its own aspects. But it is not self-sufficient." (1967: 93-4).
71. Cf., for instance, the eight Duino Elegy (1923).
72. Cf. 2010a.
73. Cf. 2002.
74. Cf. 2011.
75. Cf., for example, 1987.
76. For a development of the metaphysical import of the plan d'immanence, see Bensusan & Cardoso (2012).
77. Met. Z-7.

78. The current use of the word automaton suggests something very different, something that is built so that it follows external rules. As Latour (2013: 222) points out, there is nothing more heteromaton than an automaton.
79. Cf. Poem, DK 4-9.
80. Cf. 1964, 1985.
81. Cf. 2009: chap. 1.
82. See Severino 1985.
83. Soph., 285b.
84. Soph., 285c.
85. Throughout the book I refer to the anarcheologies of chapter 2 as "Anarcheology" followed by their number (1-3) and then followed by an indication of the referenced section, by letters or numbers.
86. Cf. 2008: 97.
87. Op. Cit.: 94.
88. Souriau (2009: 114-129) explores things and phenomena as two (specific) modes of existence.
89. Cf. Met. Λ, 6, 1071b. 5.
90. Cf. 1985: 111.
91. Cf. Met. M, 3.
92. See Met. Δ, 2.
93. Cf. Routley 1980, Priest 2005.
94. Cf. Harman 2010: 11.
95. Cf. 1986.
96. Cf. KrV B 625-630.
97. Cf. 1905.
98. Cf. 1948/9.
99. Cf., for example, Zimmerman 1998 for a review.
100. Examples from Quine 1948/9.
101. This has to do with why Aristotle thought that ousia protai to onton or why Kant (P, note 24) insists on the importance of a putative fix holder for passing predications. One way to see how contingent predicates seem more acceptable is to consider the anomalous predicates considered by Goodman (1983). "Grue," as much as "green," is a predicate that we can contingently ascribe to emeralds, for we depend on an induction to project our current observations onto the future. It is not evident why we prefer "green" to "grue." Goodman, however, doesn't consider a predicate like, say, "dexist" for something that exists before, say, tomorrow, and doesn't exist thereafter. It seems that the permanence (and the non-contingency) of what exists is more often taken for granted.
102. Cf. 2013.
103. Cf. 2013: 2.

104. Cf. Op. Cit.: 8.4.
105. Cf. 2013: 7.
106. See 2013: cap. 2. Williamson believes the development of a metaphysics goes hand in hand with the development of logical tools. "In each case," he writes, "a deviant metaphysics corresponds to a deviant logic." And he proceeds, "[a]ny logical principle has persuasive force in some dialectical contexts and not in others" (2013: 146). His main arguments for necessitism rely on enabling modal logic to have more inferential power without having to appeal to free logic or other resources that he takes to be deviant. But he sees logic and metaphysics as intertwined, and he rejects the view that logic is a neutral arbiter of metaphysical disputes.
107. Cf. Op. Cit. 1.6.
108. Cf. 1975: 722-3.
109. Cf. 1987, Plateau 10.
110. Lucretius (RN), Book II, sections 216-224.
111. Cf. Souriau 2009, Latour 2013.
112. Cf. 2009: 165-194.
113. Peter Handke, in his *Essay on Tiredness* (1994), speaks of the heartlessness of his attempt to content himself with investigating the images that a problem engenders and translating it as heartlessly as possible into language with all its twists and turns and overtones. He plays down contrast – an image created by a story-teller is not to be contrasted with any other before being fully appreciated. Telling a story is to avoid attention to be drawn to anything but the intensity of the image being drawn. It should play on affirmations. Negation, in storytelling, is not a non-picture, is another picture with specific details to it.
114. 114   Cf. 2013.
115. Cf. 2005: §7, §19, §25, §34.
116. Cf. 2013.
117. Cf. 2010.
118. Cf. 1957: 56.
119. Anarcheology is not a dictionary word. It has been used sporadically. The primary uses of the term here will be related to Bensusan et al. 2012.
120. Cf. 1987.
121. Cf. 1995.
122. Cf. 2013: 47-51.
123. In a class about the notion of anarcheology he invited me to give in his course of "Arabe pour les philosophes" in 2011 at the University of Paris 8.
124. See fragments 177b*, 286 and 286a* in the an-archeology below, Anarcheology 2/277b*, 2/286 and 2/286a*. Digging tunnels is another (perhaps xenoarcheological) way to deal with archés: use them for architecture.
125. Cf. https://www.youtube.com/watch?v=1BDBcKW72Oc
126. Cf. 2005.

127. Cf. 1977.
128. Moore's poem "Poetry" has many versions itself since its first appearance in 1919. In more recent versions, the words above don't appear. For the original version of the poem cf. Kreymborg (1920)
129. Cf. 1988. Although Irréductions is the second part of the book, it somehow stands alone, or so I thought when I photocopied only this second part and bound it for my trip to Ethiopia.
130. A sauce served with injera, Ethiopian flat bread.
131. The Ethiopian term both for the European and for white people in general.
132. This refers to the great soul of the world, in the Zulu tradition. It is sometimes compared to the Christian God.
133. Nenaunir is an enchanted serpent. Its priests are called Mungos.
134. Cf. Bensusan et al. 2012.
135. See Sahagún 2013.
136. See Léon-Portilla 2002.
137. See Léon-Portilla 2006.
138. See, for example, Sahagún 2006.
139. Sacred place, sacred mountain – like Coatepec for the Mexicas.
140. The sacred word.
141. The burning of Nanahuatzin is the event that marks the rise of the Fifth Sun.
142. 142   Cf. Leibniz's Dm, LAC and Mon.
143. Couturat's interpretation of Leibniz's system (Couturat 1901) renewed interest in Leibniz in the early twentieth century. He claimed to have found in Leibniz's unpublished materials elements of a doctrine that contrasted with most of what was commonly ascribed to Leibniz. More recent research has found the distance between the published and the unpublished doctrines to be smaller (see, for example, Deleuze 1992, Wilson 1999).
144.   In fact, Leibniz is adamant his system is a combination of determination and contingency. Replying to Pierre Bayle's suspicions which were similar to those raised by Arnauld, Leibniz attempts to make a clear distinction between necessity and determinacy in the Theodicy (Theo). He takes anything to be contingent if its negation is not a contradiction. Leibniz holds that whatever takes place in the world was chosen together with the wisest possible choice of a best possible world. This choice was made based on a simulation in God's head of the possible interaction of all monads. Once the world is chosen, whatever happens (including God's miracles) is determined. Yet, everything is contingent. It is clear that contingency has nothing to do with indifference or with what is random. Leibniz (cf. Theo 303-324) clearly distances himself of the idea of a random sway of the determined orbits that would constitute the Epicurist clinamina. Every act is determined by the nature of the substances involved which were chosen as part of the chosen world. Contingency requires no momentary lapse of connection with the rest of the world.
145. See footnote to section Turning ontologically towards contingency in chapter 1.

146. Cf. PP 51-54.
147. Leibniz has slightly different systems of substances in different texts. For simplicity here, I will consider monads as simple substances, like it seems to be the case in the Monadology (Mon).
148. Cf. Mon. 65-67.
149. See Three speculative accounts of contingency in chapter 1 above.
150. Cf. Op. Cit. section 71.
151. Cf. Schaffer (2010a) and Bohn (2009).
152. In previous presentations, they occupy the space of a point, that is, a dimensionless space.
153. I won't go into the discussion about materialism here, but matter itself is understood in many different ways, and whether it is active or merely passive is a relevant discussion. As for the role of matter in processes of ontogenesis, it is interesting to consider the Naturphilosophie tradition – as in Hamilton Grant (2006). Rosi Braidotti (2012) made suggestive approximations between "matter" and "mother."
154. Cf DE AA VI, 3, 588.
155. Cf. Schaffer (2010a) for the distinction. Schaffer himself considers Leibniz to be a priority pluralist.
156. Cf., for example, Tarde (1999), Whitehead (1985) and Latour (1988).
157. Cf. 1988 1.1.7, 1.1.8 and 1.5.1.
158. Cf .Deleuze (1992) for an analysis of Leibniz's monadology in terms of a baroque concerto grosso.
159. Cf. 1988 1.1.2, 1.1.4, 1.3.2 and 1.3.5.
160. Or as examples of what Meillassoux (2008) labeled metaphysics of subjectivity.
161. See chapter 1 above, Three speculative accounts of contingency.
162. Cf. 1985: 19.
163. Cf. 1988 1.1.9, 1.2.1, 1.1.14.1, 1.2.5.1 and 1.2.6.
164. Cf. 1985: 28-20. Whitehead builds some of his categories of explanation in terms of prehensions (perceptions and "negative perceptions" or perceptions of what is something's absence) such that the rejection of vacuous actuality is central. The notion of vacuous actuality, he remarks, is close to that of "inherence of quality in substance". In other words, what is inherent to an actual entity is its connections with others through prehensions.
165. Cf. 1988 1.1.5.3.
166. Cf. 1988 1.2.3.
167. Cf. 1985: 60.
168. Cf. Nagel 1999. A translation: I think therefore I know.
169. I am therefore I know.
170. Compare with Heraclitus, fragment 210, Anarcheology 2/210.

171. Cf. 1988 1.2.3.1.
172. Cf. 2013: 417.
173. Cf. 1992.
174. 1985: 19.
175. Cf. 1985: 23.
176. Cf. 1988: 2.4.7.
177. Cf. 1988: 1.2.2.
178. In Whitehead God Himself is open to the improvement and this can be achieved by worldly deeds. God, and not only the world, is therefore conceived as up for grabs.
179. Cf. Mumford (2004), Mumford & Anjun (2011).
180. Cf. Molnar (2003).
181. Cf. Ellis 2002).
182. Cf. Bird (2007).
183. Cf. Harman (2009: 112-116).
184. Cf. 2010, 2010a.
185. Cf. 2010: 348-351.
186. Cf., for example, Quine (1951) and Davidson (1974, 1983).
187. Cf. 1983, 1991, 1991a.
188. For an exploration of epistemological holism, see Bensusan & Pinedo (2014a).
189. Cf. 1984, 1994.
190. I won't go into this at length here, but see Bensusan and Pinedo (2014a) or Ramberg (1991) for a more thorough presentation.
191. Cf. Borgoni & Palomo (2006).
192. Cf. 2010.
193. Cf. 2013.
194. See 2010, ch. 1; but also 2009: 107ff., 143ff., 169ff.
195. Cf. 2010: 81.
196. Cf. 1995, 2005.
197. Cf. 2010: 16.
198. 1995: 157, my translation. Original text: [...] il faudrait supposer que la science ne sera jamais achevée, parce que cette science est une relation entre des êtres qui ont par définition le même degré d'organisation : un système matériel et un être vivant organisé qui essaie de penser ce système au moyen de la science. [...] la relation entre la pensée et le réel devient relation entre deux réels organisés qui peuvent être analogiquement liés par leur structure interne.
199. Cf. 1988: 1.2.3.
200. Cf. 2009: 113-4.

201. Cf. 2009a.

202. The cathedral of Santo Domingo was built from 1559 onwards over the foundations of a Wiracocha palace, the Kirswarkancha. Most of the stones of the cathedral walls were taken out of the Saqsaywaman building, a strong construction that probably had been used for defensive purposes.

203. Cf. 1960.

204. The comparison of metaphysical composition and language composition is perhaps a chapter of an effort to draw metaphysical lessons from what was achieved in the linguistic turn. Manuel de Pinedo and I (in a talk presented in the 2009 Nottingham Conference on the Metaphysics of Science) called this effort "a linguistic turn of 360 degrees." There, we focused mainly on a metaphysical reading of Wittgenstein's Investigations (2009), in particular the idea of predicates as only definable through family resemblance, and on contextualist semantics for demonstratives and dispositional predicates. We argued that we can use some of the insights of the philosophers of language working in these areas to introduce the idea that properties are themselves both dependent on family resemblance and context-sensitive.

205. Cf. 1999: 173.

206. Cf. Latour (1988a).

207. Cf. 1985: 39-40.

208. Cf. Fine 2005a and McTaggart 1908.

209. See, for example, Markosian (2004), Sider (2003).

210. For a more detailed exploration of the relation between reality and perspectives, see my article "The cubist object," Bensusan (2011).

211. It is interesting also to compare this monadology, with its existential trialism, with Markus Gabriel's ontology of fields of sense (see Gabriel 2014).

212. See Anarcheology 2/212 and 2/214.

213. Cf. 2010: 117 ff.

214. Cf. 2010: 119.

215. Cf. 2004.

216. Cf. 1983.

217. The attraction force of the virtual – which is different from the possible in that it is never actualized – is important for Deleuzian realism about the non-actual. For a good analysis of attractors as virtuality, within the scope of Deleuze's ontology, see Delanda 2002: 41-59.

218. Cf. Deleuze & Guattari (1987) and Garcia (2011).

219. Cf. Bataille (1945).

220. Cf. 1992.

221. Cf. 1995: 178-179.

222. Cf. 1982: 29, my translation. Original text: .on ne peut pas interroger que le pouvoir, le non-pouvoir est la question même.

223. For recent accounts of truth as identity see, for example, Hornsby 1997, David 2001. Wittgenstein points at this continuity between the contents of facts and the contents of thoughts on several occasions. In the Investigations (2009), section 95, he says that our thought can be such that it doesn't "stop anywhere short of the fact." John McDowell (1994) has explored this to set the stage for his version of an identity theory of truth.

224. Cf. for example, Pritchard (2005).

225. Cf. 1995.

226. Cf. 1963.

227. There is much discussion of the connection between beliefs and holding something to be true. The most interesting ones revolve around what is called the paradox, introduced by Wittgenstein (2009a, 10). The paradox arises when someone asserts both that "p" and that "I currently believe that not-p" or variations thereof.

228. Cf. PH.

229. Cf. 2009: 351-352.

230. Cf. McDowell 1994.

231. Cf. PH, I, 210-12.

232. Cf .Polito (2004).

233. Cf. Conche (1994) and Bett (2000).

234. Cf. Conche (1994: 60).

235. Cf. Conche (1994: 225).

236. It seems that Wittgenstein himself ascribed to the issue a measure of indetermination; see his Remarks on the Foundation of Mathematics (1978, section VII-41). For discussion, cf. McDowell 1984, Bensusan 2007, Bensusan & Pinedo 2014.

237. Cf. Heidegger & Fink (1979).

238. Cf. 2008.

239. Cf. Wittgenstein 1969 and Davidson 1974, 1983, 1991.

240. Cf. 1969.

241. This is Frede's (1997) reading of Sextus – he understands Sextus as an urban skeptic who appreciated the need for sharing some contents with people in his community while not entertaining any beliefs. This is why, apart from suspension of judgment, the urban skeptic would also recommend that some contents are accepted but not believed (that is, not held as true).

242. Cf. for example, Pritchard (2012).

243. Cf. for example, Martin (2002).

244. Cf. 2006.

245. Cf, new fragment 131, Anarch. 2/131.

246. The metaphysics of some is the ontological correlate of a holistic epistemology sketched by Davidson and developed further in Bensusan & Pinedo (2014a).

247. The qualifications account for the difference between the first two and the last formulation of the ontology of doubts. The last formulation is noncommittal about whether doubts are in the world – as it is noncommittal about whether there are only determinations in the world.

248. Cf. 1992.

249. For further discussion on the ontology of antennas, see Borges & Bensusan (2013).

250. Cf. 1995: 70-82.

251. Recapitulation was a popular idea at the origins of the theories about the evolution of species (see Oken, St.-Hilaire, Buffon and also Schelling). One of the prevailing marks of recapitulation is Haeckel's thesis, according to which ontogeny recapitulates phylogeny: the phases of development of an embryo repeat those of its species. Deleuze (especially with Guattari in 1987) draws on recapitulation to sketch the idea of a geological epidemiology. A rhythm-oriented ontology also draws on the idea that recapitulation has no borders.

252. Lucretius's clinamina, RN, Book II, sections 216-224.

253. Cf. 1980, see also chapter 1 above.

254. Cf. 2002.

255. Cf. Op. Cit. 94.

256. Cf. Phy. VI, 6, p. 238.

257. Cf. 1969.

258. Cf. 1967.

259. Consider time without change as in the Shoemaker thought experiments (1993).

260. Cf. 1973.

261. Cf. 1991.

262. Tropes are abstract particulars, not located in space or time but not universal like properties; examples of tropes are: this white, the red of this bottle of wine, etc. See Campbell (1990)

263. In order to show how our notions of objectivity are spatial and ultimately visual, Strawson (1959) presents a being whose experience is wholly auditory. Such being's navigation has to be guided by elements that have nothing to do with he inner and the outer – or the deeper and the apparent (see Evans 1985).

264. See chapter 1, Fragments, compositions and composers: a monadology

265. An issue that emerges here is the complexity of an entraining rhythm. A rhythm can always be viewed as a sequence of beats and intervals, but beats are themselves rhythmic. One approach to the issue is to start with the minimum sequence that can provide the rhythm and take this sequence to measure its complexity (as it is done to consider the Kolmogorov-complexity of something; see, for example, Li and Vitanyi 1993). Such an approach, nonetheless, cannot do much more than measure the complexity of a rhythm as it is heard – as it entrains something else. The matryoshka character of each beat makes it feature a specific complexity.

266. Cf. 1995, 2005.

267. Cf. KrV B 75.

268. Cf. 1999. McDowell has recently distanced himself from this formulation.
269. Cf. 2009.
270. Some readers of Wittgenstein, influenced by Sellars (like Brandom and McDowell), seem to espouse the idea that without a language – and the concepts that come with it – there would be nothing to be said. That is, content depends on language. Within a rhythm-oriented perspective, conceptual content appears in a broader context. It is, to be sure, one of the many rhythmic signals that is to be transductively exploited.
271. Cf. Bensusan (2008).
272. Cf. 1931.
273. At Martin-Gropius-Bau, in Berlin, 2014.
274. See section Three anarcheologies in chapter 2.
275. Cf. 1978: 378.
276. Cf. 1986.
277. Harman distinguishes the attempts to deconstruct objects from below, through their components, matter or elementary particles, and attempts to deconstruct them from above, through sensory qualities, impressions or aggregates. He describes the former as strategies to undermine objects and the latter as overmining them.
278. Cf. 1887.
279. Cf. 1797.
280. Cf. 1962.
281. Cf. 2014.
282. Cf. 1979.
283. Cf. 1980, plateau 3.
284. Cf. Op. Cit: 65-6.
285. It is remarkable how close the early part of this Plateau is close to some of the central tenets of Lovelock's Gaia hypothesis. For him too, there is no interior or exterior of life understood as a separating border. Gaia is alive because it is infected from being the environment of many forms of life.
286. It is interesting to compare the double articulation as the surface of animation with the recent work of Elizabeth Povinelli that tries to go beyond what she calls the carbon imaginary of life (2014).
287. Harman (2014) compares Whitehead (and Latour) on the one hand and Deleuze (and Simondon) on the other placing the former in school X and the latter in school Y. The difference between these two schools of process philosophy envisaged by Harman is that in school X, but not in school Y, the emphasis is on individual entities and not on becomings. One could then say that while the monadology of fragments is in school X, rhythm-oriented ontology is in school Y. (Simondon's partial monadologies would be clearly in Y.)
288. Cf. Deleuze & Parnet 1987: I, 1.

289. Compare with verses 17-38 of the first part of the Sahagún Colloquia above (Anarcheology 3/VI-1016-17 to 38).

290. Cf. 2005.

291. Cf. 2008.

292. Cf. 1989: 22.

293. Rorty's image of metaphysics seems to be related to necessary connections. To place something in the realm of sheer contingency, as he intends to do with the world and with language and mind, is to place it outside the scope of any metaphysics. Contingency, for him, is the antidote to metaphysics. This is the limit of the convergence between this book and Rorty's endeavors.

294. Cf. 2013: Introduction.

295. Cf. 1972: 135.

296. Cf. 1972: 135-6.

297. Cf. 1986.

298. Cf. Bensusan & Costa Leite (2012).

299. See Blanché (1966) for an initial analysis of the geometry of opposition. In the triangle formed by a logic, its antilogic and its counterlogic, two sides express relations of contradiction and contrariety, and the third expresses subalternity (provided that some restrictions to the original logic apply).

300. Most of our results up till recently are in Bensusan, Costa-Leite & Souza (2015). The study of galaxies has been primarily carried out with my colleague Alexandre Costa-Leite. He himself has worked on how contingency interact with epistemic operators (Costa-Leite 2006). We have also developed a way to think about contradictions in the world in terms of galaxies (Bensusan & Costa-Leite 2013). Recently we are developing a general approach to universal logic based on the framework of galaxies (and other sets of possible worlds). See Trafford (2014) for a somewhat similar research.

301. Cf. Béziau (2005).

References

Agamben, Giorgio. *Che cos'è il commando?* Roma: Nottetempo srl, 2013.

Anscombe, Elizabeth. *Intention*. Cambridge, MA: Harvard University Press, 1957.

Aristotle. *Organon.* (Org.) *The Works of Aristotle, Vol. I.* Translated by David Ross. Robert Maynard Hutchins, ed. London: Encyclopaedia Britannica, 1952.

_____ *Metaphysics (Met.)* 2 vols. Translated by David Ross. Oxford: Clarendon Press, 1908.

_____ *The Physics (Phy.), The Basic Works of Aristotle*. Translated by Rhys Roberts and Ingram Bywater. McKeon, Richard, ed. Random House, New York, 1970. Pages 218-394.

_____ *De Anima (Ani.)* Translated by Mark Shifmann. Newburyport: Focus, 2011.

Bataille, Georges. *Sur Nietzsche*. Paris: Gallimard, 1945.

Bennett, Jane. *Vibrant Matter: A Political Ecology of Things*. Durham: Duke University Press, 2010.

Bensusan, Hilan. *Excessos e Exceções*. São Paulo: Ideias & Letras, 2008.

_____ "Pode Deus determinar o valor de PI?". *Kriterion*, 68 (2007): 47-66.

_____ "The cubist object". *Speculations II* (2011): 169-186.

Bensusan, Hilan, Leonel Antunes & Luciana Ferreira. *Heráclito: Exercícios de Anarqueologia*. São Paulo: Ideias e Letras, 2012.

Bensusan, Hilan & Tomás R. Cardoso. "Por uma metafísica de tramas: o mundo sem arché." *Kriterion*, 53 (2012): 281-298.

Bensusan, Hilan & Alexandre Costa-Leite. "Antilogic, Counterlogic and the square of opposition", presented at the 3rd World Congress on the Square of Opposition, 2012, Beirut, June 26-30.

_____ "Dialetheism and Galaxy Theory", presented at the 4th World Congress on Universal Logic, 2013, Rio de Janeiro, April 3-7.

Bensusan, Hilan, Alexandre Costa-Leite & Edelcio de Souza. "Logics and their galaxies". Studies in Universal Logic, The Road to Universal Logic, 2 (2015): 243-252.

Bensusan, Hilan & Manuel de Pinedo. "Soft Facts". *Daímon*, 61 (2014): 7-21.

_____ "I only know I know a lot: Holism and knowledge", *Epistemologia*, XXXVII (2014a): 234-254.

Bird, Alexander. *Nature's Metaphysics: Laws and Properties*. Oxford: Oxford University Press, 2007.

Bett, Richard. *Pyrrho, his Antecedents, and his Legacy*. Oxford: Oxford University Press, 2000.

Béziau, Jean-Yves. *Logica Universalis - Towards a general theory of logic*. Basel: Birkhauser, 2005.

Blanché, Robert. *Structures intellectuelles, essai sur l'organisation systématique des concepts*. Paris: Vrin, 1966.

Blanchot, Maurice. *L'Écriture du Désastre*. Paris: Gallimard, 1980.

Bohn, E. "An argument against the necessity of unrestricted composition". *Analysis* 69.1 (2009): 27–31.

Borges, Fabiane & Hilan Bensusan. "The Antenna Rush (Nature Hacking and the Ontology of Satellites)". *O-Zone: A Journal of Object-Oriented Studies*, 1 (2013): 22-26.

Borgoni, Cristina & Jesús Palomo. "Humildad Davidsoniana: Conocimiento e Ignorancia como Precondiciones de la Interpretación Radical," *Actas del V Congreso de la SLMFC*, Granada, Ediciones Sider S.C., 2006, Pages 105-109.

Braidotti, Rosi. "Interview with Rosi Braidotti." In: *New Materialism: Interviews & Cartographies*. Dolphijn, Rick & Iris van der Tuin. Ann Arbor: Open Humanities Press, 2012.

Bryant, Levi R., Nick Srnicek & Graham Harman (Eds.). *The Speculative Turn: Continental Materialism and Realism*. Melbourne: Re.press, 2011.

Campbell, Keith. *Abstract Particulars*. Oxford: Blackwell, 1990.

Cartwright, Nancy. *How the Laws of Physics Lie*. Oxford: Oxford University Press, 1983.

Choi, Sungho. "Finkish Dispostions and Contextualism." *The Monist* 94 (2011): 103-120.

Churchland, Paul. *Scientific Realism and the Plasticity of Mind*. Cambridge: Cambridge University Press, 1979.

Cleland, Carol. "On the individuation of events." *Synthese* 86.2(1991): 229 -254.

Conche, Marcel. *Pyrrhon ou l'apparence*. Paris: Presses Universitaires de France, 1994.

Costa-Leite, Alexandre. "Combining modal concepts: philosophical applications." *The Logica Yearbook 2006*, Academy of Sciences of Czech Republic.

Couturat, Louis. *La logique de Leibniz: d'après des documents inédits*. Paris: Félix Alcan, 1901.

D'Alessandro, H. *El Cucaracho (y otras aventuras)*. Mexico: EyC, 2012.

David, Mariam. "Truth as Identity and Truth as Correspondence." In: *The Nature of Truth: Classic & Contemporary Perspectives*. Lynch, Michael, ed. Cambridge, MA: MIT Press, 2001. Pages 683-704.

Davidson, Donald. "On the Individuation of Events." In: *Essays in Honour of Carl G. Hempel*. Nicholas Herscher, ed. Dordrecht: Heidel, 1969, Pages 216-234.

_____ "On the Very Idea of a Conceptual Scheme." In: *Proceedings and Addresses of the American Philosophical Association* 47 (1974): 5-20.

_____ "A Coherence Theory of Truth and Knowledge." in D. Henrich (ed.), *Kant oder Hegel?* Stuttgart: Klett-Cotta, 1983.

_____ "First Person Authority." *Dialectica* 38 (1984): 101-111.

_____ "Three Varieties of Knowledge." In: *A. J. Ayer Memorial Essays: Royal Institute of Philosophy Supplement,* 30. A. Phillips Griffiths, ed. Cambridge: Cambridge University, 1991.

_____ "Epistemology Externalized." *Dialectica* 45.2-3 (1991a): 191-202.

_____ "Knowing One's Own Mind." In: *Self-Knowledge.* Quassim Cassam, ed. Oxford: Oxford University Press, 1994. Pages 43-64.

Debaise, Didier. *Un Empirisme Spéculatif: Lecture de Procès et Realité de Whitehead.* Paris: Vrin, 2006.

DeLanda, Manuel. *A Thousand Years of Nonlinear History.* Cambridge, MA: MIT Press, 1997.

_____ *Intensive Science and Virtual Philosophy.* London and New York: Continuum, 2002.

Deleuze, Gilles. *Difference and Repetition.* Translated by Paul Patton. London and New York: Continuum, 1995.

_____ Interview with Robert Maggiori. In *Libération*, September 2 and 3, 1986.

_____ *The fold: Leibniz and the Baroque.* Translated by Tom Conley. London: Anthlone Press, 1992.

Deleuze, Gilles & Félix Guattari. *A Thousand Plateaus: Capitalism and Schizophrenia.* Translated by Brian Massumi. Minneapolis: University of Minnesota Press, 1987.

Deleuze, Gilles & Parnet, Claire. *Dialogues.* Translated by Hugh Tomlinson and Barbara Habberjam. New York: Columbia University Press, 1987.

Derrida, Jacques. *Spectres de Marx: l'*état de *la dette, le travail du deuil et la nouvelle Internationale.* Paris: Galilée, 1993.

Descartes, René. *Principes de philosophie* (PP). Paris: Vrin. 1993.

Descola, Philippe. *Beyond Nature and Culture*. Translated by Janet Lloyd. Chicago: University of Chicago Press, 2013.

Ellis, Brian. *The Philosophy of Nature: A Guide to the New Essentialism*, Montreal, McGill-Queen's University Press, 2002.

Englander, Nathan. *For the Relief of Unbearable Urges*. New York: Vintage, 2000.

Esposito, Roberto. *Termini della politica. Comunità, immunità, biopolitica*. Milano: Mimesis, 2008.

Evans, Gareth. "Things Without the Mind." In: *Collected Papers*. Oxford: Clarendon Press, 1985. Pages 249-291.

Ewing, Alfred. *Idealism: a Critical Survey*. New York: Methuen & Co, 1934.

Fine, Kit. "Tense and Reality." In: *Modality and Tense: Philosophical Papers*. Oxford: Oxford University Press, 2005. Pages 261-320.

_____ "The varieties of necessity." In *Modality and Tense: Philosophical Papers*. Oxford: Oxford University Press, 2005a. Pages 235-260.

Ford, Lewis. *The Emergence of Whitehead's Metaphysics, 1925-1929*. Albany: State University of New York Press, 1984.

Frede, Michael. "The Sceptic's Two Kinds of Assent and the Question of the Possibility of Knowledge." In: *The Original Sceptics: A Controversy*. Burnyeat, Myles and Michael Frede, eds. Indianapolis: Hackett, 1997. Pages 127-152.

Gabriel, Markus. *Fields of Sense – A New Realist Ontology*. Edinburgh: Edinburgh University Press, 2014.

Galatzia (2014). *Mi cuerpo es touchscreen*. Web, 21 September, 2015. <http://www.youtube.com/watch?v=We-VukNWvq4>.

Garcia, Tristan. *Forme et objet: Un Traité des choses*. Paris: PUF, 2011.

Gettier, Edmund. "Is Justified True Belief Knowledge?" In: *Analysis*, 23.6(1963): 121-123.

Goodman, Nelson. *Fact, Fiction, and Forecast*. Cambridge, MA: Harvard University Press, 4th edition, 1983.

Gould, Stephen Jay. *Wonderful Life: The Burgess Shale and the Nature of History*. New York: W. W. Norton & Company, 1989.

Grant, Iain Hamilton (2006). *Philosophies of Nature After Schelling*. London and New York: Continuum.

———— "Does Nature Stay What-it-is?: Dynamics and the Antecedence Criterion." In: *The Speculative Turn: Continental Materialism and Realism*. Bryant, Levi R., Nick Srnicek and Graham Harman, eds. Melbourne: RePress, 2011. Pages 66-83.

Han, Byung-Chul. *Müdigkeitsgesellschaft*. Berlin: Matthes und Seitz, 2010.

Handke, Peter. "Essay on tiredness." In: *The Jukebox And Other Essays On Storytelling*. New York: Farrar Straus Giroux, 1994.

Harman, Graham. *Prince of Networks: Bruno Latour and Metaphysics*. Melbourne: RePress, 2009.

———— *L'objet quadruple*. Paris: PUF, 2010.

———— "Whitehead and schools X, Y and Z." In: Gaskill, Nicholas and Adam Nocek, eds. *The Lure of Whitehead*, Minneapolis: University of Minnesota Press, 2014.

Heidegger, Martin. "Wozu Dichter." In: *Holzwege*, Gesamtausgabe Band 5. Frankfurt am Main: Vittorio Klostermann, 1977. Pages 269-320.

———— Über den Anfang. In: *Gesamtausgabe Band 70*. Frankfurt: Vittorio Klostermann, 2005.

———— *Poetry, Language, Thought*. Translated by Albert Hofstadter. New York: Harper & Row, 1971

Heidegger, Martin & Fink, Eugen. *Heraclitus Seminar*. Translated by Charles Seibert. Tuscaloosa: University of Alabama Press, 1979.

Heraclitus. *Fragments* (Frag). London: Penguin, 2009.

Hornsby, Jennifer. "Truth: The Identity Theory." *Proceedings of the Aristotelian Society, New Series*. 97(1997): 1-24.

Hume, David. *A Treatise of Human Nature* (Tre). Oxford: Clarendon Press, 1896

_____ *An Enquiry Concerning Human Understanding* (Enq). Oxford: Clarendon Press, 1975.

Jabès, Edmond. *The Book of Questions.* Translated by Rosmarie Waldrop. Middletown: Wesleyan University Press, 1977.

_____ *Le petit livre de la subversion hors de soupcon.* Paris: Gallimard, 1982.

_____ *Les deux livres: aigle et chouette.* Paris: Fata Morgana, 2005.

Jankélevich, Vladimir. *Le Je-ne-sais-quoi et le Presque-rien,* Paris: Seuil, 1980.

Kant, Immanuel. *Kritik der Reinen Vernunft* (KrV). Sämtliche Werke. Leipzig : Verlag von Felix Meiner, 1919.

_____ *Prolegomena zu einer jeden künftigen Metaphysik, die als Wissenschaft wird auftreten können* (P). Sämtliche Werke. Leipzig: Verlag von Felix Meiner, 1920.

Kaplan, David. "How to Russell a Frege-church." *Journal of Philosophy* 72.19 (1975): 716-729.

Karkowski, Zbigniew. (1992). "The Method Is Science, The Aim Is Religion." Web, 21 September, 2015. <http://www.desk.nl/~northam/oro/zk2.htm>.

Kim, Jaegwon. "Causation, Nomic Subsumption, and the Concept of Event," *Journal of Philosophy* 70 (1973): 217-36.

Kreymborg, Alfred. *Others for 1919: An Anthology of the New Verse*, New York: Nicholas L. Brown, 1920.

Kripke, Saul. *Naming and Necessity.* Cambridge, MA: Harvard University Press, 1972.

Laruelle, François. *Principes de la non-philosophie.* Paris: PUF, 1996.

Latour, Bruno. "Irreductions." In: *The Pasteurization of France.* Translated by Alan Sheridan and John Law. Cambridge, MA: Harvard University Press, 1988. Pages 153-239.

_____ *The Pasteurization of France.* Translated by Alan Sheridan and John Law. Cambridge, MA: Harvard University Press, 1988a.

_____ *Pandora's Hope: Essays on the Reality of Science Studies*. Cambridge, MA: Harvard University Press, 1999.

_____ *Politics of Nature: How to the Bring Sciences into Democracy*. Translated by Catherine Porter. Cambridge, MA: Harvard University Press, 2004.

_____ *An Inquiry into Modes of Existence*. Translated by Catherine Porter. Cambridge, MA: Harvard University Press, 2013.

Leibniz, Gottfried. "Discours de métaphysique" (DM). Lestienne, Henri, ed. Paris: Alcan, 1929.

_____ "De existentia" (DE). In: *Sämtliche Schriften und Briefe*, herausgegeben von der Deutschen Akademie der Wissenschaften zu Berlin, Darmstadt (1923 on), Leipzig (1938 on) and Berlin (1950 on). AA VI, 3.

_____ "Correspondance avec Arnauld" (LAC). In: *Discours de Métaphysique et Correspondance avec Arnauld*. Paris: Vrin, 1957.

_____ *La Monadologie* (Mon.). Boutroux, Emile, ed. Paris: LGF, 1991.

_____ *Essai de Theodicée* (Theo.) Amsterdam: Chez François Changuion, 1710. (*Theodicy*, Chicago and La Salle: Open Court, 1985).

Lemmon, Edward. "Comments." In: *The Logic of Decision and Action*. Rescher. Nicholas, ed. Pittsburgh: University of Pittsburgh Press, 1967. Pages 96-103.

Leon-Portilla, Miguel. *Bernardino de Sahagún: First Anthropologist*. Translated by Mauricio Mixco. Norman: University of Oklahoma Press, 2002.

_____ (2006). "Estudio Introdutório." In: *Nuestros dioses han muerto?* Leon-Portilla, Miguel, ed. Mexico: Jus. Pages 7-38.

Lewis, David. "Finkish Dispositions." in *The Philosophical Quarterly* 47.187(1997): 143–158.

_____ *On the Plurality of Worlds*. Oxford: Blackwell, 1986.

Li, Ming & Paul Vitányi. *An Introduction to Kolmogorov Complexity and Its Applications*. New York: Springer, 1993.

Lovelock, James. *Gaia – A New Look at Life on Earth*, Oxford: Oxford University Press, 1979.

Lucretius. *On the Nature of Things* (RN). New York: Cosimo, 2009.

Malabou, Catherine. *Ontology of the Accident: An Essay on Destructive Plasticity*. Translated by Carolyn Shread. Cambridge and Malden: Polity Press, 2012.

Maalouf, Amin. *Le premier siècle après Béatrice*. Paris: Editions Grasset & Fasquelle, 1992.

Markosian, N. (2004). "A defense of presentism." In: *Oxford Studies in Metaphysics*, Zimmerman, Dean, ed. Oxford: Clarendon. Pages 47-82.

Martin, Charles B. (2007). *The Mind in Nature*. Oxford: Oxford University Press, 2007.

Martin, Charles B. & John Heil. "The Ontological Turn," *Midwest Studies in Philosophy* 23 (1999): 34-60.

Martin, Michael. "The Transparency of Experience," *Mind and Language*, 17 (2002): 376–425.

McDowell, John. *Wittgenstein on following a rule*. Synthese, 58.3 (1984): 325-363.

_____ "Functionalism and anomalous monism." In: *Actions and Events: Perspectives on the Philosophy of Donald Davidson*. LePore, Ernest & Brian McLaughlin, eds. Oxford: Blackwell, 1985. Pages 387-398.

_____ *Mind & World*. Cambridge, MA: Harvard University Press, 1994.

_____ "Knowledge and the internal." In: *Philosophy and Phenomenological Research* 55 (1995): 877-893.

_____ "The scheme-content dualism and empiricism." In *The Philosophy of Donald Davidson (The Library of Living Philosophers)*, Hahn, Lewis, ed. Chicago: Open Court, 1999. Pages 87-105.

McTaggart, John. "The unreality of time." *Mind* 17 (1908): 457-73.

Meillassoux, Quentin. *After Finitude: An Essay on the Necessity of Contingency*. Translated by Ray Brassier. London and New York: Continuum, 2008.

_____ "Excerpts from *L'inexistence divine.*" In: Harman, Graham, *Quentin Meillassoux: Philosophy in the Making*. Edinburgh: Edinburgh University Press. Pages 175-238.

Molnar, George. *Powers: A Study in Metaphysics*. Oxford: Oxford University Press, 2003.

Morton, Thimothy. *Hyperobjects: Philosophy and Ecology after the End of the World*. Minneapolis: University of Minnesota Press, 2013.

Mumford, Stephen. *Laws in Nature*. London: Routledge, 2004.

Mumford, Stephen & Rani Anjum. *Getting Causes from Powers*. Oxford: Oxford University Press, 2011.

Nagel, Thomas. "Davidson's new cogito." In; *The Philosophy of Donald Davidson (The Library of Living Philosophers)*. Hahn, Lewis, ed. Chicago: Open Court, 1999. Pages 195-207.

Nietzsche, Friedrich. *Zur Genealogie der Moral. Eine Streitschrift.* Leipzig: C. G. Naumann, 1887.

Parmenides. *Parmenides: A Text with Translation, Commentary, and Critical Essays* (Poem). Tarán, Leonardo, ed. Princeton: Princeton University Press, 1965.

Plato. "The Sophist" (Soph). *Plato in Twelve Volumes, Vol. 12*. Harold Fowler, ed. Cambridge, MA: Harvard University Press, 1921.

Polito, Roberto. *The Sceptical Road – Aenesidemus and the Appropriation of Heraclitus*. Leiden: Brill, 2004.

Povinelli, Elizabeth. *"Native life: Or, being outside the carbon imaginary."* Talk at Oxford Martin School, March 7, 2014.

Priest, Graham. *Towards Non-Being. The Logic and Metaphysics of Intentionality*. Oxford: Clarendon, 2005.

Pritchard, Duncan. *Epistemic Luck*. Oxford: Oxford University Press, 2005.

_____ *Epistemological Disjunctivism*. Oxford: Oxford University Press, 2012.

Quine, Willard van O. "Two dogmas of empiricism." *The Philosophical Review*, 60.1(1951): 20-43.

_____ *Word and Object*. Cambridge, MA: MIT Press, 1960.

_____ "On What There Is." *Review of Metaphysics* 2 (1948-9): 21-38.

Ramberg, Bjorn. *Donald Davidson's Philosophy of Language*. Oxford: Wiley-Blackwell, 1991.

Rilke, Rainer Maria. *Duino Elegies*. Frankfurt: Insel, 1923.

_____ *Letters Volume II*. Translated by Greene, Jane & Herter Norton. New York: WW Norton & Company, 1947.

Rini, Adriane & Max Cresswell. *The world-time parallel: Tense and modality in logic and metaphysics*. New York: Cambridge University Press, 2012.

Rorty, Richard. *Contingency, Irony, and Solidarity*. Cambridge: Cambridge University Press, 1989.

Routley, Richard. *Exploring the Meinongian Jungle and Beyond: An Investigation on Noneism and the Theory of Items*. Canberra: Australian National University Press, 1980.

Russell, Bertrand. "On Denoting," in *Mind*, New Series, 14.56 (1905): 479-493.

Sahagún, Bernardino de. *Nuestros dioses han muerto*. Leon-Portilla, Miguel. Mexico City: Jus, 2006.

_____ *General history of the affairs of New Spain. Books X-XI: Aztec's Knowledge in medicine and botany*. Kupriienko, Sergii, ed. Kiev: Vidavets Kuprienko, 2013.

Santos, Lucio. *La Rhythmanalyse*. Rio de Janeiro: Société de Psychologie et de Philosophie, 1931.

Sartre, Jean-Paul. *L'Être et le néant. Essai d'ontologie phénoménologique*. Paris: Gallimard, 1943.

Schaffer, Jonathan. "The Internal Relatedness of all Things." *Mind*, 119 (2010): 341-76.

_____ "Monism: The Priority of the Whole." *Philosophical Review* 119 (2010a): 31-76.

Schelling, Friedrich. *Ideen zu einer Philosophie der Natur.* Leipzig: Breitkopf und Haertel, 1797.

Severino, Emanuelle. "Ritornare a Parmenide." in *Rivista di filosofia neoscolastica*, LVI.2 (1964): 137–175.

_____ *Il parricidio mancato.* Milano: Adelphi, 1985.

Sextus Empiricus. *Outlines of Scepticism (PH)*, Julia Annas & Jonathan Barnes. eds. Cambridge: Cambridge Unversity Press, 2000.

Shoemaker, Sydney. "Time without change." in Robin Le Poidevin and Murray MacBeath (Eds.), *The Philosophy of Time*. Oxford: Oxford University Press, 1993.

Sider, Ted. *Four-Dimensionalism: An Ontology of Persistence and Time*. Oxford: Clarendon Press, 2003.

Simondon, Gilbert. *L'individu et sa genèse physico-biologique*. Grenoble: Jerôme Millon, 1995.

_____ *L'individuation à la lumière des notions de formes et d'information.* Grenoble: Jerôme Millon, 2005

Souriau, Etienne. *Les différents modes d'existence*. Paris: PUF, 2009.

_____ "Du mode d'existence de l'oeuvre à faire". In *Les différents modes d'existence*. Paris: PUF, 2009a.

Sousa, Eudoro de. *Horizonte e Complementariedade*. Brasília: Editora Universidade de Brasília, 1975.

Strawson, Peter. *Individuals: An Essay in Descriptive Metaphysics*. London: Routledge, 1959.

Szymborska, Wislawa. *Sól*. Krakow: Państwowy Instytut Wydawniczy, 1962.

Tarde, Gabriel. "Monadologie et sociologie." In: *Oeuvres de Gabriel Tarde*. Alliez, Eric, ed. Paris: Seuil, 1999.

Trafford, James. "Expanding the universe of Universal Logic." In: *Theoria*, 81 (2014): 325-345.

Viveiros de Castro, Eduardo. *Métaphysiques Cannibales*. Paris: PUF, 2009.

Whitehead, Alfred. *Process and Reality*. New York: The Free Press, 1985.

_____ *Science and the Modern World*. New York: Free Press, 1967.

Williamson, Timothy. *Modal Logic as Metaphysics*. Oxford: Oxford University Press, 2013.

Wittgenstein, Ludwig. *On Certainty*, Oxford: Blackwell, 1969.

_____ *Remarks on the Foundations of Mathematics*. Revised Edition. Translated by Elizabeth Anscombe. Oxford: Basil Blackwell, 1978

_____ *Philosophical Investigations*. 4th edition revised. Translated by Elizabeth Anscombe, Peter Hacker and Joachim Schulte. Oxford: Wiley Blackwell, 2009.

_____ *Philosophy of Psychology: A Fragment*. In: *Philosophical Investigations*. 4th edition revised. Translated by Elizabeth Anscombe, Peter Hacker and Joachim Schulte. Oxford: Wiley Blackwell, 2009a.

Woodard, Ben. *On An Ungrounded Earth: Towards a New Geophilosophy*. New York: Punctum, 2013.

Woese, Carl. "A New Biology for a New Century." *Microbiology And Molecular Biology Reviews*, 68.2(2004): 173–186.

Zimmerman, Dean. "Distinct indiscernibles and bundle theory." In: *Metaphysics: the Big Questions*. Peter Van Inwagen & Dean Zimmerman, eds. Oxford: Blackwell, 1988. Pages 58-66.

www.ingramcontent.com/pod-product-compliance
Lightning Source LLC
Chambersburg PA
CBHW051047160426
43193CB00010B/1092